PRIME MINISTERS'
WIVES
— AND ONE HUSBAND

By the same author

Great Britain and Europe 1815–1914
The Troubled Century 1914–1993
Oscar Wilde's Last Chance: The Dreyfus Connection

PRIME MINISTERS'
WIVES
– AND ONE HUSBAND

Mark Hichens

PETER OWEN
London and Chester Springs

PETER OWEN PUBLISHERS
73 Kenway Road, London SW5 0RE

Peter Owen books are distributed in the USA by
Dufour Editions Inc., Chester Springs, PA 19425-0007

First published in Great Britain 2004
© Mark Hichens 2004

ISBN 0 7206 1203 9

A catalogue record for this book is available from the British Library.

Printed and bound in India by Replika Press

ACKNOWLEDGEMENTS

I have had generous help in writing this book. Shelagh Montague-Browne was kind enough to read through the chapter on Clementine Churchill and made some valuable suggestions; and the late John Grigg went through with great care the part on Margaret Lloyd George and made a number of helpful and apposite comments. I am especially indebted to Anne Armitage (de Courcy) for extensive guidance and encouragement. The book has been much improved and facilitated by her assistance.

CONTENTS

ILLUSTRATIONS

INTRODUCTION

Great Britain has been well served by the wives of her Prime Ministers. Nearly all have been loyal, conscientious and discreet. With a few exceptions their marriages have been soundly based, and there have been no divorces – although Dorothy Macmillan pleaded with her husband for one and David Lloyd George gave his wife ample grounds for separation. There has been one legal separation – between Caroline and William Lamb (later Lord Melbourne), and for most of their married lives Robert and Catherine Walpole lived apart as did the Duke and Duchess of Wellington. Moreover, relations between Henry and Margot Asquith were not always on an even keel. Otherwise, with the usual ups and downs, the marriages have been loving and lasting.

It might have been expected that among the forty or so spouses there would have been a few who would have been power-hungry and unscrupulous and sought to be the power behind the throne, but this has not been the case. There have been no Marie Antoinettes or Tsarina Alexandras breathing pernicious advice into their husbands' ears. Of course some wives have been powerful and influential: Emily Palmerston was certainly the most powerful woman in the country in her day and so, some believed, was Lucy Baldwin. But their power was exercised benignly – on behalf of their husbands or their charitable causes and not themselves. The majority of the wives have not been politically minded and have been content to remain in the background, managing their homes, caring for their families and providing for their husbands a calm and happy domestic base where they could relax and do the things they enjoyed most. It was perhaps the most important quality in a wife that she should be a good listener, as the great need of politicians is for someone to whom they can pour out their concerns and in whom they can confide with complete trust. No great political sophistication is required of them, but they should at least be be attentive and ready with down-to-earth advice and, in particular, be good judges of people's character; in this some have been more shrewd than their husbands.

Not many Prime Minister's wives have felt themselves capable of speaking out candidly when they thought their husbands might be acting unwisely. Of course in public they must back their spouses up and stand squarely behind them, but in private there are times when the best service a politician's wife can render is some plain speaking. This was Clementine Churchill's great strength, notably in 1940 when Winston's popularity and prestige were at their height and she wrote him an outspoken letter saying, in effect, that power was going to his head. Years later Denis Thatcher, too, was ready to speak frankly. Usually he kept out of politics, but at carefully judged moments he would intervene to calm his wife and introduce a note of reality or, in his own words, 'to tell her what the hell was going on'.

A thorny problem for wives has been coping with the media. Journalists will always seek them out for their views on every sort of topic as well as titbits of information on their private lives. Any communication is dangerous: all too often their lightest word will be distorted and taken out of context and they suddenly find themselves in the midst of controversy. Because of this most have found it the safest course to give no interviews at all, even to the friendliest correspondent. But they cannot escape that easily. Journalists are constantly on the look-out for the least indiscretion or slip of the tongue, and they have to be humoured and treated with courtesy, whatever the provocation. In the twentieth century it has been the aim of nearly every consort – Margot Asquith being the main exception – to keep out of the limelight and say as little as possible, and in this, on the whole, they have been successful. But of course there is nothing they can do when the satirists decide to make them the butt of their jokes, as *Private Eye* did so successfully with Mary Wilson and Denis Thatcher. All they can do then is to go along with it and seem to enjoy the fun.

The wives have come from different backgrounds: some, but not many, from the aristocracy – Dorothy Macmillan, Catherine Gladstone, Caroline Lamb – but most from business and professional families. It is notable that of the last two aristocrats to be Prime Minister, Lord Salisbury and Lord Rosebery, the former married the daughter of a judge and the latter the daughter of a banker. It is likely, therefore, that the wives would have been very different from one another in their personalities, interests and lifestyles. A few have been keen political activists, ready to play their parts behind the scenes, drawing people out, soothing ruffled feelings and building bridges. In this Emily Palmerston was supreme, but Margot Asquith in her idiosyncratic way and Hannah Rosebery less conspicuously were no mean performers. Others were essentially homebodies and did the minimum of political entertaining but undertook extensive charitable works (notably Catherine Gladstone, Lucy Baldwin and Norma Major). Apart from Audrey Callaghan and Cherie Blair none had had careers of their own. Most were domestically minded, although only Mary Anne Disraeli considered that her sole task was to see to the comfort and well-being of her husband.

In recent times the role of the Prime Minister's wife or consort has begun to change. Before arriving in Downing Street Audrey Callaghan's career had been in local government. Denis Thatcher had been a successful businessman, and although he had retired before Margaret became Prime Minister he continued to lead his own independent life. Cherie Blair pursues a successful legal career as well as being the first wife for a hundred years to give birth to a baby while in Downing Street.

Much is expected of Prime Ministers' wives. They are constantly in the public eye, and some of their duties are arduous and uncongenial. But there are some perks – including the right to live in 10 Downing Street. No house in the country is so rich in history. It is the centre of government and a place to which most people love to be invited. But not all wives have found it an unmixed blessing; as a home it has certain disadvantages. It may contain splendid rooms with historic associations, but the Prime Minister's living quarters are plain and somewhat cramped. The house is constantly overrun by officials and politicians, and, with an office and household staff of over a hundred, for those who value their privacy and a quiet life it is not ideal.

It is paradoxical that London's most famous address should be a relatively undistinguished building. Its façade is unexceptional, and it has a long history of major structural faults. Certainly its origins were unworthy, even murky. At the restoration of Charles II in 1660 the site fell into the hands of an unprincipled adventurer, one George Downing, who had been a soldier in Cromwell's army and had ingratiated himself with the King by the zeal with which he hunted down his former comrades in arms and brought them to the scaffold. For this he was awarded what was then King Street, which he demolished, replaced with jerry-built houses and renamed Downing Street. It was not then a prime location, being in the middle of marshland and one of the more sleazy parts of Westminster, abounding in brothels and gin palaces. However, it was well placed for the Houses of Parliament, and by 1732 it had been acquired by King George II and offered to his First Lord of the Treasury – the title of Prime Minister was not used until later – Robert Walpole, who accepted it only on condition that it became the home of each succeeding First Lord of the Treasury. Walpole himself lived there for six and a half years, but on his demise it did not straight away become the London home of his successors, who preferred to live in their own more palatial residences. However, it was occupied by Lord North at the time when the American colonists were freeing themselves from British rule and later by Pitt the Younger during the war with Napoleon. Pitt was a bachelor, and in spite of the fact that he employed some twenty-seven servants (or perhaps because of it) his domestic arrangements were chaotic, and at the end of his twenty-four years' occupancy his successor, Lord Grenville, described the place as 'uninhabitable'. By then the shoddy building work and inadequate foundations were becoming evident and the first of many major overhauls became necessary.

During the nineteenth century most Prime Ministers preferred their own houses to 10 Downing Street, which they regarded as shabby and inconvenient, and it was used only for offices or residences for junior ministers. However, in 1877 Disraeli, by then a widower and in some financial straits, decided to move in. He found the place 'dingy and depressing' and had a major battle with the Ministry of Works about an adequate refurbishment.[1] A few years later his great rival W.G. Gladstone, during his second ministry, also moved in and found it 'a wilderness and a chaos' and had the same difficulties with the Ministry of Works. After him it was spurned by Lord Salisbury and Lord Rosebery, and the next Prime Minister to occupy it for any length of time was Henry Asquith, who was not a rich man. His wife, Margot, later recorded her impressions of the place while waiting in a car in Downing Street, as he was about to become Prime Minister:

> The street was empty and but for the footfall of a few policemen there was not a sound to be heard. I looked at the dingy exterior of Number Ten and wondered how we would live there.

Later she wrote that the building was 'liver-coloured and squalid', and she was amazed how little known it was – even taxi drivers did not know how to get there. The inside, too, was dismal: 'inconvenient with three poor staircases'. And her stepdaughter, Violet, was astonished to find hardly any bookcases or baths. 'Did Prime Ministers', she wondered, 'never read and never wash?'

During the twentieth century it became the custom for all Prime Ministers to move into Number Ten, but not all of their wives were happy to do so. Dame Margaret Lloyd George had no love for the place and made little effort to make it homely or comfortable. A contemporary wrote that 'the housekeeping was very ramshackle and that it was as if a small suburban household was picnicking there'. For Ramsay MacDonald, the first Labour Prime Minister, moving into Downing Street presented special problems. He was a widower and not at all wealthy and was dismayed to find that he was expected to provide some of his own furniture as well as all linen, cutlery and crockery. His twenty-year-old daughter Ishbel did her best to make the house habitable for him and his five children, but she later wrote:

> For us Number Ten was just a colony of bed-sitting rooms with a large communal dining room where we met for breakfast at eight o'clock.

Both Winston and Clementine Churchill had a deep love for Number Ten and gave it great distinction, but during the Second World War, following heavy bomb damage, it became necessary for them to move out into the Number Ten annexe in nearby Storey Gate, which was better protected. Clement Attlee, the next Labour Prime Minister, also liked Number Ten and found it 'very comfortable', but this enthusiasm was not shared by his wife, Violet, who became distraught by the way their living quarters were overrun by officials and Members of Parliament. This dislike was shared by the next Labour Prime Minister's wife, Mary Wilson, who also found Number Ten oppressive and who during her husband's second premiership refused to live there. Some reluctance to move in was also shown by Labour Prime Minister Jim Callaghan who would have liked to have stayed in their modest south London flat, but his competent and businesslike wife Audrey insisted on living there and coped with all problems admirably.

By the time Margaret Thatcher arrived Number Ten had expanded considerably, consisting of some sixty rooms, three staircases and office space for 140 people. Her daughter Carol has described the private flat on the top floor as 'an extended railway carriage with four bedrooms, a modest dining-room, drawing-room and small kitchen'. No staff were provided and the Prime Minister had to make her own domestic arrangements, with the result that meals for the family and visitors were often sparse potluck affairs. When the Blairs arrived there in 1997 they soon realized that Number Ten would be too small for their young family, so it was exchanged for the Chancellor of the Exchequer's larger flat at Number Eleven.

Today, with the threat of international terrorism, Downing Street and the neighbourhood is under close security guard. But it is still a focal point for most tourists, still the nerve centre of government and host to an endless stream of home and foreign VIPs. For three hundred years it has had an extraordinary history and has been through many vicissitudes: at times it has been stormed by angry mobs threatening to destroy it, at others by cheering crowds come to rejoice and give thanks; it has also been under bombardment from both Hitler's Luftwaffe and the IRA. Inside its walls historic decisions have been taken and many dramas enacted. Who in the early eighteenth century would have foretold such a future for a nondescript house in a Westminster backwater?

If 10 Downing Street has not always provided unalloyed joy for Prime Ministers' wives, few of them have felt anything but affection for Chequers, the other prime ministerial residence. A historic country house set in the Buckinghamshire Chilterns, Chequers was a gift to the nation from Arthur Lee (later Lord Lee of Fareham) and his beautiful and wealthy American wife Ruth. The estate consisted of a mansion of Elizabethan origins (with Gothic additions made in Victorian times) along with some twelve hundred acres of farmland and gardens.

The Lees had acquired a life lease of the estate in 1909 and immediately set about repairing the mansion and restoring it to its Elizabethan splendour. In this they spared no expense, and in addition they lost no opportunity to buy pictures and other works of art with any connection to the place's history (including a death mask of Oliver Cromwell). They were naturally proud of what they had achieved at Chequers and were concerned about its future. They had no children and wanted to bequeath it to the nation, but this was not possible until 1917 when they were able to obtain the freehold of the property.

Arthur Lee was a Conservative Member of Parliament in the early years of the twentieth century and during the First World War had held office in the coalition government of Lloyd George for whom he had a fervent admiration. Working in close contact with him, he had witnessed the tremendous strain under which Lloyd George laboured, and it was as a result of this that Lee conceived the idea of providing for Prime Ministers a house of peace and quiet where they could relax and recuperate. As the wartime pressure on Lloyd George became more intense Lee and his wife decided that they must set the project up at once, which was an act of great unselfishness as they had both become deeply devoted to Chequers and would have loved to spend the rest of their lives there. Before the property could be legally transferred an Act of Parliament was necessary and this would take time, but Lee made it clear to Lloyd George that he could start using the house at once, which he did quite frequently, especially for high-level conferences with war leaders.

The house was not finally made over until 1921 and, although according to the Act the Lees had the right to remain in it during their lifetime, they decided to move out at once; this they did quietly and unobtrusively after a grand celebratory dinner attended by the highest in the land.

In the years that followed, Prime Ministers and their wives quickly came to appreciate the value of Chequers. It was somewhere to which they could escape and unwind, with all their needs attended to by a highly efficient domestic staff for which they had no responsibility. (Since the Second World War it has been manned by volunteers retired from the Services.) It is not surprising then that some of them came to love the place dearly and were greatly distressed when they had to leave it.[2] Some would have loved to leave their mark there, but they were limited in this by the Chequers Trust, drawn up by the Lees, which aimed to prevent any major changes. All that was allowed to Prime Ministers was to leave a memorial window in the house and a tree planted in the grounds (although Churchill was allowed, uniquely, to plant an avenue of beeches known as Victory Drive).

Since 1917 Chequers has been the scene of great events. During the Second World War it was much used by Winston Churchill and became something of a fortress, surrounded by barbed wire entanglements, sandbags, anti-aircraft guns and Nissen huts containing a company of the Guards, but on moonlit nights it was considered too prominent a target from the air and Churchill would move to another country house, Ditchley Park in Oxfordshire.

After the war Chequers remained a great favourite of Prime Ministers' wives, who welcomed a break from domestic responsibilities and the hurly-burly of Downing Street. Not that there was always peace and repose there, for on occasions it would be used for harbouring visiting heads of states, and then there would be frenetic activity. When President Clinton dropped in for a visit of only a day he had a retinue of over a hundred, including a doctor, nurse, kitchen steward and various political advisers as well as a host of Secret Service men. In addition to exhaustive arrangements about protocol and security visitors had to be entertained in a thoroughly English way; they were shown round the house and briefed on its antiquities (including the Prison Room, where the unfortunate Lady Mary Grey, younger sister of Lady Jane the Ten-Day Queen, was locked away on the orders of Queen Elizabeth I for the offence of making an unsuitable marriage); they were taken for a walk in the garden and grounds where they might plant a tree and then on to a local pub where they would drink tepid beer; and in the evening there might be a performance by a peripatetic opera company.

Just before he left Lord Lee wrote in the Chequers visitors' book: 'This house of Peace and Ancient Memories was given to England as a thanks-offering for the deliverance in the Great War 1914–1918 and as a place of rest and recreation for her Prime Ministers for ever.'

Few will dispute that the Lees' bequest has been an unqualified success.

Notes

1. Even a bath was considered inessential.

2. Strangely, the one exception was Lloyd George. Although fulsome in his thanks and praises to the Lees, he confided to his secretary (and second wife) that he felt uneasy in Chequers and that it was full of ghosts of dull people. His wife, Margaret, also disliked it, but then she could never love anywhere that was not in North Wales.

1

FROM CATHERINE WALPOLE TO ANNE NORTH

An empty, coquettish, affected woman, anything rather than correct in her own conduct, or spotless in her fame, greedy of admiration.' – Lady Mary Wortley Montague on Catherine Walpole

Caress the favourite, avoid the unfortunate and trust nobody. – Advice of Mary Bute to her husband

CATHERINE WALPOLE

Although Robert Walpole is generally accepted to have been the first English Prime Minister, it is not a title he himself would have acknowledged, and it did not come into official use until a century later. His position was that of First Lord of the Treasury, but he was the first man to be head of a government consisting entirely of his own supporters, with powers, previously exercised by the sovereign, to appoint them and fire them as he wished.

As well as being the first he is also the longest-serving Prime Minister, holding office for over twenty years. In many ways this is surprising: in an aristocratic age he was no aristocrat, nor was he a great orator or inspirational politician. The reason he was able to stay in office for so long, in spite of strong, sometimes vitriolic, opposition, was his hard head for business, his great capacity for work and a keen insight into human nature; to this should be added the wholesale corruption of Parliament.[1]

He was the third son of a Norfolk landowner and as such would, in the normal course of events, probably have been put into some trade or profession or, possibly, the Church. But with the death of his two elder brothers his father set about grooming him as heir to his estate, and this included finding him a suitable wife. In this Robert had no part; he was expected to accept his father's choice, which was for a lady of a different class, the daughter of a well-to-do Kentish timber merchant, who was also the granddaughter of a former Lord Mayor of London.

Catherine Shorter brought with her a handsome dowry but was otherwise an unfortunate selection. She had little interest in politics and none at all in country life, with a particular distaste for Norfolk. Her aspirations lay in the world of fashion. Such things as clothes, jewellery, gossip and cards were what absorbed her. To achieve her ends she could be recklessly extravagant, and for much of their marriage Walpole was heavily in debt. Her physical charms were considerable and for a time Walpole went along with her modish lifestyle, but he soon tired of it. He was never a courtly figure: to the end of his life he had a rustic air about him that was out of place in high society. And so after six years their marriage had virtually broken down, and most of the time they went their separate ways: Robert to the life of a Norfolk country squire – farming, hunting, shooting, carousing – while Catherine dabbled in the more brittle delights of London and Bath. During those years each gave the other ample grounds for divorce, but there was never any question of this or even a legal separation. They continued to see each other from time to time to keep up the pretence that their marriage was still intact, and they were unbothered about each other's activities while they were apart.

During the last thirty years of their marriage Robert sired at least two illegitimate children, including one by Maria Skerrett, who became his regular mistress and then his second wife after the death of Catherine.

Meanwhile Catherine's life, too, had been licentious and her lovers had included, so it was rumoured, the Prince of Wales (the future George II). When in 1717, eleven years after her last child, she gave birth to a son there was considerable speculation as to his paternity. In time Horatio, or Horace as he was better known, was to become one of the great wits and writers of his age. In almost every way, in looks and character, he was quite unlike Robert, and the general belief was that he was the son of Carr, Lord Hervey, with whom he had much in common, notably a polished literary style and a waspish tongue. This was stated positively in one of her numerous letters by a leading light of society, Lady Mary Wortley Montagu.[2] Robert, however, always accepted Horace as his son, although it was noticeable that he had little to do with him.

Catherine was not without her successes in society life, but it seems that generally she was not highly regarded. Lady Mary was scathing about her: 'an empty, coquettish, affected woman, anything rather than correct in her own conduct, or spotless in her fame, greedy of admiration'. Certainly it is easy to find fault with her, but in fairness it should be remembered that she had had a difficult life: married to a man with whom she had little in common and with whom she had had six babies or miscarriages in six years. And being the mother of Horace redeems much.

By the time of Catherine's death Robert had been living with Maria Skerrett for ten years. He married her at once, but she died of a miscarriage five months later. Robert by then was sixty-one and did not marry again. Maria had been the great love of his life. Although no great beauty, she was clearly a remarkable lady. Lady Mary Wortley Montagu was fulsome in her praises, writing of her 'sweetness of temper and many agreeable qualities'. Robert was inconsolable at her loss, but she had given him ten years of happiness. He died eight years later.

HENRIETTA NEWCASTLE

The revolution of 1688, which overthrew James II and replaced him with William III and Mary, is generally recognized as marking the predominance of the powers of Parliament over those of the monarchy, and for this reason has become known as 'glorious'. But what happened to Parliament soon afterwards was far from glorious. The House of Commons, once the great upholder of constitutional rights and personal liberty, was systematically corrupted so that it became the servile instrument of the Whig oligarchy. This became possible partly by means of outright bribery but more especially by what was known as jobbery; that is, providing supporters with comfortable, well-paid jobs on which they came to depend for their livelihood. At elections votes were easily procured – in the so-called rotten boroughs there was often only a handful of voters who could usually be bribed or otherwise coerced into voting for the candidate of the local aristocrat. There was no secret voting at that time, and if a voter stepped out of line he would soon pay the penalty by being ousted from his home or job or both. The result of this was that the House of Commons was filled with abject placemen out for what they could get. As Walpole so bitterly remarked: 'All these men have their price.'

In this field of jobbery and corruption no one played a more prominent and flagrant role than Thomas Pelham-Holles, Duke of Newcastle. He owned estates in eleven English counties and had enormous political influence, which he exercised to the full. Not a particularly gifted or intelligent man, he yet brought political patronage to a fine art, so that for over forty years he held high offices of state, including that of First Lord of the Treasury, and no government was possible without his support.

At an early stage in his career Newcastle realized that it was necessary for him to make a prestigious marriage. Love would not come into the matter. Station and influence were everything. And, casting around, his eyes fell on Henrietta (usually known as Harriet) Godolphin, of no great beauty or vivacity but of impeccable antecedents. One of her grandfathers, the first Earl Godolphin, had held high office under four monarchs, and the other was the great Duke of Marlborough. Negotiations were opened and on Harriet's side these were carried out by her grandmother, the formidable Sarah, Duchess of Marlborough. Some hard bargaining ensued over the size of Harriet's dowry, on which at first the two sides could not agree. A mediator was found in Sir John

Vanbrugh, the architect, who had done work both at Blenheim Palace and at Newcastle's stately home at Claremont in Surrey, and he reported back to Newcastle that 'as in all her other traffick, so in a husband for her Grand Daughter, the duchess would fain have him good and cheap'. Eventually, however, a compromise was reached, Newcastle looking forward (vainly as it proved) to founding a family descended from the Duke of Marlborough, and Duchess Sarah realizing that the physical charms of her granddaughter were not great.

Although at first there was no love in their marriage this was to come in time; Thomas and Harriet became deeply devoted to each other and found a number of interests in common. These did not, however, include politics, to which Thomas was passionately devoted but in which Harriet took only a passing interest. She would not go electioneering, nor did she become a great political hostess. When Thomas was away from home, which he was frequently, he wrote to her every day, but the content of his letters was not weighty matters of state but rather gossip, or tittle-tattle as he called it, which he knew would amuse her. The great sadness of their marriage was that it brought no children. After one miscarriage Harriet had no further pregnancies. It may be that one reason for this was Harriet's health, which was always precarious. She seemed to suffer interminably from one complaint after another, and most of her visits away from home were for treatment at Bath or some other spa. On these, as at all times, a troupe of doctors and apothecaries were in attendance with fancy cures that almost certainly did more harm than good.

It must not be supposed, however, that Harriet led an idle life, dabbling in the arts and fretting about her health. She took an active part in the management and development of the Claremont estate and in particular helped her husband by keeping meticulous accounts. She seems to have inherited a clear head for money in part, perhaps, from her grandfather, the first Earl Godolphin, who was a distinguished Lord of the Treasury, and also from her grandmother, Sarah, whose parsimony and cupidity were legendary. And this hard head was badly needed, for her husband's personal finances were always in chaos. He might have been immensely wealthy in land and electoral influence but ready money was always in short supply. He was forever in debt with creditors clamouring for settlements.

In spite of her ill health and the ministrations of quack doctors, Harriet was to survive her husband by eight years.

HESTER CHATHAM

After the accession of George III, Prime Ministers (or First Lords of the Treasury, as they were still called) came and went in quick succession. For the most part these were undistinguished men who were not always the most powerful member of the government. This was notably the case when William Pitt, later Lord Chatham, was a minister, for whatever post he held he was always the dominant force in the Cabinet.

William Pitt was a phenomenon. The odds against his achieving high office were long. In an aristocratic age he was the younger son of a commoner, without great wealth and, initially, with no powerful connections. Moreover, he had a great capacity for making enemies: most leading statesmen were ill disposed towards him, and both George I and George II detested him. And yet he succeeded in imposing himself on both kings and the ruling clique. All governments dreaded his opposition and sought, sometimes cravenly, to gain his support. For with all his disadvantages Pitt did have unique qualities. Outstanding among these was his magnificent oratory. Perhaps no other British statesman has ever had such a hold over Parliament – and not only Parliament. At his most powerful most of the country came under his spell. He was War Minister during the Seven Years War, and opinions may have differed as to his ability as an administrator or strategist, but few would deny the electrifying effect he had on those who came in contact with him and that he more than anyone was responsible for winning one of Britain's most successful wars and establishing the first British Empire.

Pitt's great popularity in the country was due not only to his oratory; of equal importance were his independence and integrity. In Parliaments full of placemen and timeservers he stood out as being his own man with a reputation for being scrupulous about money and refusing to rely on any form of patronage.[3] In a country where the great majority of the people were unrepresented in Parliament he came to be regarded as their spokesman against the deeply entrenched ruling caste; hence his sobriquet 'the Great Commoner'.

For whatever reasons, Pitt did not marry until he was forty-six, when his choice of wife was Lady Hester Grenville, the offspring of a marriage between two powerful and ambitious Buckinghamshire families: the Grenvilles of Wotton and the Temples of Stowe.[4] Lady Hester was thirty-three and had probably known William Pitt for at least fifteen years, so it would not seem to have been a particularly romantic marriage, but neither was it just a dynastic match. All the evidence is that they were in love, and the marriage never faltered, producing five children including the brilliant William, known to history as 'Pitt the Younger'. Credit for the strength of the marriage must go to Lady Hester. It is never easy to be married to a genius, and William was more difficult than most. In the first place, he suffered from appalling health. Since childhood he had been afflicted with gout, which today is mainly associated with pain in the feet but in the eighteenth century was used to describe a variety of symptoms, and Pitt was affected all over including in his bowels. He seems to have been in almost constant pain, endlessly seeking relief by drinking the waters at various spas and by taking the advice of doctors with imaginative but unscientific cures. His nervous system, too, was prone to violent lapses, when he would be plunged into the deepest depressions; his mind would become clouded and he would become obsessed with wild and impractical ideas.[5] Despite all these torments Lady Hester was a tower of strength, never failing in her love and devotion. As far as possible she pandered to his whims and was always soothing and supportive. Particularly trying must have been his theatricality. For Pitt was essentially a great actor and, like most great actors, was never off-stage. Everything, even the most trivial details such as the arrangement of his bandages and bedclothes, had to be invested with drama when visitors were expected. Never did Hester lose sight of the fact that she had the care of a great man, whom it was her bounden duty to protect and sustain.

She did not meddle much with politics, being fully occupied with her husband and five children. She did, however, perform valuable services as an intermediary especially when, as quite often happened, her husband had shut himself up in his room and would communicate with no one but her. In 1761, after William's resignation as Secretary of State, Hester was created a baroness in her own right, an honour that was surely hard won and well deserved.

MARY BUTE

When, at the age of twenty-two, George III came to the throne he was full of lofty ideas about purifying the political scene and ridding the country of the venal Whig oligarchs who had for so long been in power. In this ambitious aim he had been inspired partly by his mother, Princess Augusta, and partly by his tutor. John Stuart, Earl of Bute, for years an impecunious Scottish nobleman on the make, had been greatly favoured by fortune. Almost by chance he had been taken into the household of Frederick, Prince of Wales, George's father, and had then established an intimate relationship with Princess Augusta. This may or may not have been of an amorous nature,[6] but it is certain that, on the premature death of Frederick, Bute became the dominant influence in Augusta's life, and she appointed him personal tutor to her son, then, at the age of fourteen, heir to the throne.

Bute had good looks, some erudition and a compelling personality, and it was not long before he had gained a complete ascendancy over the young prince, a somewhat callow, indolent youth with no particular interests or ambitions. Under Bute's tutelage, however, this would change completely: he became filled with moral fervour and an urge to improve himself in every way. This was all to the good, but less beneficial was his devotion to and complete dependence on Bute.

When George III came to the throne he lost no time in making Bute Secretary of State and in the following year Prime Minister in place of the Duke of

Newcastle. The year 1761 was indeed an *annus mirabilis* for Bute, for it was then, too, that he became a rich man. In 1736 he had married the daughter of a very wealthy but niggardly Yorkshire landowner, Edward Wortley Montagu, whose wife, Lady Mary, was the famous scholar and traveller. Both parents had strongly opposed the marriage, as at the time Bute had seemed to be a penniless peer without prospects. It had been necessary, therefore, for the couple to elope. In time, however, as Bute's prospects improved they came to terms with him, and when Edward died in 1761 he left his large fortune to his daughter.[7] As well as great riches this also brought Bute the potential for powerful electoral influence, as he became the owner of at least nine rotten boroughs. In the same year, following the death of the Duke of Argyll, Bute inherited control of the forty-five Scottish members of the Commons, so that as a borough-monger Bute was almost on a par with the Duke of Newcastle. With this number of parliamentary seats at his disposal, great powers lay within his reach, but he proved unable to grasp them. He was not an adept politician and did not remain long in office. Besides his rapid rise to high office, his Scottish birth and his suspected liaison with Princess Augusta had made him many enemies. London mobs frequently demonstrated against him, bearing aloft a boot (a mispronunciation of his name) and a petticoat (as a protest at undue feminine influence).

For a time after his resignation he continued to have influence with the King, but this was to decline. His wife, Mary, had by then borne him eleven children as well as providing almost limitless money. She had watched over his rise to power with some acumen: 'Caress the favourite, avoid the unfortunate and trust nobody' had been her worldly advice to him. In recognition of her services she was created a peeress in her own right as Baroness Mountstuart of Wortley.

ANNE NORTH

The government that lasted longest during the early years of George III's reign was that headed by Lord North, a name for ever associated with the loss of the American colonies and one of England's most disastrous wars. Posterity has not been kind to him: he is usually represented as obstinate, foolish and out of control. But he was in fact an able parliamentarian, a good administrator and a man of great charm and wit. If his prime ministership had come to an end before the American entanglement he might have been regarded as an outstanding peacetime holder of that office. His fault was that he felt it his duty to carry out the wishes of his King and stand by him through thick and thin, even though this meant supporting a policy which in his heart he knew to be wrong and heading for disaster. For this he came under ferocious attack from most of the great orators of that time (including William Pitt, Charles James Fox and Edmund Burke), attacks that he bore with great courtesy and good humour.

Throughout his long ordeal it is doubtful that even he could have survived without the devoted support of his wife and family. At the age of twenty-four he had married Anne Speke, the daughter of a Somerset landowner, who was reputed to be a lady with great expectations. But, in the event, these did not materialize, and for most of his life North lived in straitened financial circumstances, dependent on the salary he obtained from his public offices. This was not necessary as his father, the Earl of Guildford, was very wealthy but also, unfortunately, very niggardly and long lived, so that North came into his inheritance only in the last two years of his life.

Little is known of Anne Speke, but there seems to have been general agreement that she was no great beauty, although, like her husband, sensible and sweet-tempered. She was also a prolific bearer of children – altogether seven, five of which in ten years. One of their daughters later recorded that during their thirty-six years of marriage she had never heard an unkind word between them.

North died in 1792 at the age of sixty, by then completely blind and heavily overweight. Anne died five years later.

Notes

1. More of this later. See p. 19.

2. A famous eighteenth-century bluestocking. As well as a scholar and a poet she was also a prolific diarist and scandalmonger.

3. This was not perhaps altogether deserved. In Parliament for a time he represented the most corrupt of rotten boroughs, Old Sarum, an almost entirely deserted site. He also found it necessary in order to maintain himself in office to come to terms with the Duke of Newcastle, the great wielder of patronage.

4. The descendants of whom were to become Dukes of Buckingham.

5. Particularly in the matter of gardens in which he had a consuming interest, and he would suddenly demand sweeping and impossible changes to the landscape.

6. Characteristically Horace Walpole (see p. 18) had no doubts about it.

7. This was after disinheriting his wildly eccentric son, whose aberrations included converting to Islam and marrying a Nubian.

2

FROM URSULA ADDINGTON TO MARY GREY

She has grown ugly by Jove. – Wellington about to propose to Kitty
after an absence of nine years

URSULA ADDINGTON

In 1800 the English political scene was dominated by William Pitt the Younger.
He had become Prime Minister in 1783 at the age of twenty-four and held
that office with one intermission until his death in 1806. He was unmarried.

While Pitt was out of office between 1801 and 1804 his place was taken by
Henry Addington, competent and businesslike but a dull speaker and an unin-
spired personality – a marked contrast to Pitt.[1] While he was Prime Minister
peace was made with Napoleon by the treaty of Amiens ('a peace of which everyone was glad and no one proud'). When the war was renewed he was forced to
resign and make way for the return of Pitt. Soon afterwards he was created Lord
Sidmouth and held high office in various governments. He lived until the
age of eighty-seven, by which time he had sunk into obscurity where he has
remained ever since.

His marriage to Ursula Mary Hammond of Cheam was a completely happy
one, although they were of widely differing temperaments. Where Ursula was
lively, outgoing and humorous, Henry was sombre and buttoned up. But they
were deeply devoted to each other and Ursula was able to draw Henry out in
a way no one else could; only with her was he able to feel relaxed and at ease.
Their marriage was blighted by tragedy: Ursula had at least two miscarriages and two children died in infancy; later their eldest son suffered a mental
breakdown from which he never recovered. When Ursula died in her fifties
Henry was devastated and went into a mourning that some found excessive.
Twelve years later he married again at the age of sixty-six – a widow some
thirty years younger than him who, like Ursula, was able to bring some warmth
and humour into his life. She predeceased him by two years.

ANNE GRENVILLE

On the death of Pitt a coalition government was formed known as 'the Ministry of All Talents'. At the head of this was George, Lord Grenville, a politician of wide experience and considerable ability but not well liked. Cold and aloof, he made little effort to contain his natural arrogance. At the age of thirty-three he proposed marriage to Anne Pitt, daughter of Thomas Pitt, younger brother of Lord Chatham. This was considered a highly advantageous match by the relatives of both parties, as it would form an alliance between two eminent Whig families; but at the age of seventeen Anne was somewhat overawed by the overtures of this grand, alarming figure whom she hardly knew and for a time held back. Then, after parental and other pressures had been brought to bear, she relented. There was little question at first of it being a love match, but in time the two became deeply devoted and found a number of interests in common, although these did not include politics. In spite of being the niece of Pitt the Elder and the cousin of Pitt the Younger, Anne kept aloof from them. They had no children.

DOROTHY PORTLAND

The Ministry of All Talents was followed in 1807 by another makeshift coalition, headed by the elderly Whig grandee William Bentinck, third Duke of Portland, a man of great stature and erudition but few political skills. By 1807 he was sixty-nine, in poor health and not at all anxious to take on the tasks of Prime Minister; but he was persuaded that it was his duty, and for two years in the middle of the war against Napoleon he struggled to keep some control over the disparate groups in his Cabinet.[2]

His wife, Dorothy Cavendish, was the daughter of the fourth Duke of Devonshire. Dorothy and her three brothers had been brought up in great splendour but amid much family discord. Their grandmother, wife of the third Duke, had strongly disapproved of the marriage of Dorothy's mother and father and would have nothing to do with the children, even when they were left orphans; and so they were cared for somewhat coolly by uncles and aunts.

After her marriage Dorothy kept in close contact with her brother, the fifth Duke of Devonshire, and tried to support him through his troubled marriage to Georgiana Spencer. In middle age she had become an imperious lady and took a strongly censorious view of her sister-in-law's peccadilloes (particularly her gambling debts), at one time urging that she be sent to Coventry by the Devonshire family. Throughout her life Dorothy was a staunch and active Whig and when, at the time of the French Revolution, her husband showed signs of gravitating towards the Younger Pitt and the Tories, she held him in check; it was not until after her death from cancer in 1794 that he felt able to make such a move.

JANE PERCEVAL

When the Duke of Portland's health finally broke down there were several brilliant men who might have succeeded him, but in the event the choice fell on Spencer Perceval – capable, courageous, honourable but a political mediocrity. He was the second son of the Earl of Egmont and on his mother's side was related to the Earl of Northampton. Being a younger son without an inheritance it was necessary for him to earn his own living, which he did at the Bar, eventually with considerable success.

At the age of twenty-five Spencer fell deeply in love with Jane Wilson, the nineteen-year-old daughter of a reasonably prosperous ex-army officer. Jane returned his love, but her father, considering that Spencer, although the son of an earl, was impecunious, forbade the match. Two years later, however, when Jane came of age, he could forbid it no longer, and she and Spencer were married in 1790. By then Spencer's prospects at the Bar were improving, but his finances were still stretched and they began their married life in lodgings above a carpet shop in Bedford Row. In time his earnings increased considerably, but so, too, did his family – at an alarming rate, eventually numbering ten.

In 1794 at the age of thirty-four Spencer was elected to Parliament, where he soon made a name for himself by his oratory and debating skills, but his career was always held back by shortage of money. When in 1809 he was offered the premiership it was something of a poisoned chalice, as the Tory Party at the time was bitterly divided and the war against Napoleon was at a critical stage. It was no mean achievement on his part that for three years he held the party together and kept the country on course in the European war. It is doubtful that he would ever have become a great Prime Minister, but this was not put to the test as in 1812 he was assassinated outside Parliament by a lunatic with a grievance.

After her husband's death Jane and her large family were reasonably well provided for by Parliament, and two years later she married again – to an army officer with adequate means. She died thirty years later at the age of seventy-six.

LOUISA LIVERPOOL

Spencer Perceval was succeeded as Prime Minister by Robert Jenkinson, second Earl of Liverpool, apparently another man of no great distinction. But he was more able than might appear. Disraeli's judgement of him as 'the arch mediocrity' was surely not justified. He was to remain Prime Minister for fifteen years (longer than any other Prime Minister except Walpole). His government brought the war against Napoleon to a victorious conclusion and was to survive, although with bitter criticism, the troubled times at home which occurred in the years that followed. And when he died, still in office, there was a major split in the Tory Party.

In 1798 Robert Jenkinson, as he then was, married Louisa Hervey, the youngest daughter of the notorious Earl of Bristol, also Bishop of Derry – an unusual combination even in the eighteenth century. The marriage, although childless, was a happy one, and, unlike those of most of Louisa's nearest relations, did not break up. In reaction perhaps to the 'dissipation, vice and folly' she found all around her, and particularly in her own family, Louisa was noted for her strict Evangelical piety and works of charity among the poor. Towards the less righteous members of her own class she tended to be outspokenly censorious and had a reputation in some quarters for prudery.

JOAN CANNING

On the death of Lord Liverpool the Prince Regent, overcoming a strong distaste for him, chose George Canning as the next Prime Minister. Canning, on the progressive wing of the Tory Party, was a brilliant but controversial character. In wit and intelligence he was unsurpassed, but he was also arrogant and malicious, which had made him many enemies. For several years he had been an outstanding Foreign Secretary, but he was to occupy the premiership for only seven months before he died.

Canning had a turbulent childhood. His father, a ne'er-do-well Irish lawyer, died when George was a baby, leaving his mother virtually penniless, so that for a time she was compelled to earn her living as an actress, at that time considered a dubious profession. Later George was taken under the wing of a wealthy uncle who saw to it that he went to Eton and Oxford and was then elected to Parliament, where his skills as a speaker attracted the attention of the Younger Pitt, who gave him office.

Great as were Canning's abilities, however, he would not have gone far in politics without financial backing, which at first he did not have. But in 1799, at the age of twenty-nine, he fell in love with Joan Scott, a lady of beauty and charm as well as considerable wealth. Her father, a Scottish general, had made a substantial fortune, so it was said, as a professional gambler. In 1799 he was no longer alive, nor was his wife, but his three daughters had been left well endowed. Of these, the elder two had married heirs to dukedoms (Portland and Moray), and it might have been expected that Joan would follow suit, but instead she succumbed to the overtures of George Canning, brilliant but impecunious and something of a political adventurer. Inevitably it was thought by many that George had married Joan for her money, but it is certain that his love for her was genuine. Until then his life had not been chaste and he had had love affairs with various ladies including, improbably, a dalliance with the coarse and voluptuous Princess of Wales.[3] But these had been transitory, and with Joan Scott he was never in doubt that it was true love at last.

Certainly the marriage proved a happy one and survived successfully Canning's stormy political career. It is evident that Joan had no great addiction to politics and did not aspire to be a great political hostess. She was content to be her husband's confidante and listen to him pouring out his woes with occasional words of sympathy. It seems she made no great impression on the *beau monde*. A contemporary described her as 'a pretty woman with a large fortune and of very pleasing manners', and, if this is to damn with faint praise, at least she neither gave rise to any scandal nor caused her husband serious embarrassment.

Canning died in 1827 at the age of fifty-seven, his life almost certainly shortened by strain and overwork. In spite of faults of temperament he was widely lamented. It was felt that an exceptionally bright light had gone from the political firmament. Even George IV, at one time a bitter enemy, relented and, as a mark of respect, created Joan a viscountess in her own right.

CATHERINE WELLINGTON

For a time after the death of Canning his followers on the left of the Conservative Party remained in the ascendant under the premiership of Lord Goderich. But 'Goody Goderich', as he was known, was no leader. Reputed to be 'as firm as a bulrush', he resigned after a few months, when the leadership passed to the Duke of Wellington on the hard right of the party. Wellington's genius on the battlefield did not extend to the political arena. Under him there was a major split in the Tory Party, and later he was forced to accept most of the changes he was pledged to resist – notably Catholic emancipation and the reform of Parliament. Wellington's marriage, too, was a failure.

No Prime Minister's wife has had such an unromantic and unhappy marriage as Catherine Pakenham, later first Duchess of Wellington. Kitty, as she was known, was the daughter of Lord Longford and in her young days was said to be 'of a sweet disposition and an indefinable beauty'. At the age of twenty she had attracted the attention of a young army officer, Captain the Hon. Arthur Wesley,[4] who formally proposed to her, but his suit was rejected. Arthur was the younger son of the Earl of Mornington but had no financial resources apart from his army pay, which was considered inadequate for the upkeep of a wife. Also at that time, strangely, in view of what he later became, he had a reputation for being fickle and unambitious. There is little evidence of Wesley's heart being broken by this rejection, but he did let it be known that if something occurred to make Kitty and her brother (then head of the family) change their minds, 'my mind will still remain the same'.

Three years later Arthur left England for India, where his brother Richard was soon to become Governor-General. During the next nine years Arthur would gain military renown in the wars with the French and their Indian allies as well as great wealth from prize money, and when he returned to England in 1805 he was already something of a national hero.

While he was away it does not seem that he had had many thoughts of Kitty. Certainly he never wrote to her or mentioned her in any of his other correspondence. Nor on his return was he in any hurry to resume his suit; but when it was intimated to him that Kitty was still unmarried and might be responsive to his overtures he decided that he must propose to her again. It seems he did this out of a sense of duty, feeling beholden to her because of the undertaking he had given twelve years before. And so without setting eyes on her he sent off a formal proposal by letter, which Kitty with some nervous misgivings accepted. He had been warned that she was much changed since he had last seen her, but he chose to ignore this. However, when he arrived in Ireland for the wedding it struck him forcibly. 'She has grown ugly, by Jove,' he is said to have murmured to his brother. Soon after the wedding it became evident that it was not only her looks that had changed: the lively and attractive twenty-year-old had grown into a somewhat maladroit lady of thirty, timid and incompetent and with a tendency to faint at moments of stress.

After the briefest of honeymoons Arthur made his own way back to England, leaving Kitty to follow later. There then followed two years of uneasy married life in London during which the differences between them became more marked. Kitty was clearly frightened of Arthur, which annoyed him as did her unpunctuality and irresponsibility about money. It was plain that all love for her had perished.

In 1808 Arthur left England for Portugal and Spain, where for the next five years he was to conduct the Peninsular War, at the victorious conclusion of which he became in England and in most of Europe the great conquering hero, and even more so after the Battle of Waterloo. Honours poured in on him and he was everywhere in demand for great occasions. His need was for a sparkling, worldly-wise wife at his side, but Kitty could not measure up to this. She was overawed by his greatness and dreaded being in the limelight. In 1814 Arthur was appointed ambassador to France under the recently restored King Louis XVIII, and he wrote to Kitty suggesting – and perhaps hoping – that she might not feel equal to the demands of being an ambassador's wife and might prefer to stay at home. But she insisted on coming and, of course, was hopelessly inadequate; among the gorgeously gowned beauties of Europe she sat at the head of his table, dressed unsuitably in white muslin, chatting cluelessly and indiscreetly and forever gushing about her husband, which was anathema to him. However, somehow they managed to keep up appearances and there was no question of a divorce or legal separation, even though Arthur was by no means unresponsive to the many advances from the beautiful women around him.

After Waterloo thirty-seven years of life still lay ahead of Arthur. During this time he was Prime Minister from 1828 to 1830, and then and later he incurred great unpopularity because of his opposition to all reform. At times London mobs shrieked abuse at him and tried to smash the windows at Apsley House, which moved him no more nor less than the wild cheers that had greeted him after Waterloo. It was during a scene of this sort, at the age of fifty-nine, that the unfortunate Kitty died.

MARY GREY

Following the fall of the Duke of Wellington's government in 1830, due to a split in the Tory Party, the way was at last open to the Whigs and Lord Grey with his programme of electoral reform. Charles Grey had been advocating reform for many years. During the great repression that had descended on England after the French Revolution, when anyone proposing even the mildest change was liable to be branded a dangerous revolutionary and packed off to Botany Bay, Grey had been foremost among the small group of Whigs who, at some danger to themselves, had kept the flag of freedom flying and stood out against the harsh laws the government of Pitt had passed to keep revolutionary tendencies in check. It had been a seemingly hopeless struggle and at one point Grey had despaired and withdrawn to his estate in Northumberland, saying he would not return to the political arena until there were signs that the English people had taken up 'seriously and affectionately' the reform of the voting system by which rich men were able to control the membership of the House of Commons.

This is not the place to tell the story of the passing of the Great Reform Bill and how perhaps the most radical measure ever passed by Parliament was instigated and carried through by a wealthy nobleman descending from his eyrie in the north, presiding over the fray of the parliamentary battle, seeing it to a successful conclusion and then withdrawing from the scene.

Lord Grey of the Reform Bill, as he came to be known, ranks high in the pantheon of liberal reformers, but his honourable political career was not matched by his private life. In his youth he had a passionate love affair with Georgiana, Duchess of Devonshire, seven years his senior, who bore him a daughter. Their affair came to an end abruptly when, without a word to Georgiana, Grey married Mary Elizabeth Ponsonby. Such behaviour, even in that indulgent age, was considered shocking. A contemporary described him as 'a fractious, exigent lover, a man of violent temper and unbounded ambition'.

Mary Ponsonby was the daughter of a wealthy Irish landowner. She was to prove a faithful and supportive wife to Charles and bore him no fewer than fifteen children. Seven years after their marriage a bachelor uncle presented Charles with an estate in Northumberland of rare beauty. At Howick Charles and Mary established an exceptionally happy family home, one which Charles became increasingly unwilling to leave for the political turmoil in London, and great persuasion was often needed to make him do so. During these absences it was usually necessary for Mary to remain at Howick to look after their large family, but she did have an interest in politics and was quite ready to contribute her opinions. In particular she was one of the people who most strongly urged Charles to come out of retirement and return to the fray. In 1816 she wrote: 'I really cannot express how much I regret the determination you seem to have taken entirely to give up all interference in politics. My dearest Charles, the subject is become a very sore one with me, and adds very much to the depression for which you scold me so unmercifully.'

While in London Charles did not lead a solitary and chaste life. It was not long before he had resumed his relationship with Georgiana. Brazen though this might seem, incredibly Mary seems to have been unaware of their love affair and of their illegitimate daughter, and she and Georgiana became good friends. And it was not only with Georgiana that Charles consorted: he also had a liaison with the second wife of the playwright Richard Brinsley Sheridan, who was not one to keep the affair to herself. Such behaviour was too much for Georgiana's close relatives. Her sister, Harriet Lady Bessborough, wrote at the time: 'From first to last his conduct has been abominable' and that she 'had admired too much one who, whatever he is among men, is anything but honourable among women'.

But these deviations did not affect the Grey's marriage: he and Mary were too deeply in love and bonded by their family and devotion to Howick. After finally retiring from office in 1834 Grey lived for a further eleven years, for the most part years of peace and happiness. There were occasions when Mary's health gave cause for concern, when Charles, sometimes to her irritation, became immoderately solicitous. But he need not have worried. Mary was a woman of great stamina. In spite of the rigours of the Northumbrian climate and having given birth to fifteen children she was to outlive Charles by sixteen years to the age of eighty-five, with more than thirty grandchildren.

Notes

1. Famously described in a doggerel verse by George Canning: 'Pitt is to Addington as London is to Paddington.'

2. Not always successfully, as hostility between two of its members, Canning and Castlereagh, became so intense that they fought a duel.

3. The estranged wife of the future George IV. If this liaison had involved adultery Canning could, by a medieval law, have been guilty of treason, still punishable by death.

4. Later the spelling was changed to Wellesley.

3

CAROLINE LAMB

A creature of caprice and impulse and whim . . . her manner, her talk, her character shifted their colours as rapidly as those of a chameleon. On fire for the dramatic, the picturesque, the ideal, openly at war with the tame and the trivial, at every turn she flouted convention. She seemed more alive than other people, and heightened their sense of life by her presence. – Lord David Cecil, *The Young Melbourne*

The cleverest, most agreeable, absurd, amiable, perplexing, dangerous, fascinating little being that lives now or ought to have lived 2000 years ago. – Lord Byron on Caroline

No Prime Minister has had a more tormented marriage than William Lamb, second Viscount Melbourne. His wife, Caroline Lamb (she did not live to become Lady Melbourne), was brilliantly gifted but unbalanced and ultimately deranged: at once the delight and despair of all who knew her. She came from an exalted aristocratic background: her father was the third Earl of Bessborough, and her mother, Henrietta, was the daughter of Lord and Lady Spencer and sister of Georgiana, Duchess of Devonshire.

Caroline's childhood was unsettled. Her mother was a woman of outstanding beauty and charm but suffered from ill health, which required her to spend much time in gentler climates abroad, usually Italy. She was devoted to her daughter and insisted on taking her along, but then left her for long periods with a nurse while she went back to England. Why Caroline was separated in this way from the rest of her family, including three elder brothers, is not clear, but at the age of eight it was decided she should return to England to go to school – a small exclusive establishment in London for girls of her class. But Caroline had no love for school and lost no time in making this clear, showing for the first time signs of the temperament that was to become notorious. The benevolent but ineffectual gentlewoman who ran the school found her quite unmanageable, and it became necessary to take her away. It was then decided that she should be lodged in Devonshire House with her cousins, who were of the same age, in the care of a governess, and it was there that Caroline spent her early formative years.

Devonshire House was the most splendid of all the great aristocratic London houses. A palace in Piccadilly overlooking Green Park, it was the favourite resort of the Whig aristocracy, who gathered there to talk politics and take their pleasure. It was dominated by the Duchess, the illustrious and much loved Georgiana, who created an incomparable atmosphere. This has been described lyrically by Lord David Cecil in his masterpiece *The Young Melbourne*:

> It passed in a dazzling, haphazard confusion of routs, balls and parties, hurried letter writings, fitful hours of talk and reading. But in its own way it was also unique. Rare indeed is it to find a real palace inhabited by a real princess, a position of romantic wealth and splendour, filled by figures as full of glamour as the location itself. Moreover in Devonshire House the graces were cultivated in the highest perfection. Here in the flesh was the exquisite eighteenth century of Gainsborough, all flowing elegance, and melting glances and shifting silken colour.

But beneath the glittering surface all was not well at Devonshire House. There was tension and much unhappiness and the family set-up was bizarre – dominated by a *ménage à trois* of the Duke, the Duchess and Lady Elizabeth Foster. The Duke, a morose and reclusive character, had never been in love with Georgiana and had made it plain to her that her principal function was to produce a son and heir, which for many years she was unable to do. Georgiana, for her part, took refuge from a loveless marriage in a number of lovers and in entertaining on a magnificent scale. By the time Caroline arrived on the scene, however, she was in decline. She was as charming and warm-hearted as ever, but her looks were fading and her figure overblown, and she suffered dreadfully from headaches, jaundice and bilious attacks. She had also become addicted to gambling and had built up enormous debts. Her great comfort in her last years was the passionate friendship she had formed with Lady Elizabeth Foster, who was also the mistress of the Duke and who in due course became the second Duchess.

Lady Elizabeth was the daughter of the notorious Earl-Bishop (of Bristol and Derry respectively) whose debaucheries had earned him a scandalous reputation all over Europe (where he is still commemorated by a number of hotels named after him).[1] She had married an unprepossessing Irish landowner by whom she had had two sons before parting from him. Subsequently she was to have two more children by the Duke of Devonshire, while Georgiana, too, was to have a child out of wedlock (by the future Lord Grey of the Reform Bill), so that the Devonshire nursery into which Caroline was thrust at the age of nine consisted of a number of children of dubious parentage; and the ambience was unsettled and unreassuring.

In this milieu Caroline was not unhappy but was determined, as always, to have her own way and be the centre of attention. She had learned at school that this could be achieved by throwing tantrums, and these became more frequent and more violent – not only screams of rage but glass and china and any objects handy being hurled at those who crossed her. These outbursts were not at first taken seriously by her doting mother, who referred to them lightly as *petites sauvageries*, but later she became concerned and called in a child specialist, who gave fatal advice: her difficulties arose, he said, from an over-active brain, and her main need was for quiet and relaxation. She must not, therefore, be made to learn anything against her will and she was far too sensitive for any kind of discipline.

Inevitably this made matters worse: her rages increased rather than diminished as they went unchecked and she found she could always get her way by them. More regrettably her education was neglected, and she was allowed to do only those things which took her fancy at that moment. Left to herself, she spent most of her time in a world of fantasy: at one moment a pathetic, misunderstood little girl, the next a rumbustious tomboy riding bareback at full speed. Ordinary life was too dull for her; she had to have drama and excitement and, above all, admiration. Certainly she was not an easy child to live with, but in between her fits of temper she could be very beguiling; she was intelligent and artistic and, although no great beauty, had sparkling charm and winning ways, particularly with men. Women tended to be less susceptible.

At the age of thirteen Caroline, while on a visit to a country house, caught the eye of one of the outstanding young men of his generation, William Lamb, the second son (putatively) of Lord Melbourne. She, in turn, was attracted by him but was much too young for any thoughts of marriage; and in any case the only daughter of an earl would be considered above the expectations of the second son of a parvenu Irish viscount (see p. 53). However, they made a lasting impression on each other, and seven years later the situation was transformed when William's elder brother died and he became the heir to a viscountcy and a large fortune. This emboldened him to propose, but at first Caroline held back, saying her temper was too violent for marriage and suggesting that, instead, she should disguise herself as a boy and act as William's clerk; predictably this whimsical idea found no favour with William.[2] In spite of his changed circumstances he was still looked at askance by the Bessborough family. He had the reputation of being a cynic and disbeliever and often caused offence by his rough and ready manners and blasphemous speech. Besides, Lady Melbourne and Lady Bessborough could not abide each other. However, no one could deny William's great charm and intellect; it was certainly apparent that he and Caroline were deeply in love, and Lady Bessborough may well have dreaded the rages that would have ensued had she stood in Caroline's way. And so consent was forthcoming, and they were married in a private ceremony in the Bessborough London house simply and quietly but not entirely without incident, when Caroline was overcome at the thought that she was about to leave home for ever.

The first years of William and Caroline's marriage were blissfully happy. They lived for each other and complemented each other perfectly. Caroline was aware of how inadequate her education had been and longed to learn, while William loved to teach. They were utterly in love and had little time for anyone else. 'They flirt all day,' a visitor remarked. And after two years (and two miscarriages) Caroline was delivered of a son, Augustus, to whom they were both devoted. But this was too good to last. A man of William's ability could not be expected to commit himself indefinitely to the whims of a child bride, and such a life would not for ever satisfy the wayward and capricious Caroline. She could not sustain the role of dutiful wife and would soon be longing for drama in her life. Greatly as she loved William, she found him too staid and tranquil. Instead of being enraged by her tantrums he treated them with amused tolerance. Whatever she did, he was calm and passive; he could not be provoked into anger, and she was made to feel like a pampered child rather than an adult equal.

As their passion for each other subsided and William separated himself more into a life of his own, so differences began to appear. For Caroline married life became hard to bear. There had always been stresses. She had never got on well with the Melbourne family, particularly her mother-in-law, and although she had her own establishment she was expected to live in an apartment in Melbourne House. Also, because of her sexual immaturity the physical side of marriage caused her anguish; and William's bluff, somewhat coarse attitude to the matter jarred. Later she was to complain that he had instructed her in 'things she did not need to have known'. And she was shocked, too, by his offhand attitude to religion. 'Things are coming to a pretty pass,' he once remarked, 'when religion is allowed to invade private life.' More and more it was borne in on her that married life was not unalloyed joy. She had been devastated by her two miscarriages, and, although the safe delivery of a son had brought her great happiness, it was not long before there was anxiety about the child's mental condition, which was not normal.

As always, when life became oppressive, Caroline took refuge in a world of fantasy. Instead of the role of wife and mother she sought to present herself as a woman of the world and *femme fatale*. On this she sought advice from the Countess of Oxford, who was well qualified to give it. Married to Edward Harley, the fifth Earl, she had spread her favours freely, so that her five children had become known as 'the Harleian Miscellany'. She, then, undertook to initiate Caroline into the ways of the world. Her first need, she told her, was for a lover, and here her choice was not well judged. Sir Godfrey Webster was the son of the great Whig hostess Lady Holland, by her first marriage; and his charms, such as they were, were purely physical. A soldier of some distinction, hard drinking and hard gambling, mentally he was a nonentity. Such a liaison brought

Caroline little kudos, and she made a crucial mistake. It was the unwritten law of Whig society that while extramarital affairs were tolerated they should be conducted with discretion. Caroline made no attempt at this but rather blazoned it abroad, causing great outrage, particularly to her mother-in-law, Lady Melbourne, and to Sir Godfrey's mother, Lady Holland – two dominating figures in society. On her husband, however, her affair had no effect. William refused entirely to play the part of the enraged, jealous husband. Instead he looked on it with amusement and said that it would soon blow over. Of course such nonchalance infuriated Caroline and left her more frustrated than ever and dreaming of a demon lover more outlandish than Sir Godfrey. He was soon to appear.

George Gordon, sixth Lord Byron, came from a turbulent family. It was believed that it lay under a curse originating from the closing of the monasteries in the sixteenth century, when Sir John Byron bought Newstead Abbey in Nottinghamshire from Henry VIII and evicted the monks with great brutality; but not before they had thrown all their treasures into the lake and laid a curse on the Byron family for ever. In subsequent years there was much evidence of the potency of this curse, as successive Lords Byron were plagued by misfortune and were notorious for wickedness and vice.

It soon became clear that George Gordon had not escaped the monks' curses. He was born with a club foot and his upbringing had been woeful and tempestuous, with a somewhat hysterical mother, a freebooting father and painful and humiliating sexual experiences with both sexes. Caroline first met him when he was at the height of his fame soon after his return from a long Mediterranean odyssey in the course of which he had experienced life to the full, consorting with all sorts of men and women and encountering at first hand the mysteries of the Orient. During this time he had also written a long semi-autobiographical poem to which he had given the title 'Childe Harold'. This describes the wanderings of a melancholy, disillusioned youth, sensuous and rebellious and at war with mankind. Byron himself seems to have attached no great importance to it and was reluctant for it to be published, as it revealed too much of himself, but when it was it caused a furore. London society went wild about it and Byron, from being an unknown, found himself overnight a literary lion and the most sought-after man in London. The popularity of 'Childe Harold' was something of a phenomenon. It is, surely, not such a great poem, but it struck a sensitive chord in London at that time. For years, during the French Revolution and the war against Napoleon, the mood in Britain had been reactionary and repressive, people were ready for a change, and the rebelliousness, eroticism and mystery of 'Childe Harold' made a tremendous impact. And this was stirred up all the more when it became known that the author was beautiful, wicked and a lord. And so he became the cynosure of all eyes as society hostesses vied with each other for his company. All of which left Byron bemused, as he was totally unprepared for such a reception and was, in reality, a very different character from the hero of 'Childe Harold'. Far from the fearless, romantic figure depicted there, he was shy, ill at ease and with a sexuality that was (to put it mildly) maladjusted. But at first nothing could abate the 'Byromania' which swept London, and foremost in the fray was Caroline Lamb.

Their first meeting was an anticlimax. Caroline played hard to get and was unconcerned and dismissive; she wrote afterwards that he was 'mad, bad and dangerous to know' – words that summed him up exactly (and herself to some extent), and if she had heeded them she would have been spared much suffering. But she had no intention of shying away, and their second meeting was much more emotional. Of it Caroline wrote: 'That pale face is my fate', and soon afterwards their affair was launched on its turbulent course.

For all of nine months the two were besotted with each other: Byron moody, in turn passionate, tragic, enigmatic and pouring out his life story and the afflictions that had beset him; Caroline, fascinated and eager and contributing her own tales of woe. No attempt was made to keep the affair private. On the contrary, it was blazoned abroad. They went everywhere together – making love, quarrelling, reconciling, all in public view. This was foolhardy as it was an accepted tenet of the Whig aristocracy that such affairs had to be *sub rosa*, and such a blatant display might have led to social ostracism, but such was the high social standing of Caroline and the idolization of Byron that this was not their fate. On youth, rank and genius an indulgent eye was turned.

While the affair was in full swing it was expected that William would take robust, masculine action, but as before he was not to be moved, treating the whole matter with apparent indifference. He let it be known that he thought it too ridiculous to be taken seriously and that it would soon peter out. And up to a point he was right. It was not long before the passion began to subside and tensions and irritations became more pronounced. And it must be doubted that they were ever truly in love. Byron was bewitched by Caroline's charm and vitality, and it flattered his vanity to have conquered such a glittering, high-born lady, but having done so it was not in his nature to stay put; he was ready to move on to fresh fields. And while Caroline, for her part, was thrilled by Byron's reputation and romanticism and loved to show off her capture of such a celebrity, her feelings did not go deep. It is likely that physical relations between them were limited. Byron was not greatly attracted by thin women, favouring those more sensuous and full-blown. In any case, his sexuality was ambivalent. Caroline's, too, was not clear-cut: whatever her pose of the moment she was inherently modest and sex-shy. It could well have been the case, then, that their legendary love affair was something of a charade, performed flamboyantly and erotically by two actors of beauty and genius, but essentially egotistical and concerned only with image.

Byron's ardour was the first to languish. He soon became weary of Caroline's ploys and tantrums and found her too neurotic and possessive; and it greatly irked him to be monopolized in public and put on show. Caroline had not entirely lost her hold on him, but for most of the time he wanted to be rid of her, and in this he had help from an unexpected quarter. Lady Melbourne had been appalled by what she considered the brash and vulgar behaviour of her daughter-in-law. Love affairs she herself had had in plenty – but prudently (see pp. 53–4). Relations with Caroline had always been fraught: she well knew her capacity for play-acting and was convinced that in the Byron affair there was little true love, only a compelling desire to create a sensation. She was also desperately anxious as to how much Caroline's scandalous behaviour might damage William's career prospects. It seemed to her, therefore, that she must do everything she could to bring the affair to an end, and her methods were characteristically oblique.

She was sixty-two, thirty-six years older than Byron, but still good-looking and of formidable charm and personality, her ability to understand and manage men as consummate as ever. She decided, then, that she must establish a relationship with Byron – not romantic, certainly not sexual but kindly, good-humoured and infinitely understanding. She knew well how to manage a shy, maladroit young man with genius but no self-confidence; there would be no tears or scenes or pleas to his better nature, only intimate talk and gentle prompting. And, of course, Byron found this irresistible. He was put at his ease at once and poured out his torments and troubles to her uninhibitedly. Pointless for him to pose with her as the heroic Childe Harold; she would see through all pretence. With her the mask could be dropped and he could be himself – weak, sensual and bewildered – and she would never be shocked and never fail to understand and to soothe. Later he was to say of her: 'The best friend I ever had in my life. The cleverest of women, if she had been a few years younger what a fool she would have made of me, had she thought it worth her while.'

Lady Melbourne, no doubt, was flattered that she had conquered so completely the great literary lion of the day but, cool and level-headed as always, she never lost sight of her main objective, which was to wean him away from Caroline, and this she did with great deftness – nothing forceful or direct, but by artful humour and insidious mockery Caroline was made to look ridiculous and, by implication, Byron, too, if he persisted with her.

Such methods had their effect and at times Byron was desperate to end the affair. 'This dream, this delirium of two months must pass away,' he wrote to Caroline; but she was not ready to let him go. She still imagined him as the great love of her life and still had dreams of an elopement, concocting all sorts of madcap ploys to keep him. The most dramatic of these occurred when, after a blazing row with her father-in-law at Melbourne House, she ran away into the night with the intention, it later transpired, of pawning her jewellery and making for Portsmouth where she would set sail for some far-distant land. However, before this could happen she was run to ground in a surgeon's house in Kensington where she had been given refuge after telling a tale of piteous woe. After that her family became seriously concerned for her sanity and wanted to remove her a long way from London and possible contact with Byron. The Bessborough estate in Ireland seemed suitable. At first Caroline flatly refused to go, saying she could not possibly risk the journey as she was pregnant; but when this proved a fantasy she was finally persuaded.

Meanwhile, Byron had fallen under the spell of that predatory siren Lady Oxford, who had taken him under her wing and was harbouring him at her country house. His feelings for Caroline continued to fluctuate. Never was his duplicity and weakness of will so evident. At one moment he was writing to her passionately: 'I again promise to vow, that no other, in word or deed, shall ever hold the place in my affection which is, and shall be, most sacred to you till I am nothing.'

But at the same moment he was telling Lady Melbourne that he was having nothing more to do with Caroline and that 'it is necessary to write all manner of absurdities to keep her quiet'. Soon afterwards he wrote to Caroline: 'I love another . . . my opinion of you is entirely altered, and if I had wanted anything to confirm me, your . . . levities, your caprices and the mean subterfuges you have lately made use of while madly gay – of writing to me as if otherwise, would entirely have opened my eyes. I am no longer your lover.'

As a result of this letter Caroline was plunged into depression and, while in Dublin, made a suicide attempt, saying she was dying of a broken heart and had no wish to live longer. Soon afterwards she was brought back to England where her behaviour became ever more unbalanced.[3] At times she still yearned for Byron, writing him passionate letters declaring her undying love. Then for a time she decided they must separate for ever and wrote demanding the return of all her letters and presents, and when these did not come she organized a fantastic outdoor extravaganza in the country to show the world that their love affair was at an end and to reveal Byron's heartlessness and infidelity. For this a local band was engaged as also was a chorus of village maidens, decked out in virgin white, who sang and danced while an effigy of Byron was burned and a small page recited an incantation composed by Caroline for the occasion. The only audience for this was a small crowd of bemused rustics, but word of it spread abroad and Caroline's sanity was increasingly called into question.

An even greater public scandal occurred soon afterwards at a ball given by Lady Heathcote, Caroline encountered Byron and after some waspish exchanges seized a knife and made another suicide attempt. The knife was wrested from her but not before she had cut herself and stained her clothes with blood. She was taken back to Melbourne House, where she received scant sympathy from her mother-in-law, who had no illusions that it had all been play-acting: 'I could not have believed it possible', she wrote later, 'for anyone to carry absurdity to such a length. I call it so for I am convinced she knows perfectly well what she is about all the time.' In spite of these exhibitions and histrionics, however, Byron and Caroline could not entirely rid themselves of each other. Byron was always vulnerable to her frailty and helplessness, while Caroline was for ever haunted by 'that beautiful pale face'. In between declaring their mutual hatred and vowing never to meet again they continued to correspond. On one occasion Caroline managed to get into Byron's rooms when he was not there and scrawled across an open book the words 'Remember me', which provoked from Byron his most bitter excoriation:

> Remember thee! remember thee!
> Till Lethe quench life's burning stream
> Remorse and shame shall cling to thee
> And haunt thee like a feverish dream!
>
> Remember thee! Aye, doubt it not,
> Thy husband too shall think of thee,
> By neither shalt thou be forgot,
> Thou false to him, thou fiend to me!

And yet the affair lingered on. During this time Byron's life was becoming desperate. He had been unable to sell Newstead Abbey, and his debts were becoming ever more pressing. At the same time his health was failing as his way of life became more dissolute, and his popular glamour, too, was dwindling. He was no longer the idol he had once been. People had been shocked by his treatment of Caroline and deeply disturbed by rumours of his private life. Young women who had once swooned at the sight of him now drew away their skirts from the ground on which he had trodden. His affair with Lady Oxford had come to an abrupt end when she went abroad with her husband without a word of farewell. And then came his involvement with his half-sister, Augusta Leigh. To the other complexities of his sex life came a deep and physical love for his nearest living relative.

During Byron's affair with Lady Oxford Caroline had been agitated and desperate to know what was going on and had corresponded distractedly with both parties; but during his relationship with Augusta, perhaps because she could not believe it possible, she was comparatively restrained. Yet she still wrote him emotional and demanding letters, and Byron wrote to her while at the same time swearing to his friends that he was having no contact with her. To Lady Melbourne he wrote: 'All that bolts, bars and silence can do to keep her away are done daily and hourly.' And again: 'I beg to be spared from meeting her until we be chained together in Dante's Inferno.' Still he could not bring himself to break with her completely. Usually they only met on public occasions, but they did have one last meeting together when Byron poured out to her all the details of his seamy sex life. This was certainly meant to hurt her and shock her but it also had the effect of killing her love. In her diary she wrote: 'He told me things I cannot repeat and all my attachment went.' But, of course, she did repeat some of them, as Byron must surely have known she would, and as more and more rumours of his private life were spread abroad those closest to him became convinced that his only salvation lay in marriage. Reluctantly, Byron himself came to agree with them.

Byron's attitude to marriage was unromantic in the extreme. Money was the main consideration; his bride must have plenty of it. Also she must be demure and virtuous, not, it might be supposed, because he had any great regard for these qualities but because it gave him satisfaction to mock them and defile them. As for looks, these were of no great matter. The lady should be 'quite pretty enough to be loved by her husband without being so glaringly beautiful as to attract too many rivals'. Nor did he look for romance; mutual esteem and confidence, he wrote, were of more importance. Impossible to believe that these were the thoughts of the creator of Childe Harold.

In casting around for a lady who might fulfil these requirements his eyes were directed towards a niece of Lady Melbourne – Annabella Milbanke. She seemed to fit the role ideally. She was certainly rich and, having been brought up in the country, she was unsophisticated and unfashionable with a strong distaste for the social scene. She was also chaste and demure. A more unlikely bride for Byron it is impossible to imagine. The two could hardly have been more different – and yet they were drawn towards each other. Byron by Annabella's virtue and godliness, which he sought to debase; Annabella by Byron's evil ways, which she sought to reform.

It was never possible that such a marriage could survive. The wonder is that it lasted as long as it did. Annabella was a woman of strong character, but life with Byron was more than any wife could bear. At the end of a year she sued for a legal separation for which there were ample grounds including homosexuality and incest, but the only one mentioned in the Deed of Separation was 'that he had acted in a most foul manner upon the person of his wife'. Exactly how was not specified.

Byron had no option but to agree to this and immediately afterwards he left England for ever. For a time he found consolation in Genoa with an Italian countess who loved him passionately, but he left her to become infatuated with a Greek youth of fifteen who treated him with the scorn and indifference he had shown to his female lovers. In 1824 he set out to achieve what he had always craved, military glory and fame as a man of action. The idea of striking a blow for Greek independence from the Turks appealed to him irresistibly. But by then his body had become a wreck and on the way to Greece he contracted marsh fever from which he died, at the age of thirty-six.

At the time of Byron's marriage to Annabella there was great anxiety as to how Caroline would take the news of it. Tears and tantrums were expected; but these did not come. Instead she wrote an equable and apparently guileless letter of congratulations and made no attempt to undermine the marriage or pour scorn on it. And later, when word was going round that it was breaking up, she urged reconciliation on both parties. At first her sympathies were with

Byron. She warned him of the scurrilous reports about him that were being circulated and told him to deny everything. She also gave him a pledge:

> If letter or report or ought else has been malignantly placed in the hands of your wife to ruin you, I am ready to swear that I did it for the purpose of deceiving her. There is nothing, however base it may appear, that I would not do to save you and yours.

Later, however, when Byron failed to respond she found herself being drawn towards Annabella. Both women had been abused and betrayed by Byron, and, although still not completely free from his spell, were seeking revenge on him. And both of them had dark secrets, which it was in their power to reveal. Caroline wrote to Annabella: 'I will tell you that which if you merely menace him with the knowledge shall make him tremble.' Finally, then, Caroline did have some part in the ending of Byron's marriage, although her love for him was still not dead.

There was some irony in the fact that at the same time as Byron's marriage was foundering, the first steps were being taken towards a legal separation between Caroline and William. Throughout Caroline's follies and deviations William had been endlessly patient and considerate. He avoided all scenes and would not listen to the advice of his family that he should take her to task and separate from her. For Byron he had a strong dislike, but it never occurred to him to confront him or 'demand satisfaction'. It seems that the only occasion on which he felt serious anger towards him was when he was said to have treated Caroline cruelly. It has to be questioned, however, whether his attitude, magnanimous though it might be, was the most fitting. It could have been that a more forceful hand would have brought Caroline to her senses; and it seems that Caroline herself was aware of this. 'He cared nothing for my morals,' she wrote. 'I might flirt or go abroad with whatsoever men I pleased. He was privy to my affair with Lord Byron and laughed at it.' She wanted him to be furious about it, not amused.

But in time William's forbearance came under too much strain. He began to find her moods and outbursts unendurable; her childish frolics no longer amused him and her behaviour in public was a grave embarrassment. In 1815 they visited the battlefield of Waterloo and then went on to Paris, where Caroline disported herself characteristically, Fanny Burney remarking caustically that 'she was dressed or rather not dressed so as to excite universal attention'.[4] The hero of the moment was, of course, the Duke of Wellington, and Caroline was fulsome in her attentions to him. The Iron Duke, always susceptible, was charmed by her but declared her to be 'as mad as a March hare'.

Back in England Caroline's moods were as unpredictable as ever – at one moment in a frenzy with glass and china flying in all directions, the next meek and submissive, proclaiming how in future she was going to be 'gentle, amiable and healthy'. But this was beyond her. In particular, her health continued to deteriorate as she drank more, ate less and became increasingly dependent on laudanum (a tincture of opium). The strain on William became ever greater, and his family urged him strongly to obtain a judicial separation. But from this he still held back; in spite of everything he continued to feel strongly protective towards her, and in certain moods she never failed to enchant him.

In 1816, however, she overstepped the mark and did something for which there could be no forgiveness: without a word to William she published a highly indiscreet and offensive novel. *Glenarvon* was a bitter satire of London society, regarded by some as her revenge for the way it had treated her. It was published anonymously, but the style and content left no one in doubt as to who was the author. The characters in the book, too, were unmistakable. Glenarvon, heroic but wicked, was obviously Byron, while the heroine, Calanthar – innocent, impulsive and misunderstood – was clearly Caroline. Others were also thinly disguised, such as the great hostesses Lady Holland and Lady Melbourne, who were held up to ridicule and contempt. From a literary point of view the book was worthless, but, providing as it did a peephole into the ways of the aristocracy, it was assured of wide sales, and edition after edition were sold out. Inevitably many enemies were made, and from then on Caroline was considered by society to be beyond the pale. Hardest hit of all was William. That his wife should write such a brazen and vulgar book left him devastated, and that he was unaware that she had done it made him look foolish. The arguments for a legal separation became overwhelming: it was borne in on him that if he did not seek one he would be thought to be condoning what his wife had written.

And so a Deed of Separation was drawn up, and the family was assembled for the signing; then, at the last moment, William relented. He had been caught alone with Caroline and she had put on one of her piteous, defenceless acts, and once again his heart had melted. 'Caroline,' he had told her, 'we will stand and fall together.' Byron, too, had found, Caroline was 'at her most dangerous when humblest'. Once more, then, William tried to humour her, to cope with her moods and keep her on the rails. He encouraged her to keep writing and helped her with two further novels, but as these were discreet and inoffensive they attracted little attention, and Caroline sought fame in other fields.

For a time she found solace as an intellectual and surrounded herself with *bien pensants*, including William Blake, the poet, and William Godwin, a fashionable left-wing philosopher of no great profundity who, like others of his ilk, was not averse to being taken up by a high-born lady. But Caroline was no scholar. She was content to listen to them briefly but preferred discoursing to them. There on her sofa she would lie, swathed in becoming folds of muslin and surrounded by souvenirs of Lord Byron, talking by the hour of the great people she had known and the ardours and endurances of her life of passion.[5]

But she soon wearied of her listeners. They were of a different class and she found their manners unattractive. 'These sort of people', she said, 'are not always agreeable, but vulgar, quaint and formal. Still I feel indebted to them, for they have one and all treated me with kindness when I was turned out.' To get back into society was her great wish, but after *Glenarvon* and the scene at Lady Heathcote's ball this was impossible.

Caroline was also to find diversion in politics. In 1819 her brother-in-law, George Lamb, sought election to Parliament in that most democratic of boroughs, Westminster, where years before her aunt, Georgiana, Duchess of Devonshire, had gained notoriety by her uninhibited support of Charles James Fox, bestowing kisses on butchers and bakers and anyone else with a vote. Now Caroline decided to take a leaf out of her book and threw herself into the fray with all her usual abandon. Braving abuse and missiles, she plunged into the murkiest taverns, dancing and drinking with the electors. 'What else she did', commented Princess Lieven,[6] darkly, 'is shrouded in mystery.' How much her activities contributed to George Lamb's victory cannot be estimated, but it should be noted that in the election the following year, in which she took no part, he was defeated.

It was Caroline's tragedy that not one of the roles she adopted was she able to sustain. They did not satisfy her for long, and after brilliant beginnings they faded out. This was especially the case in the part she most coveted, that of romantic heroine. Like another enchantress a hundred and fifty years later she aspired to be a Queen of Hearts. To sustain her morale love affairs were of the essence, and these she had with all and sundry. The most prominent was with an aspiring young man of letters, Edward Bulwer Lytton – emotional, naive and half her age. Predictably it ended in tears and she had to console herself with her doctor and her son's tutor, a gentle diffident academic who in taking the post had little idea of the storms and scenes he would encounter.

As might be expected, the death of Byron caused an emotional upset. She had had no correspondence with him for eight years, but on hearing the news she collapsed in a state of shock and took to her bed for two months. Subsequently she sought to find out what had been his last words, but these were not of her – only of his wife and daughter and the Greek youth who was spurning his love. She also had an opportunity of seeing his memoirs before they were burned, but in these she was only mentioned caustically: 'Caroline possessed an infinite vivacity of mind and an imagination heated by reading novels which made her fancy herself a heroine of romance and led her to all sorts of eccentricities.' There is a story that, out riding one day, she encountered by chance Byron's funeral cortège on its way to his ancestral home and this, too, disturbed her deeply.

As all Caroline's attempts to find happiness and fulfilment came to nothing her life became increasingly wayward and disordered. She gave up regular meals and had trays of food left about the house for her to nibble at when she felt inclined. Her bedroom was a shambles of odd bits and pieces – an altar cross, a crucifix, a bottle of brandy and plates of uneaten food. And she was still prone to the wildest eccentricities – dressing up as a page boy in silver-lined jacket and scarlet pantaloons and having herself borne into the dining-room (naked, according to some accounts) on an immense silver salver. She did whatever she felt like doing at whatever time of day or night. When he was with her William did what he could to soothe her and control her, but it was becoming too much for him; his patience was exhausted and he was becoming totally exasperated

He had much else to bear at that time. Apart from Caroline's lunatic ways he was being forced to the conclusion that his dearly loved son, Augustus, was not going to change and would always have mental problems. There was also the death of his much-loved mother and the relapse of his father into a condition that was seldom more than an alcoholic haze. His great comfort came from his sister, Emily, who continued to urge him to separate from Caroline, and to this, eventually, after twenty years of married torment, he was persuaded to agree. But even then he dragged his heels and left all the arrangements to Emily while he took himself off abroad. The details were not settled without acrimony. There was disagreement about the financial terms, and at one stage Caroline made wild, outrageous accusations against William – that he had kept her short of money, had corrupted her innocence and had frequently used violence against her. Matters were made worse by the intervention of Caroline's brother, William Ponsonby (described by Emily as 'an ass and a jack-anapes'), who wrote William a foolish letter in which he abused him and accused him of marrying Caroline only for reasons of social prestige.

For a time Caroline held out doggedly against a formal Deed of Separation but was worn down in the end by Emily, who was quite ready, as she put it, 'to bully the bully'. The Deed required Caroline to leave Brocket (the Melbournes' country home), which eventually she did but not without drama. 'Shall I go abroad?' she wrote to a friend. 'Shall I throw myself upon those who no longer want me or shall I live a good sort of half kind of life in some cheap street a little way off the City Road, Shoreditch, Camberwell or upon the top of a shop – or shall I give lectures to little children, and keep a seminary and thus earn my bread?' In the event none of these fates overcame her but, to the immense relief of the Lamb family, she took herself off to Paris where they hoped she would be out of reach of William, who, they feared, was still wobbling and inclined to take her back.

On the way to France she had a particularly rough crossing, which caused Emily to express the hope that 'she had been so sick as to feel little anxiety to cross the water again directly'. She was nevertheless back in England after two months, complaining bitterly about the misery of her plight, and, as always, this did not fall on deaf ears. Once again William felt he could not forsake her and allowed her to return to Brocket, which appalled his brothers and sister, especially when he started visiting her there. By then, however, a comparative calm had descended on Caroline. She had become less fretful and riotous, no longer the angry, spoiled child forever seeking the limelight. And at the same time her frenzied vitality began to ebb, as all she sought was rest and peace. She was still haunted by memories of Byron, who would always be the romantic hero of her dreams, but more and more it was William who occupied her thoughts: William who had always been more of a father than a husband to her but who had always stood by her and tried to keep her steady. 'My husband', she wrote, 'has been to me as a guardian and I love him most dearly.'

In 1827 at the age of forty-two Caroline became seriously ill with dropsy, and perhaps other illnesses, too, which doctors at that time could not diagnose. As a result her body swelled grotesquely and she was in great pain. She was in no doubt that her hour had come. In this extremity there appeared a new Caroline: gone was the egotism and hysteria and in its place came calmness, acceptance, consideration for others and courage. She seemed overcome with guilt at the way she had wasted her life and the suffering she had caused, particularly to William; her great wish now was to make amends and behave as he would wish her to.

At that time William had just accepted his first major political appointment – as Chief Secretary for Ireland – a demanding post that required all his attention, and Caroline was intent that he should not be distracted by cares on her behalf. Her attitude, so different from before, amazed those around her. Her doctor wrote to William in Ireland: 'Her conduct has been very amiable, indeed her behaviour of late has altered very much in every respect for the better. She appears convinced she cannot ultimately recover, but with feelings of perfect resignation she does not mind to die.' To her sister-in-law, Lady Duncannon, Caroline wrote: 'I consider my painful illness as a great blessing. I feel returned to my God and my duty and my dearest husband; and my heart which was so proud and insensible is quite overcome with the great kindness I received. I have brought myself to be quite another person and broken that hard spell which prevented me saying my prayers.'

The reality of Caroline's condition could not long be kept from William, but he was totally immersed in his responsibilities in Ireland and could not easily get away. His letters, however, were full of love and care:

> My heart is broken that I cannot come over directly; but your brother, to whom I have written, will explain to you the difficult situation in which I am placed . . . How unfortunate and melancholy that you should be so ill now and that it should be at a time when I, who have had so many years of idleness, am so fixed and held down by circumstances.

Soon afterwards Caroline's condition became critical and it was clear she would not live much longer. Then at last she pleaded: 'Send for William. He is the only person who has never failed me.' And he did not fail her now. He came from Ireland immediately and was with her a few days later when she died peacefully and without drama.

Just as in her last years there had been a transformation in Caroline, so, too, was there in William. As she declined he burgeoned. With his accession to office he took on a new stature, and this continued to grow. No longer was he the compliant, cuckolded husband, the ineffective, dithering politician, but a force to be reckoned with. Marriage had been a daunting ordeal for him, yet he had come through bloodied but unbowed, buoyant and unembittered. For the time being it was to be uphill all the way: Home Secretary, Prime Minister and the much loved and trusted mentor of the newly enthroned Queen Victoria. But the memory of Caroline haunted him always. 'In spite of everything,' he wrote in later years, 'she was more to me than anyone ever was or ever will be.' And at the mention of her name tears would fill his eyes.

Notes

1. Her sister, Louisa, was married to Lord Liverpool, the long-serving Prime Minister. (See p. 28.)

2. Dressing up as a boy became an obsession with Caroline which lasted into middle age. It may have derived from a deep desire to have been a boy and been one of the causes of her disturbances.

3. One of her ploys was to send Byron a lock of her pubic hair. He, for his part, sent her a lock of hair from Lady Oxford's head.

4. Courtier and novelist.

5. *The Young Melbourne* by Lord David Cecil.

6. See Chapter 5, note 1.

4

FROM JULIA PEEL TO CATHERINE AND HARRIET ABERDEEN

Certainly one of the most stupid persons I ever met with. – Lord Aberdeen after his first meeting with his second wife

You must be head of the most moral and religious government the country has ever had. – Advice of Lady Russell to her husband

JULIA PEEL

Julia Lady Peel was one of the great beauties of her time, a beauty commemorated in two famous portraits by Sir Henry Lawrence. She came from a military family and her father, General Sir John Floyd, served for some years in India, where she was born.

Her husband, Sir Robert Peel, was the dominant figure in politics for many years, with an extraordinary record of achievement including the establishment of the Metropolitan Police, the abolition of over two hundred death penalties, Catholic Emancipation and the repeal of the Corn Laws. He was once described as 'the best man of business who was ever Prime Minister'. He was of a different background from his wife, being the son of a very rich Lancashire cotton-spinner, and throughout his life, in spite of having been at Harrow and Oxford, he retained a slight Lancashire accent. He had a public reputation for being cold and aloof, but this was due to political caution, rather than being in his nature, which was warm-hearted and forthcoming with a fondness for broad Lancashire jokes – rather too broad for some of his listeners.

To Julia politics were a closed book. She never professed to understand them and never attempted to. She found plenty to occupy herself in running two stately homes, one at Tamworth in Staffordshire and another in Whitehall Gardens in London, as well as bringing up seven children.

In 1850 she was suddenly left a widow when her husband died as a result of a riding accident, a death that caused widespread grief among all classes of people. Julia herself was inconsolable. 'He was the light of my life,' she wrote, 'my brightest joy and pride.' She died nine years later.

FRANCES RUSSELL

Lady John Russell (née Frances Elliot) was the daughter of the second Earl of Minto, a Whig politician of some eminence. She was one of a family of ten and had an idyllically happy childhood in the glorious countryside surrounding Minto House in Roxburghshire. Lady Fanny, as she was known in her youth, was of great intelligence and provided herself with an admirable education from being given a free run of her father's extensive library and from listening to the talk of his many distinguished visitors.

Lord John Russell, her future husband, was a leading light of the Whig Party when she was still a child. The third son of the Duke of Bedford, he had come to prominence when he introduced the Great Reform Bill of 1832 into the House of Commons. At the age of forty-three he had married a widow who died three years later leaving him with four stepchildren and two young children of his own. In 1840 he proposed to Lady Fanny, who was taken by surprise and initially refused him. She might well have hesitated to marry a man, however eminent, nearly twice her age and with six children under his wing. However, almost at once she had second thoughts and in the following year when he proposed again she accepted.

Lady John Russell (she became Countess Russell when her husband was raised to an earl) was a political wife with a keen interest in politics and strong views of her own which she was ready to put forward and which were not necessarily in accord with those of her husband. And the advice she gave him was always of a high moral tone. When he became Prime Minister for the first time in 1846 she wrote to him from her sick-bed that he must be 'head of the most moral and religious government the country has ever had'. She had no wish to be involved in the everyday machinations of politics and never became a great political hostess, scheming and intriguing on her husband's behalf.

The Russells' marriage was entirely happy, and during the thirty-seven years it lasted she bore him three sons and one daughter. During her widowhood of twenty years she took care of grandchildren who had become orphans. To these she showed great love and took pains to imbue them with the Puritanical tenets of the Church of Scotland. But on one of them at least these had little lasting effect. Bertrand Russell was to become in time an avowed and outspoken free thinker as well as a world-famous mathematician and philosopher and dispenser of views on multifarious subjects.

Lady Russell died in 1898 at the age of eighty-three.

CATHERINE AND HARRIET ABERDEEN

Although George Gordon, fourth Earl of Aberdeen is one of the lesser-known Prime Ministers, in his lifetime he was respected and admired as much as any other contemporary statesman. The magisterial Sir Robert Peel said of him that he estimated him higher than any of the men of exceptional talent who surrounded him. And the great Duke of Wellington told him: 'You have only to give your attention to any subject, however irksome and disagreeable to you, to do it better than others.' Gladstone said of him: 'He is the only man in public life of all others whom I have loved.'

And yet his reputation today does not stand high. He is remembered mainly as the Prime Minister who allowed the country to become involved in the Crimean War, which he then conducted with little competence.

Throughout his life Aberdeen was dogged by misfortune. At the age of eleven he was left an orphan with five younger brothers and sisters, who looked on him as a father figure. During the rest of his life he was to lose two wives and four daughters, all before their time and in tragic circumstances.

Aberdeen's first wife was Catherine Hamilton, daughter of the Marquess of Abercorn. The seven years of their marriage were blissfully happy; Catherine was a woman of great beauty and character, and he never recovered from her early death, mourning her on a scale that even some Victorians found excessive.

In spite of his devotion to his wife's memory Aberdeen nevertheless felt the need to marry again, if only for the sake of the three young daughters with whom he had been left. Soon after Catherine's death her elder brother, Lord James Hamilton, also died, leaving a widow and three young children, and it seemed to Lord Hamilton's father, the Marquess, that it would be a good arrangement if Aberdeen were to marry James's widow, Harriet, and unite the two families. At first Aberdeen was reluctant. His first impression of Harriet had been unfavourable. 'Certainly', he told his brother, 'one of the most stupid persons I ever met with.' But in time the idea grew on him. He knew how much importance his father-in-law attached to it, and he was able to persuade himself that he was in love with Harriet, who was certainly in love with him. Their marriage, which occurred in 1815 (three weeks after the battle of Waterloo), was to prove stormy, however.

Harriet was a woman of moderate beauty and limited intelligence, and it was soon borne in on her that she would never occupy the same place in George's heart as Catherine had done. This caused her obsessive jealousy, which she took out on Catherine's daughters, who, she knew, were now their father's great love. George struggled to keep the peace and assure Harriet of his love for her, but she was not to be soothed and was a malevolent stepmother.

The marriage was made no easier by Harriet's refusal to have anything to do with Haddo, the Aberdeen estate in the north of Scotland. This was wild, somewhat barbaric country and George himself had avoided it until he came of age, spending his entire youth in England. But he developed an affection for the place and set in motion all manner of improvements – planting trees, cultivating gardens, draining marshes and building churches and schools. In this Catherine had shared his enthusiasm and insisted on going with him on his annual visit. But nothing would induce Harriet to make the five-day journey; she preferred to enjoy bad health in the balmier air of Brighton.

Although Aberdeen's second marriage was often under stress, it was not an entire failure as it produced four sons and one daughter. It was to last for sixteen years but, as so often in Aberdeen's life, was stricken with tragedy. Between 1822 and 1829 all three of Catherine's daughters fell victim to tuberculosis. Four years later Harriet herself died, followed soon after by her and George's daughter, also called Harriet. Although she had long been a trial to him and they had been leading increasingly separate lives, George was greatly upset by her death. He was no more than forty-nine at the time, but he did not marry again.

After 1834, when he no longer had to nurse his wife and daughters through fatal diseases, which he had done devotedly, George's political career took off. In the 1841 to 1846 government of Sir Robert Peel he was Foreign Secretary, and in 1852 he became Prime Minister of a coalition government of Whigs and Peelite Conservatives. It was tragic that his ministry was overshadowed by the Crimean War for which he was much blamed, by no one more than himself. He died six years later.

5

EMILY PALMERSTON

Head held high, always smart and sparkling and looking so well in her diamonds. – Contemporary description of Lady Palmerston

You mustn't deceive yourself about it. If you do this you must take the consequences. – Warning from Lord Melbourne to his sister Emily when she was about to marry Lord Palmerston

Lady Palmerston was one of the greatest of political hostesses. The sister of one Prime Minister, the wife of another and the close confidante of both, she had as much political influence as any woman of her time.

Emily Mary Lamb was born in 1787, the sister of William Lamb (see p. 35). Her father, Peniston, first Lord Melbourne, was a man of great wealth and some social standing but not of aristocratic descent. His fortune derived from his father and grandfather, who had been shrewd and acquisitive lawyers from the Midlands. As well as great wealth, he had also inherited from them a country estate, Brocket Hall, a baronetcy and a seat in Parliament. However, their industry and acumen was not passed down to him, and his life had been one of indolence and dissipation. Avaricious mistresses and unbridled gambling took much of his time and money, and although a Member of Parliament for forty years he was only known to have spoken on one occasion.

Very different from this ineffective wastrel was his wife, Elizabeth Milbank, the daughter of a Yorkshire landowner and a lady of strong character and steely determination. Married to Peniston at the age of nineteen, she had lost no time in furthering her ambitions – to rise in the social hierarchy and become one of London's leading hostesses. A fashionable house in Piccadilly was acquired from the Holland family and redecorated and refurbished at prodigious expense. Her entertainments there were lavish and perfectly managed, and it was not long before she had made a great impression on London society. This was due in part to the scale of her hospitality and in part to her undoubted beauty and charm, but more especially to her intelligence and personality and her ability, which she developed to a fine art, to manipulate people, particularly (but not solely) men; most men, blithely unaware that they were being beguiled, found her soothing and sympathetic. She was also completely discreet, was never shocked and never threw tantrums – the perfect confidante. Nor was she chaste, although she understood and observed the rules of the Whig aristocracy scrupulously. In the course of her life she was to have many lovers and their identity was no secret, but they were never openly flaunted. Her choice of lovers tended to be dispassionate and calculating, the main consideration always being what they might be able to do for her. And so it was that a year after her marriage her husband was granted an Irish barony, in due course raised to a viscountcy and in time to an English peerage – not bad going for a life almost entirely devoid of achievement.

Elizabeth was equally ambitious for her children. They were to have every advantage and incentive to rise in the world. Essentially, she was a managing and possessive mother, but she had the wisdom not to let this show, and she believed that it was in the children's best interests to be given as much latitude as possible. And so at Brocket Hall they were allowed to run wild, and some visitors were shocked by their unrestrained talk and boisterous behaviour. 'It is like getting among savages,' one once remarked. As a family they were happy and close-knit, and this in spite of the fact that their paternity was diverse. Only the eldest son, Peniston, was known to be the son of Lord Melbourne. Of the others, William, the future Prime Minister, was widely held to be the son of Lord Egremont, Lady Melbourne's foremost lover; George was thought to be the son of the Prince Regent (the future George IV), and of the others, including Emily, there were various candidates, which did not, according to general opinion, number Lord Melbourne among them.

And so Emily, the only surviving daughter, was brought up in an atmosphere of freedom and exuberance and the enjoyment of the good things in life – riding, fishing, dancing, games and lively company. For her brothers there was an interruption to this when they were sent away to boarding-school, but there was never any question of this for Emily. Like other young ladies of that time she was kept at home and put in the charge of governesses, who did not overburden her with learning – a little French, perhaps, some religious knowledge, good manners and deportment. Of greater importance was what she learned for herself in her father's library and from the contact she had with their eminent visitors. An idyllic existence certainly, but it was to come to an end when at the age of seventeen she was married to a neighbouring nobleman, Lord Cowper. Lord Cowper, like Lord Melbourne, was very rich, unambitious and compliant and, although no fool, was said to be 'of slow pronunciation and slow of gait and pace'. He was not to be the great love of Emily's life, but they were married contentedly for thirty-four years and she bore him three children.

Like her mother before her Emily lost no time in establishing herself as a leading political hostess both at Pansanger Hall, the Cowper country home, and in a London house off Hanover Square. In some ways she resembled her mother – as manipulative and politically minded, but more spontaneous, warmer and less predatory. Nevertheless she had a sharp tongue and gossiped maliciously, and there were those who questioned her good nature. Her brother William, who loved her dearly, used to refer to her as 'that little devil Emily'.

Lord Cowper, like Emily, had been brought up a Whig, and their houses were often a gathering place for Whig politicians, but Emily did not confine herself to these; she cast her net wide and, according to one observer, her parties were 'full to the brim of vice and agreeableness, foreigners and roués'. But what fascinated her was the political scene, where she could intrigue and bring into play her undoubted beauty and charm. At all times she had many interests at heart, especially those of her own family, and the one that predominated was the advancement of the political career of William. He was recognized as being the cleverest and great things were expected of him, but for many years his political career failed to take off. He had been brought up a Whig, but at the beginning of the nineteenth century the party was in disarray, some members supporting William Pitt in the war against Napoleon, others in opposition. William's loyalty was always to that most charismatic of Whig leaders Charles James Fox, and when he died in 1806, a year after William entered Parliament, William was left adrift, languishing in the political wilderness for more than twenty years. During this time he did not cut an impressive figure: he made no great mark in Parliament, failed to take a firm line on most issues and had all the appearance of a political dilettante. His attitude appeared to be seen most clearly when at one time he stood down from re-election, announcing that 'it did not suit my views to run the slightest risk of failure'.

Emily was driven to distraction by his lassitude and irresolution. She was convinced he had it in him to achieve greatness and was determined to put some backbone into him. 'William is so lazy and undecided,' she wrote to their brother Frederick. And again: 'William wants energy so much and somebody at his back to push him.' She was particularly vexed by his indecisiveness and tendency to sit on the fence. 'William's speech in Parliament', she wrote, 'was twaddling and foolish, speaking on one side and voting on the other . . . such milk and water. I wish he would join one side or the other.'

In the years after her marriage Emily's status as a political hostess climbed steadily, and this was marked by her election to the committee of London's most exclusive club. Almack's was ruled imperiously by a body of eminent ladies who saw to it that membership was confined to the greatest and best and that its strict rules were obeyed meticulously. It was known as 'the ambition and despair of the middle classes'. It was described by a contemporary writer as 'That most distinguished and despotic conclave, composed of their Mightinesses the Ladies Patronesses of the balls at Almack's, the rulers of fashion, the arbiters of taste, the leaders of tone and makers of manners whose sovereign sway over the world of London has long been established on the firmest basis, whose decrees are laws and from whose judgement there is no appeal.'

Increasingly Emily became involved in the in-fighting of politics: the jock-eying for places, the allaying of ill will, the forming of alliances and the furthering of careers. Here, as always, William was her prime concern and she felt it her duty to direct sharp criticisms at him, sometimes of a personal nature. 'William looks cheerful and gay', she wrote, 'but is much too fat.' She also took a strong line in his tempestuous matrimonial affairs. She had no love for the wayward Caroline Lamb and, like all her family, strongly urged William to separate from her. 'He is an ass', she wrote, 'for having borne her as he has done.' She always spoke with the utmost candour as she knew that nothing she said would diminish his love for her. No doubt he heeded her with what Charles Greville, the diarist, described as 'his lazy, listening, silent humour'.

Other family troubles, too, claimed Emily's attention. In 1818 her mother died. The circumstances of her death were tragic – wracked with mortal illness, in great pain, grossly overweight and heavily doped – a ghastly end for one who had been at the pinnacle of the social scene and had entranced the highest in the land. Her relationship with her husband had always been ambiguous, but after her death he went to pieces completely, making little attempt to remain sober. Emily wrote of him in despair: 'However little he drinks he contrives somehow or other to be drunkish . . . It must be the fog which makes him so.' He was to linger on for another ten years.

Like her mother Emily saw no need to be chaste. The Victorian age had not yet arrived. With her charm and beauty and a complaisant husband she took her opportunities as they came. But always there was one lover who prevailed over all others. When she first came to know Henry John Temple, third Viscount Palmerston, he had already embarked on his extraordinary political career. Elected to Parliament at the age of twenty-three (possible because his was an Irish peerage), he was almost immediately offered the post of Chancellor of the Exchequer, which he had the good sense to refuse as being at that time beyond his capacity. However, soon afterwards he did accept the post of Secretary at War – no mean responsibility during the war against Napoleon. At that time he was a Tory but later become a 'Canningite' and then a Whig; and in Lord Grey's government of 1830 he was appointed Foreign Secretary, a post which he was to make his own, with a few breaks, for sixteen years.

Besides being a pre-eminent politician Palmerston also had a formidable reputation for gallantry. Although Emily was his main love he did not confine his attentions to her; his lovers included at least two other patronesses of Almack's, one of whom was the notorious Princess Lieven.[1] His prowess was awe-inspiring; no woman was safe from him. Once on a visit to Windsor Castle he invaded the bedroom of one of the Queen's ladies-in-waiting, who fled screaming to take refuge with Baron Stockmar, the virtuous and high-minded political adviser of Prince Albert. Not for nothing had Palmerston acquired the sobriquet 'Prince Cupid'.

In 1837 Lord Cowper died. He had been a gentle, generous, uncomplaining husband, who had long since realized that he could not keep pace with his wife and had let her have her head. His death meant that Emily and Palmerston were at last free to marry, and Palmerston lost no time in pressing his suit. But Emily hesitated; she felt, with some reason, that marriage would expose them to ridicule. He was then fifty-five and she fifty-two, and the sight of the old roué and his mistress of thirty years coming to the altar might well have caused tongues to wag. And her children were opposed to the idea partly because of Palmerston's libidinous ways and partly because of his financial reputation, which was unsound; he had a reasonably large income but was a heavy spender and reckless gambler and was often in debt. Also opposed to the marriage, rather surprisingly, was Emily's brother William, now Lord Melbourne. He and Palmerston had much in common: they had both had a Whig upbringing, had the same sexual mores and the same bluff, bantering, aristocratic way of speaking. In 1837 they were also political colleagues in the same government, but they were never close friends. Perhaps they were too strong individualists. In any case, William felt impelled to give Emily a solemn warning: 'You mustn't deceive yourself about it. If you do this you must take the consequences.'

But it was certain that Emily would eventually succumb. Life as a widow would not have suited her. Some twenty years earlier her mother, that hard-headed realist, had roused herself on her deathbed to urge Emily to be true not to her husband but to her first and most distinguished admirer, Lord Palmerston. And so, after keeping him waiting for two years, she consented, and they were married in some style in St George's, Hanover Square, as befitted the Foreign Secretary and the sister of the Prime Minister. As expected it caused some mirth – even the demure young Queen Victoria showed some amusement – but most people were delighted by it. The general attitude was summed up by one of the *grandes dames* of the day, Lady Holland, who said 'it is the union of the best-tempered persons in the world'.

Emily's marriage to Palmerston was to be a supremely happy one. The role of wife to the country's most eminent statesman suited her perfectly and she entered into it with zest. She would certainly have known, from her brother William among others, what a contentious figure Palmerston was and that as his wife she would often find herself at the centre of storms. But she was prepared for this and was resolved that in public at least 'he is always right in everything he does'. In private, however, she was ready with advice and even reproof, telling him that there was 'too much knight errantry in his foreign policy' and that he ought to be more tactful with Queen Victoria and flatter her a little. And she was the one person to whom he was prepared to listen. Usually advice flowed over his head, but not when it came from her.

It might have been expected when they married that Palmerston at the age of fifty-five would be approaching the end of his political career, but more than twenty years of public life, most of it in office, lay ahead of him, and it became no less turbulent. In theory he was a Whig, but in reality he was a loose cannon who went his own way with little reference to party colleagues, even the Prime

Minister. A supreme individualist, some of his actions were dangerously irresponsible, and sometimes caused violent indignation in all political circles, but such were his power and prestige that he usually managed to weather the storm.

In 1855, when he was seventy-one, Palmerston became Prime Minister. It was at the time of the Crimean War when operations were going badly, and the general feeling was that only Palmerston had enough belligerence and vigour to wage the war successfully. What few people expected (or wanted) was that he would remain Prime Minister with one short break until his death ten years later. With so many people gunning for him this was an extraordinary feat. The Conservatives, led by Disraeli, were always in full hue; Queen Victoria and some of the old Whigs still looked on him as a dangerous adventurer; and even in his own Cabinet there were mutterings of discontent, notably from his latest ally William Gladstone.

That Palmerston was able to hold on to office for so long must in large measure have been due to Emily. Emily had been a political hostess since she was eighteen, but it was not until she married Palmerston that she really came into her own and acquired serious influence. For twenty-five years she was to dedicate herself entirely to her husband's interests – rallying support behind the scenes, mending broken fences and defending his every action, even the most outrageous. Every Saturday evening during the season, first at Carlton Terrace and later at Cambridge House in Piccadilly, she held receptions to which invitations were eagerly sought. For it was there that leading politicians of both parties would be gathered, scheming and propounding and testing the waters. Nowhere else could the political temperature be discerned so readily.[2] Foreigners were amazed at the way friend and foe were brought together. A French diplomat once remarked: 'What a wonderful system of society you have in England! I have not been on speaking terms with Lord Palmerston for three weeks and yet here I am on a visit to Lady Palmerston.'

Emily presided over these occasions with grace and adroitness, 'head held high, always smart and sparkling and looking so well in her diamonds', as a contemporary wrote. Everyone was made welcome and put at their ease (even sometimes gatecrashers). But they knew they were not there just for small talk and banter. From most people Emily required something – information maybe or pledges of support – and no one knew better than she how these might be elicited. Her parties were recognized as events of major political importance, and it was not unknown for parliamentary debates to be postponed if they should happen to clash. It was remarked that Lady Palmerston gave the words 'party system' a new meaning. And it was not only in London that she entertained. At Broadlands, Palmerston's country estate, she also had splendid parties attended by many statesmen from abroad; and here, too, she was a perfect hostess, with only one failing – she had no sense of time and was incorrigibly unpunctual, so much so that hungry guests sometimes despaired of ever having dinner.

And Emily had much else to do besides entertaining. She was the chatelaine not only of Broadlands but also, after her brother William's death, of Brocket Hall, and then in 1861, when Palmerston became Warden of the Cinque Ports, of Walmer Castle; and in addition there were extensive properties in Scotland and Wales. Much of the management of these she had to delegate, but she nevertheless took a close interest in them and visited them as often as she could; and whenever she did there was always a host of supplicants, tenants and staff, with entreaties and hard-luck stories, as she was well known for her kindness of heart and for being a 'soft touch'.

As they grew older the Palmerstons became more and more dependent on each other, so much so that they could not bear to be parted for even short periods. Emily was naturally delighted when Palmerston became Prime Minister, but she lamented sadly how much less she saw of him as a result. During parliamentary sittings he was hardly ever home for dinner and often as late as four or five in the morning. But their devotion to each other never wavered. In 1863, when he was seventy-nine, Palmerston found himself in the middle of a scandal, accused of improper relations or 'criminal conversations' as it was quaintly called, with a Mrs Cain. The matter gave rise to some hilarity and was treated with amused indifference by Emily, and in the divorce proceedings the case against him soon collapsed.[3]

Palmerston died in 1865 at the age of eighty-one. In the mid-Victorian age he had long been an anachronism, but he was still Prime Minister and a figure with unique personal prestige. Of his eight-one years fifty had been spent in office – nine as Prime Minister, sixteen as Foreign Secretary. As he himself had predicted, his death opened the way to all manner of new and disquieting changes.

Emily survived him by four years. Her vivacity, charm and lively interest in all that was going on remained undimmed, and in spite of the ravages of old age and the decease of old friends she remained active and high-spirited. On her death she was buried alongside her husband in Westminster Abbey.

Notes

1. Of Latvian origin, she had been brought up in the court of the mad Tsar Paul I and had then married a Russian prince who held a number of diplomatic appointments including that of ambassador in London. Here the princess, a natural intriguer, took a prying interest in all that was going on. She had a great influence on Palmerston, some thought a sinister one, and she was also a close friend of Emily. Although no great beauty, she was the mistress of several of Europe's leading statesmen and intimate with many more.

2. Eager eyes were always on the look-out for any sign that might be significant. A wag once remarked: 'One knows that there is a real crisis when Lady Palmerston forgets her rouge and Palmerston omits to dye his whiskers.'

3. Including the joke that although she was indubitably Cain was he Abel? It also caused his political opponent Disraeli to remark that on no account should the Conservatives call a General Election that year.

6

MARY ANNE DISRAELI

A striking illustration of the power the most unobtrusive of women may exercise while keeping herself strictly to a woman's sphere. – Obituary in *The Times* on Mary Anne Disraeli

If foolish and at times ridiculous, she was a splendid wife. – Society hostess on Mary Anne

A pretty little woman, a flirt and a rattle. – Disraeli's first impression of Mary Anne

Among Prime Ministers' wives there has been no success story like that of Mary Anne Disraeli. From Devon farming stock she rose to be a leading London hostess and a peeress in her own right, as well as the wife of one of England's greatest Prime Ministers. At first sight she might have seemed naive, awkward and even somewhat comic; but her appearance was misleading. She was nobody's fool and made a great success of two marriages: the first to a rich man – eccentric and morose; and the second to a man of genius – volatile, penniless and twelve years her junior.

Mary Anne was born in 1792 in the picturesque Devonshire village of Bampford Speke. Her father, John Evans, was the son of a farmer, but, like many men of Devon, had felt the call of the sea and at the age of eleven left home to join HMS *Alarm* as cabin boy to the captain, Sir John Jervis, one of the Navy's most illustrious commanders and strictest disciplinarians.[1] John Evans was a bright boy and under Jervis's tutelage rose to be a midshipman and then lieutenant. He might well have gone further and become one of the captains who served under Nelson, but in 1794 he died of malaria while in the West Indies.

John Evans's estate amounted to no more than £600 (worth some £30,000 today), so his widow, Eleanor, was left with two small children in straitened circumstances. She did have some money of her own as her family, the Vineys of Gloucester, was reasonably well off. And she may or may not have become better off when in 1810 she married a Mr Yates, variously described as a ship's surgeon and a 'master of ceremonies'. But Mary Anne's youth was one of impoverished gentility, knowing what it was to have to make ends meet and to keep up appearances. Her fortunes changed, however, when in 1815 at a ball in Clifton she met Mr Wyndham Lewis, a wealthy bachelor of thirty-four, and won his heart. Wyndham Lewis came from South Wales, where he was not only a considerable landowner but also had interests in coalmines and ironworks. The profits from these fluctuated somewhat, but never again would Mary Anne be seriously short of money, and at most times it was plentiful.

For the next twelve years her life was based in Glamorganshire where, as the wife of an eminent county figure, she entertained extensively and was involved in various charitable works. In 1820 her activities were further extended when her husband stood for Parliament in Cardiff, and she took part in his election campaign with great verve and success. In the course of her life she fought many more such battles, in which she never failed to make her mark and was only once on the losing side.

Wyndham Lewis did not remain long as Member for Cardiff. The seat was at the disposal of the Marquess of Bute, who owned most of the district, and five years later he required it for a member of his family. Lewis, however, had acquired a taste for politics and had the means to find a seat elsewhere. At the time there were still 'rotten boroughs' available to men with enough money to buy the votes of the electors. One of the most flagrant of these was Aldeburgh on the coast of Suffolk, much of which had been eroded away by the North Sea but which continued to return two Members of Parliament; and in 1827 Lewis, outbidding other contenders, became one of them. But, again, not for long, as by the Reform Bill of 1832 Aldeburgh was deprived of both its seats. Once again, then, it was necessary for Lewis to look around for another constituency, and this brought him to Maidstone, which had somehow avoided falling prey to the Reform Bill and where votes were still generally available to the highest bidder. In 1832, however, the tide was flowing strongly in favour of the Whigs, and Lewis was a Tory; and partly because of this and partly because he was having financial troubles at the time and could not disburse as much as usual he was defeated. Two years later, however, with finances restored and strenuous help from Mary Anne he was elected and remained Member for Maidstone for the rest of his life.

Lewis's election to Parliament meant that he and Mary Anne switched their main base from South Wales to London. For Mary Anne this was a welcome change. She had never felt at home in Glamorgan, the ambience of which she found very different from Devon; and, besides, she could not get on with some of her in-laws, particularly Wyndham's brother, William, an avaricious clergyman who had somehow contrived to accumulate no less than seventeen parishes, which he left in the care of curates while he devoted himself to the pleasures of the hunting field. Known in the family as 'the

Governor' he was inclined to throw his weight about, and Mary Anne found him oppressive.

In London Wyndham bought a large, opulent house at Grosvenor Gate in Park Lane, where Mary Anne soon established herself as a hostess. Her first party there was attended by some of the most illustrious figures in society, including the great Duke of Wellington, who declared it to be the best ball he had been to that Season. In the following years Mary Anne and Wyndham led a life of fashion: in London during the Season, attending a round of receptions, soirées and déjeuners; in the winter migrating with the *beau monde* to Brighton where the genial, if not very cerebral, King William IV and the prudish Queen Adelaide held court at the Pavilion, described by the diarist Greville as 'very active, vulgar and hospitable – King, Queen, princes, princesses, bastards and attendants all trotting about in every direction'. Mary Anne would have much enjoyed being part of this.

One of the advantages of a house in Park Lane was the view from its windows of the carriages in Hyde Park. Watching these was one of Mary Anne's favourite occupations, and one day her gaze alighted on a somewhat bizarre sight: a carriage occupied by an elderly lady of fashion accompanied by a young man in the most extraordinary outfit, talking and gesticulating vividly. Her curiosity was aroused and she enquired of a friend who this might be and was told that it could only be the young Benjamin Disraeli, who had made such a mark on London society by the brilliance of his talk and the eccentricity of his clothes. Mary Anne was intrigued and asked if she could be introduced to the young man, and her friend replied that nothing could be easier as he was a close friend of her husband. Mary Anne's first meeting with Disraeli was not propitious. In a letter to his sister he described her as 'a pretty little woman, a flirt and a rattle; indeed gifted with a volubility I should think unequalled and of which I can convey no idea. She told me she liked silent, melancholy men. I answered that I had no doubt of it.' And, on a later occasion, when asked by his hostess to take her into dinner he is said to have replied: 'Not that insufferable woman!'

Benjamin Disraeli came from a well-to-do Jewish family. His grandfather had made a substantial fortune out of trade, which enabled Benjamin's father, Isaac, to lead a gentlemanly life free from commerce, which was fortunate as he had a strong distaste for it, once describing it as 'the corruption of mankind'. His only interest in life was literature, and all he ever wanted was the leisure and peace to read and compile literary anthologies. His reading had made him a free thinker and he had renounced his Jewish faith. He was in fact without religious beliefs, but to be a declared atheist at that time was to incur opprobrium, so for reasons of expediency he had joined the Church of England and had had his children brought up in the Anglican faith.

At the time of his first unfriendly meeting with Mary Anne, Benjamin was striving for the success he knew his genius must one day bring him. But in this he had had setbacks. Like his father he had no head for business, and his various schemes for getting rich quickly had all ended in disaster, so that he was heavily encumbered by debt. He had had some literary success, his semi-autobiographical novels depicting high life arousing interest and some enthusiasm but not bringing much financial return. He had also achieved some social standing, his charm and wit being much appreciated, as also, in some quarters, was his flamboyant style of dress; this could be startling – canary-coloured waistcoat, green velvet trousers, lace cuffs, bright red sash often with jewelled dagger, and the whole ensemble bedecked with gold chains. This was too much for some people, but others were amused by it and thought him an 'oddity' and a sparkling entertainer who never failed to enliven their dinner parties. As a young man he was consumed with ambition to climb to the top of whatever tree he chose and had soon decided that this had to be politics. But here, too, he had had failures. He had thought that with his brilliance and éclat and undoubted gifts of oratory he could be elected to Parliament as an independent, free from party ties, but this was not how elections were won in those days when voters were less interested in oratorical brilliance than in cash hand-outs and business favours, and these Disraeli could not supply. Four times he had stood for Parliament and failed, and it seemed that his political aspirations had reached an impasse; but this was to be broken when he was taken under the wing of Mr and Mrs Wyndham Lewis.

Wyndham Lewis had become a popular and respected figure among the Tories of Maidstone. His political gifts were limited, but his pockets were full and he, and more particularly Mary Anne, spent freely. His own seat was safe for as long as he wanted it, but Maidstone returned two members; the other seat was virtually at his disposal, and in the election of 1837 (the year of Queen Victoria's accession) he nominated Disraeli as the other Tory candidate. That this was done at the instigation of Mary Anne must be certain. The coldness of their first meeting had soon thawed and her declaration that she liked 'silent, melancholy men' (the antithesis of Disraeli) was palpably untrue, probably no more than feminine provocation. It is certain that she went to some pains to cultivate his acquaintance further and became greatly impressed by him, foreseeing for him a brilliant future. These convictions were crowned with success when Wyndham and Disraeli topped the poll at Maidstone. Mary Anne was delighted at this result and from then on described Disraeli, patronizingly but affectionately, as 'our parliamentary protégé' and even 'our political pet'.

For his part Disraeli felt a great debt of gratitude to them; it was entirely their doing that he had at last achieved his life's ambition. The relationship between them grew closer and warmer; but then, suddenly, within a year, Wyndham Lewis died, and a new situation arose. He and Mary Anne had been happily married for twenty-three years; they understood each other and both their lives had been greatly enriched by their union. It is unlikely, however, that Mary Anne was inconsolable at his death – her love for him was not passionate, and he had his moods and his quirks[2] – and along with feelings of grief there may also have been a feeling of release. Certainly he left her in comfortable circumstances – a life occupancy of the London house and an assured annual income for life of some £5,000 (£250,000 by present values), and there were no conditions in the event of her remarriage. To Disraeli this must have seemed a God-given opportunity: a wealthy widow favourably disposed towards him who could give him a splendid home and political base as well as some relief from his ever more pressing financial liabilities. Later he was to admit that 'at first I was prompted by no romantic feelings and was not blind to the worldly advantages of an alliance with her'; but increasingly he was feeling greater affection for her and in time was to be deeply in love, so much so that they could joke about his earlier feelings. 'You know I married you for your money,' he told her. 'Yes,' she replied, 'but if you were to marry me again, you'd marry me for love, wouldn't you?'

It was never a disadvantage that she was twelve years older than he was, as he had always liked older women. It had been noted by a perspicacious foreign diplomat that his closest women friends were '*toutes grandmères*'. And in his youth his notions about marriage were not romantic. 'All my friends who married for love and beauty', he had once declared, 'either beat their wives or live apart from them. I never intend to marry for love which I am sure is a guarantee of infidelity.' Like many of Disraeli's aphorisms this contains much hyperbole, but it is not far from his true feelings. He loved to profess deep emotion and write flowery, amorous letters, but, as a friend noted, 'he loved without passion'. And he did not seek a wife of great beauty and wit, this was not what he required in the home; rather he looked for someone kindly and sympathetic who would be a nurse and mother to him rather than a brilliant partner. Mary Anne might have been somewhat simple and uneducated and in society sometimes a laughing stock, but otherwise she filled the bill perfectly. She was infinitely caring and supportive, she ran her household superbly, and some of her judgements were shrewd and penetrating. The more Disraeli thought of her the more he became convinced that she was the perfect wife for him.

At first after Wyndham's death he was sympathetic but restrained; but it was not long before he was showing more ardour. Only four months into Mary Anne's widowhood he was writing to her: 'You have not been a whole day absent from my thoughts.' And three months later: 'Your name is ever before me . . . the name of her who is my inspiration, my life, perhaps my despair.' Mary Anne was at first reserved in the face of these advances. It may be she was taken by surprise or was playing hard to get, but possibly she was heeding the warning of friends, for Disraeli's courtship of her had provoked much cynicism. People were amazed that someone of his sophistication could possibly consider marriage to a simple, uneducated West Country widow twelve years his senior and assumed that it could only be for her money. And, no doubt, there were those who passed these thoughts on to Mary Anne and warned her that Disraeli, although a man of great charm and brilliance, was nevertheless a penniless upstart.

Mary Anne was quite astute enough to be aware of these considerations herself and was not to be hurried, telling Disraeli that she could not consider remarrying for a year and needed time to study his character. This apparent coolness upset Disraeli, who may have divined her thoughts, and he decided to force the issue. It seems he had a somewhat stormy interview with her at Grosvenor Gate, which ended (according to him but not to her) in his being dismissed from her house for ever, and he followed this up with an angry letter in which he faced frankly the issue of money. He admitted that at first this may have been uppermost in his mind, but then gentler thoughts had prevailed and he had come to look on her as being 'amiable, tender and yet acute and gifted with no ordinary mind'. As for her fortune, it was not as great as it might be, and, in any case, as she only had a life interest in it he would not benefit from it permanently. Reaching the height of his argument he said that he would not condescend to be the minion of a princess and not all the gold of Ophir should ever lead him to the altar. Still more grandiloquently he bade her farewell:

> I will not affect to wish you happiness, for it is not in your nature to obtain it. For a few years you may flutter in some frivolous circle. But the time will come when you will sigh for any heart that could be fond, and despair of one that can be faithful. Then will be the penal hour of retribution: then you will think of me with remorse, admiration, and despair; then you will recall to your memory the passionate heart that you have forfeited, and the genius you have betrayed.

This was a bold tactic, which might have ended the affair once and for all, but in the event it proved successful, for Mary Anne capitulated at once: 'For God's sake come to me,' she wrote. 'I am ill and almost distracted. I will answer all you wish . . . I often feel the apparent impropriety of my present position . . . I am devoted to you.' And soon afterwards on 28 August 1839 they were married at St George's, Hanover Square.

At the time there were, of course, those who looked on the marriage with some levity. To the cynical it seemed impossible that Disraeli could take Mary Anne seriously. Her looks were in decline, her talk for the most part was artless prattle and she was prone to startling and embarrassing social gaffes.[3] But these left Disraeli unabashed, and nothing moved him to anger more readily than the slightest disrespect or joke at her expense; once when this happened at a country house party he left abruptly, and on another occasion when a friend ventured too far in questioning him about his feelings towards Mary Anne he replied witheringly that there was one word in the English language of which he seemed to be ignorant – gratitude.

For the thirty-three years of their marriage Disraeli and Mary Anne were to establish an entirely happy relationship. For Mary Anne her mission in life was simple: she was convinced that Disraeli would become 'one of the greatest men of the day', and it was up to her to tend him and cherish him and see to it that he was free of all domestic cares and, as far as possible, all financial worries, so that he could devote himself single-mindedly to his career. To this end she spared herself no pains; everything in the home was geared to his comfort and convenience and she attended to his every need, even to the cutting (and sometimes dyeing) of his hair.[4] In London, when Parliament was sitting, she saw to it that at whatever hour at night he came home the house was always full of light and a meal of his favourite foods was awaiting him. And when he was indisposed, which he was quite frequently, being something of a hypochondriac, she was always the most solicitous of nurses. For his part Disraeli was greatly appreciative of all her efforts and was always ready with words of praise and flattery. He never patronized or condescended and there was never any question of Mary Anne being pushed aside or treated as an encumbrance. He was at all times the most attentive of husbands and made a point of consulting her both on political matters and on his literary works. In the former Mary Anne professed herself uninterested but listened as Disraeli confided in her fully. This might have been perilous with one so forthcoming and loquacious, but his confidences were never betrayed.[5] In her husband's literary works she was much more interested. She used to refer to his books as her babies and was always ready with suggestions and criticisms as well as helping in such matters as proofreading and correspondence with publishers. The value of some of her opinions may be doubted, but they were always received with the greatest gratitude, summed up by his dedication to her of *Sybil*:

> I would inscribe this work to one whose noble spirit and gentle nature ever prompt her to sympathize with the suffering; to one whose sweet voice has often encouraged, and whose taste and judgement have ever guided its pages, the most severe of critics, but – a perfect wife.

Disraeli had hoped that once he was in Parliament his political career would immediately take off, but setbacks were still in store for him. When in 1841 a Conservative government took office under Sir Robert Peel he was not included. This was a bitter disappointment, and four years later he would lead the attack on Peel over the repeal of the Corn Laws.[6]

This caused a major split in the party, as a result of which the Conservatives would be out of office (apart from short-lived minority governments) for nearly thirty years. During most of this time the official leader was Lord Derby, but Disraeli led in the Commons, where he was the only one on equal terms with such titans as Gladstone and Palmerston. It was a hard struggle to keep the party intact and make it electable, and the brunt of this was borne by Disraeli. Among the many difficulties he confronted was the strong prejudice that still existed against him personally. Although his manner had become less exuberant and his dress less bizarre, he was still regarded by many Conservatives as a raffish outsider, a Jewish adventurer and definitely not one of them. It irked them particularly that as their leader in the Commons he was not even a landowner. This objection, however, was to some extent rectified when in 1848 he became the owner of the Buckinghamshire estate of Hughenden. The purchase of this was a gamble, as he was still heavily in debt and Mary Anne had little capital with which to help him. But in the party as well as critics he also had strong adherents who believed the Conservatives could not do without him, and they banded together to provide him with a large loan at a low rate of interest.

Hughenden was to be a delight to both Disraeli and Mary Anne; their moments of greatest peace and happiness were to be found there. Mary Anne at once undertook its refurbishment with great enthusiasm and verve if not always impeccable taste. She did, however, have a talent for gardening and landscaping, and, particularly in the extensive woodlands of the estate, she wrought great improvements. Her husband had no flair or inclination for horticulture, and she sought no help from him apart from appreciation of her efforts, which he was always ready to offer lavishly.

At Hughenden, as in London, Mary Anne's overriding concern was that Disraeli should be left free to devote himself to his career, in which, she never doubted, he would one day reach the top. But before this could happen the Conservative Party had to be saved from itself. Drastic changes were needed if it was to survive. It was no longer enough to represent only the landed interests. The Whigs were being sustained by the middle classes – industrialists, merchants and shopkeepers – and Disraeli realized that the Conservatives, too, should seek support in the fast-growing industrial cities; his belief was that this could be found among the working classes. The idea of Tory country gentlemen allying themselves with industrial workers was one that most people found astounding, but Disraeli persevered with the idea; he believed that the workers were conservative at heart and strongly patriotic. The achievement of such a task would need almost magical powers, but in the coming years he would show himself something of a sorcerer.[7]

Inevitably the strain of his labours, which were arduous and unceasing, told on his health, which was never robust, and he was liable to bouts of severe depression. It must be certain that such a burden could not have been borne without the rock-like support of Mary Anne. Not only did she take on herself all domestic responsibilities but she organized his political dinner parties, played the part of Lady of the Manor at Hughenden and accompanied him on strenuous trips abroad, somehow managing to keep pace with him despite being twelve years his senior. On occasions her sacrifices for him were heroic, as when dropping him off at the House of Commons before an important speech her finger was caught in the carriage door and in spite of excruciating pain she said nothing lest he be distracted from his speech.

She also went with him on the numerous visits to stately homes that were expected of a Tory leader. These must have been a great trial at times, as she did not fit easily into aristocratic circles, where she was regarded as something of an oddity. Generally the *beau monde* looked on her with kindly condescension. 'Dear fond woman,' wrote one great lady. 'If foolish and at times ridiculous, she was a splendid wife.' But sometimes the comments were not so kindly. 'The most extraordinary woman both in appearance and conversation,' said one, and 'Her heart is as kind as her taste is queer,' wrote another.

But in spite of her artlessness and gaucherie she was entertained in the most exalted places. In 1856 on a visit to Paris she and Disraeli were dined in state by Emperor Napoleon III. And in 1861 came the ultimate accolade when both Disraelis were invited to Windsor by Queen Victoria. This was a special honour, as the Queen was notably averse to inviting politicians with their wives, even ministers, and at the time Disraeli was in Opposition. By then, though, he had become a special favourite of the Queen. Few were more adept than he in the arts of sympathy and flattery, especially when lavishing them on older women. These had been conspicuously in evidence on the death of the Prince Consort when no one expressed sympathy or eulogized the Prince more fulsomely, and the Queen loved it, saying he was the only man who really appreciated her husband and his spotless and unequalled character. The Queen's high regard for Disraeli was soon extended to Mary Anne, for she always had a strong liking for those who were simple and direct, detesting those who were puffed up and pretentious. And so she took to Mary Anne straight away and showed her special favours on several occasions, notably when she was invited with Disraeli to the wedding of the Prince of Wales in preference to much grander people.[8]

Disraeli's first great triumph in democratizing the Conservative Party came in 1866 when during a brief minority government he persuaded its members to pass a second Reform Bill giving the vote to about one million working-class men and nearly doubling the size of the electorate. Some of his followers were very apprehensive about this (Lord Derby called it 'a shot in the dark'), but most were delighted as it made the Whigs, especially Gladstone, look floundering and indecisive.[9] On the night the Act was passed there was a great celebration at the Carlton Club, where it was the intention that Disraeli should be the guest of honour, but, typically, he declined, preferring to go home to Mary Anne who was waiting for him with a bottle of champagne and a pork pie from Fortnum and Mason. Such a simple domestic occasion was more to his taste. After supper he took Mary Anne in his arms and danced her round the bedroom, whispering in her ear that she was more like a mistress than a wife (presumably meant as a compliment).

Mary Anne was, of course, delighted by her Dizzy's triumph and even more so the following year when at last he achieved their ultimate ambition. For some time Lord Derby had been suffering increasingly from gout and by 1868 felt he could no longer continue as Prime Minister. There was little doubt, except among the most prejudiced, that Disraeli should succeed him. No other Conservative had a particle of his ability. Lord Derby therefore advised Queen Victoria to send for him as his successor, which she was very ready to do. And so at the age of sixty-four, after long and arduous years toiling in the political vineyard, he had at last 'climbed to the top of the greasy pole'. Mary Anne's cup was full. She had always known it would happen and had taken a vow that she would not attend the House of Commons until it did. Now at last she was free to go there, and for the first time to see her husband on the government front bench and hear him speak. And, of course, she had to give a splendid party in celebration. For this 10 Downing Street was considered too shabby and a room was borrowed from the Foreign Office. It was a splendid occasion, attended by the Prince and Princess of Wales and all leading politicians including William and Catherine Gladstone. But Mary Anne herself was only just able to make it. She was then seventy-six and her health was failing fast. There were already signs of the cancer that would kill her, and at times she felt desperately weak and tired. But make it she did. Although looking 'old and haggard', as one guest remarked, she was, quite rightly, the heroine of the occasion as with 'gaudy clothes and wig awry' she went into dinner on the arm of the Prince of Wales.

Disraeli's description of his progress to the premiership as 'climbing to the top of a greasy pole' proved all too apposite only a few months later. It was generally expected that with the help of the new voters he had enfranchised he would win the General Election of 1868. But it was not to be. Gladstone was nothing if not resilient, and it was his turn for a triumph, his Liberal Party being returned with a convincing majority.

After such a defeat and at his age it seemed likely that Disraeli would step down from the party leadership and withdraw from public life; but he was not ready for this. He felt his task was still uncompleted and he must battle on for some time yet. So the Queen's offer of a peerage was declined; but he did ask her as a special favour that Mary Anne should be honoured and made a peeress in her own right. This was an unusual request, but it was not without precedent, and after some hesitation Queen Victoria agreed, and Mary Anne became Viscountess Beaconsfield. It was expected that this might give rise to some derision, but generally it was accepted as a graceful recognition of her husband's services to the country and her vital part in them. Among the many letters of congratulation there was a particularly benevolent one (in typically convoluted language) from Gladstone who wrote : 'I also beg you to present my best compliments on her coming patent to (I must suppose I must still say, and never can use the name for the last time without regret) Mrs Disraeli.'

Disraeli's premiership and her own ennoblement marked the apex of Mary Anne's life, but afterwards it was suffering and affliction all the way. Usually her health had been robust and, unlike her husband, she had made light of any illnesses.[10] But she had been seriously ill in 1853, at the age of sixty-one, when Disraeli had written desperately to a friend that the physicians hardly gave him any hope and that without her everything in the home seemed to be in a state of anarchy. From this illness she was to recover, but fourteen years later (at the age of seventy-five) she was again at death's door, and there was a moving scene in Parliament when Disraeli, as leader of the House, was expected to come under heavy fire from the Opposition, but in consideration of his stress the attack was muted and Gladstone spoke words of sympathy. This was too much for Disraeli. For years he had endured Gladstone's thundering perorations with impassivity, but a little kindness and the tears came pouring down his face. From this illness there was to be some abatement but no recovery. Mary Anne well knew that cancer had set in and her days were numbered, but she was resolutely determined to keep the situation from her husband so as not to distress him. But, of course, he knew and for her sake pretended that he did not, so that the myth could be maintained that recovery was possible.

At one time Disraeli, too, became ill and they had to communicate with each other from adjoining rooms by letter. In these, as always, Disraeli was full of love and extravagant praise, saying that Grosvenor Gate had become a hospital but that a hospital with her was worth a palace with anyone else and that one of her letters to him was the most amusing and charming he had ever had and beat anything of Madame de Sevigné and Horace Walpole. No husband could have been more devoted. He spent as much time as possible with her, comforting her and always on the look-out for those things which gave her pleasure. It is possible that it was for her sake that at that time, after a lapse of twenty years, he embarked on another novel, *Lothair*, as he knew his literary works had always been of special interest to her. For her part Mary Anne always put on a brave face and did all she could to avoid becoming a burden. She tried hard to appear young and vital and to find life as interesting and exciting as ever. With great courage she accompanied Disraeli on long and exhausting official visits to Edinburgh and Manchester, where she was given a rapturous welcome. In reporting it the correspondent of *The Times* wrote that when she appeared 'the utmost deafening and enthusiastic cheers broke forth from all parts of the building'. She also sought to be with her husband at state occasions and other great functions, but these often proved too much for her and she would have to leave before the end.

In time the heroic effort became unavailing. Unable to eat and in great pain, her strength slowly ebbed away. At the beginning of 1872 Disraeli wrote pathetically: 'To see her every day weaker and weaker is heartrending, to witness the gradual death of one who has shared so long and so completely my life entirely unmans me.' In October of 1872 he brought her back to Hughenden, where even her beloved woodland walks failed to bring her joy. Already her mind had been affected by the illness, and then pneumonia set in, and on 15 December she was at last released from all suffering.

The funeral service was simple and private in Hughenden churchyard, attended only by domestic staff and farm tenants. For ten minutes in driving rain Disraeli remained bareheaded by her graveside. Tributes and messages of sympathy poured in from all over the country. These dwelled mainly on Mary Anne's great kindness and zest for life and, above all, her total devotion to her husband. Her life and achievements were summed up in stately language in the The Times: 'She stands out a striking illustration of the power the most unobtrusive of women may exercise while keeping herself strictly to a woman's sphere.' To this might have been added that this homely, warmhearted, uneducated woman had made possible one of the most brilliant of political careers.

On the death of Mary Anne, Disraeli found himself once again in financial straits. As she had had only a life interest in her first husband's estate her annuity of £5,000 came to an end as also did the lease of Grosvenor Gate, so that it was necessary for him to move out at once and take refuge for a time in a hotel, which he detested. But the situation was not desperate, as he had a Prime Minister's pension as well as some income from his books. He had also been left quite a large sum of money by a Mrs Brydges Willyams, a Jewish lady of Spanish origins who had settled in Torquay and who had formed a strong friendship with the Disraelis.

In a letter found after her death Mary Anne implored Disraeli to marry again: 'Do not live alone, dearest,' she wrote. She wished for him to be with 'someone I earnestly hope you may find as attached to you as your own devoted Mary Anne'. This he was ready to do, and within a year of Mary Anne's death he had fallen in love with the Countess of Bradford, a married lady of fifty-five. Marriage with her was not possible, as her husband was very much alive, and so he proposed instead to her elder sister, the Countess of Chesterfield, a widow of seventy-three, in the hope that this would keep him in close touch with her sister. Lady Chesterfield, however, was quite aware of the situation and was not prepared to be second best. Disraeli, therefore, had to be content with entering into a copious and impassioned correspondence with both sisters.[11] His need for an elderly lady as a confidante had not abated. He may also have considered marriage to the Countess of Cardigan, the eccentric and notorious widow of the leader of the Light Brigade. In her memoirs she recorded a proposal from him which, rather ungraciously, she said she had had to turn down because of the bad odour of his breath; but it is possible that it was she who made the going and he who backed out.

On becoming a widower Disraeli did not let up at all on his political activities, regarding these as a means of forgetting his sorrows. And his days of greatest glory lay ahead of him. In the General Election of 1874 the country signified that it had had enough of Gladstonian Liberalism, and for the first time in thirty years the Conservatives were returned with an overall majority. At last Disraeli had the power he had longed for; but it had come too late. The fire within him was burning low. As he sadly remarked: 'Power! It has come to me too late. There were days when, on waking, I felt I could move dynasties and governments; but that has passed away.'

His health was failing: he was racked with gout and suffered frequently from bronchitis. In 1876, to ease the strain, he accepted the title of Earl of Beaconsfield and moved to the comparative tranquillity of the House of Lords, leaving a House of Commons sadly bereft, many people noticing how much duller a place it had become. To his surprise and dismay the Conservatives were defeated in the General Election of 1880, and in the following year he died. Gladstone as Prime Minister at once offered a state funeral and burial in Westminster Abbey, but in his will Disraeli's instructions were quite explicit: a simple private funeral and burial in Hughenden churchyard beside Mary Anne; and these wishes were met.

At his death it seemed that he had attained all his wildest ambitions – Prime Minister, European statesman, literary figure, as well as trusted and well-loved friend of the great Queen, whom he had created Empress of the subcontinent of India. For the young Jewish adventurer – impecunious, unconnected and always struggling against the odds – surely a unique achievement.

Notes

1. He later became Lord St Vincent.

2. Disraeli once described him as 'certainly one of the oddest men that ever lived; but I like him very much'.

3. As, for example, when she announced her intention of asking Jonathan Swift (who had died a hundred years before) to dinner and when the conversation turned on Greek statuary and the beauty of the male body she told the assembled company that they ought to see her Dizzy in the bath.

4. Every lock of which was carefully preserved, and some hundreds of envelopes containing these were found after her death.

5. This was noted in dignified language by *The Times* in her obituary notice: 'Despite her habitual volubility, the instinct of her affection set a seal on her lips in the minutest matter when her talk might do him an injury.'

6. The tax on foreign corn. The Conservative Party, representing mainly the farmers and landowners, was pledged to maintain these, but Peel became convinced that they had to go.

7. A political opponent, John Bright, once said of him: 'Mr Disraeli is a man who does what may be called the conjuring for his party. He is what among a tribe of Red Indians would be called "the medicine man".'

8. Although the Queen, as always, was capable of administering acerbic advice, as when Mary Anne caught a cold and was told severely that the Queen never caught colds as she took a cold bath every morning.

9. This was perhaps the first time that a political party was said to have 'caught its opponents bathing and stolen its clothes'. Since then there have been other occasions, notably the sweeping electoral victory of New Labour in London in 1996.

10. One of Disraeli's biographers, C. Buckle, wrote that his notes to his wife from the House of Commons 'formed a constant record of indisposition'.

11. Some eleven hundred letters to Lady Bradfield and five hundred to Lady Chesterfield.

7

CATHERINE GLADSTONE

Beautiful, high-spirited and strong-willed. – Catherine Glynne described by her mother

A deranging incident has occurred. I am engaged to be married. – William Gladstone

My wife has a marvellous faculty for getting into scrapes, but also a marvellous faculty for getting out of them. – Gladstone on his wife

The marriage between William and Catherine Gladstone was a unique partnership: on the one hand, the Scottish merchant's son – dynamic, intellectual and intensely serious; on the other, the aristocrat's daughter – unconventional, disorganized, full of laughter and a touch of the saint.

Catherine was born in 1812 in the village of Hawarden (pronounced Harden) on the northern border of England and Wales. Her father had an estate of some eight thousand acres, and both he and his wife were of aristocratic lineage (with five Prime Ministers among their forebears). Catherine's childhood was happy but somewhat unsettled as her father died when she was five and her mother suffered ill health, so that Catherine and her two brothers and sister spent much time in the houses of friends and relations. In these circumstances the member of the family who might have been expected to take a leading role was the eldest son, Stephen, the new baronet, but he was of a retiring nature with no inclination for leadership, and the one who came to the fore was Catherine, the elder daughter, described by her mother as 'beautiful, high-spirited and strong-willed'. She was also inclined to be bossy, but not aggressively so, and always loving and caring, and the other members of the family – Stephen, Henry and Mary – were happy to accept her authority.

Hawarden was a wonderful place in which to grow up. There was always plenty to divert the children – riding, dancing, archery, walks in the beautiful country as well as some novel excitements such as a journey on the recently constructed railway or a ride in the newly invented steam carriage at the alarming speed of fifteen miles an hour. As was the custom of the time, the boys at the age of seven or eight were sent off to boarding-school while the girls remained at home, receiving a somewhat lightweight education from governesses. Although bright and conscientious Catherine was not a natural scholar; she did not read widely then or later in life. She was musical and had some talent as a pianist and once on a visit to Paris had the thrilling experience of a lesson from Franz Liszt. But then and throughout her life her main interest was in people – of all sorts. Her mother had a social conscience and brought her up to believe that wealth entailed responsibility, particularly towards the poor, and in Hawarden there were many of these, not only farm workers but also coalminers, among whom violence sometimes broke out. An inscription above an old mill dated 1767 read 'Poor were starving, riotous and hanged'. But Lady Glynne felt it her duty to visit them, and from an early age Catherine would accompany her. In modern times the character of Lady Bountiful, dispensing soup and scriptures, is all too readily derided, often by people with little experience of poverty, but her ministrations were surely beneficial; not only was hunger alleviated but there was, too, the human contact. One of the great differences between the British aristocracy and that of pre-revolutionary France was that the British aristocracy did not live in isolation from its workers.

Under the guidance of Catherine the Glynnes became a devoted and close-knit family – in some eyes rather too close with plenty of in-jokes, family nicknames and even their own family language known later as 'Glynnese'. Generally they were well liked, but there were those who found them clannish and aloof.

As they reached maturity none of the Glynnes seemed to be in a hurry to marry. The sisters had a number of suitors who would have made advantageous matches, but they were not to be pushed into a loveless marriage. This caused some impatience and indignation among their relations, notably their strait-laced aunt-by-marriage Lady Charlotte Neville-Granville, who wrote to Mary:

> . . . nor is it creditable or ladylike to be what is called in love. I believe that few, very few, well-regulated minds ever have been and that romantic attachment is confined to novels and novel readers, ye silly and numerous class of young persons ill-educated at home or brought up in boarding schools.

In spite of this daunting pronouncement, however, Catherine, at the age of twenty-five, did fall in love with a Colonel Harcourt. Little is known of this gentleman except that he jilted Catherine in favour of a daughter of the long-standing Prime Minister Lord Liverpool and was generally considered to have behaved badly.

It was partly to take her mind off this affair that in the following year, 1838, Catherine's mother proposed to take her family on an extended tour of Europe. This was no mean undertaking on the part of Lady Glynne, who only a few years before had suffered quite a severe stroke, as such tours in those days involved much discomfort and some rigour. It was in the course of this tour, whether by accident or by design, that the Glynne family saw much of a rising young politician – William Gladstone.

William Gladstone had been a contemporary and friend of Stephen Glynne at Oxford and visited Hawarden on one or two occasions, where he had made no great impression, Catherine once describing him, surely inaptly, as 'too matter of fact'. His was a very different background to that of the Glynnes. His family home was only ten miles from Hawarden but across the river Mersey in the outskirts of Liverpool and a world apart. William's father, John Gladstone, was a highly successful Scottish businessman who had moved down to Liverpool to be at the centre of the lucrative trade with the West Indies, where he owned extensive sugar plantations along with slaves to work them. John Gladstone was an honourable and deeply religious man who gave large sums of money to the building of churches and other charities, but he never felt guilt about being a slave owner, always defending slavery strongly on the grounds that it was countenanced in the Old Testament. Hard though he worked himself and exacting as he was in his expectations of others, he was no Scottish skinflint, treating his family with the greatest generosity. William once said of him that 'none but his children can know what torrents of tenderness flowed from his heart'.

John Gladstone soon found that William, his fourth and youngest son, was by far the most gifted member of his family, and his ambitions for him knew no bounds. William's own wish was to go into the Church, but his father was determined that he should enter politics. And so William was provided with the best education that his father thought money could buy – at Eton and Christchurch, Oxford. At both these establishments he was highly successful and blissfully happy. It seems he came in for no prejudice on account of his northern mercantile origins, but he did provoke mockery for his solemnity and intense seriousness. A contemporary at Oxford said of him: 'If he were soaked in boiling water and rinsed till he was twisted into rope, I do not suppose a drop of fun would ooze from him.' But no one could doubt the power of his intellect, and there was no surprise when he took a brilliant double first in classics and mathematics. On the political scene, too, he made an impact. At the time, under the influence of his father, he was a strong Tory, and in the recently established Oxford Union he had a great success with a resounding denunciation of the Great Reform Bill of 1832, declaring that it contained 'an element of the anti-Christ' and would certainly lead to bloody revolution and the dissolution of society.

Gladstone's strong Tory views, so forcefully and ably expounded, did not go unnoticed, and soon after leaving Oxford he was offered a safe Tory seat in a rotten borough controlled by Lord Lincoln. In Parliament he soon made his mark. His political stance was still on the right wing of the Conservative Party (the new name for the Tories) and his maiden speech contained a strong defence of West Indian slave owners, which he felt bound to undertake out of consideration for his father. On other matters, too, he showed himself of a reactionary bent, so that the great Whig historian Lord Macaulay described him at the time as 'the rising hope of those stern, unbending Tories' and another contemporary as 'an espouser of dead causes'.

Until 1835, then, life had treated Gladstone kindly: from Eton to Christchurch to Parliament progress had been smooth and swift with plaudits all the way. But this success on the political scene had not been matched in his private life. Here there had been anguish, particularly concerning love and marriage. Although he manifested a strong, even vehement sexuality, there was little romance in him and he was a heavy-handed lover. This stemmed mainly from his Evangelical upbringing, which had dwelt obsessively on sin and damnation and the dangers of life's pleasures. Of associating with women he wrote obscurely and sententiously: 'But it seems to me that female society, whatever the disadvantages may be, has just and manifold uses attendant upon it in turning the mind away from some of its most dangerous and degrading temptations.' The result of these lucubrations was that, although eager to be married and highly susceptible to the charms of women, he was ill at ease and gauche in their company.

His first attempts at courtship were impossibly maladroit. The objects of his interest were overwhelmed with his views on religion but heard little about how much he loved or esteemed them. Unsurprisingly they shied away in some alarm. These rejections were a bitter blow to Gladstone and caused much introspection. To clarify his thoughts he drew up a long thesis on the subject of 'Amusements', consisting of thirty-nine separate items, in one of which, rather strangely headed 'Essence of Balls', he examined with heart-searching thoroughness whether or not it was justifiable to attend balls, describing them sanctimoniously as 'indulgences not essentially linked with sin but opening up many channels of temptation'.

Perhaps to console himself for his recent disappointments Gladstone decided soon after to embark on a tour of Europe. This had many attractions for him, one of which may have been that he was aware that the Glynne family were in Europe at that time and he liked the idea of meeting up with them.

Whether or not Gladstone at that time was entertaining any special feelings towards Catherine is not known. What is certain is that when he first encountered the family in Naples he was in a state of deep depression. Two unsuccessful love affairs and trouble with his eyesight had taken their toll, and he wrote in his diary of 'an icy coldness in my heart' and 'walking among the splendours of the world like a dead man'. But this was to change. He was nothing if not resilient, and in a surge of physical energy he went off on a walking tour of some thousand miles in southern Italy with one companion and an intransigent donkey. The discomforts of this expedition were acute and the dangers not inconsiderable, but when he returned to Naples, where the Glynnes still were, his spirits had been restored and it became evident that his feelings towards Catherine were warming up. Soon afterwards the Glynnes moved to Rome, and Gladstone followed them; there it became certain that for the third time in four years Gladstone was in love.

It seems that William's wooing of Catherine was somewhat less discursive than his previous efforts, but it was hardly calculated to sweep a young woman off her feet. He took her to see numerous churches and to listen to a round of sermons in Italian. An ideal opportunity to propose to her occurred when they visited the Colosseum by moonlight, but Gladstone was no Don Juan and such words as came to him failed to make plain his feelings and evoke a response. A few weeks later William felt that the time had come for a direct proposal, although by letter rather than in person. This began with the admirably terse declaration that his heart and hand were at her disposal. Little more needed to be said; but it was impossible for William to be brief and there followed a rush of turgid language, focusing mainly on his unworthiness. One sentence seemed unending:

> I seek in a wife gifts better than those of our human pride, and am also sensible that she can find little in me; sensible that, were you to treat this note as the offspring of utter presumption, I must not be surprised: sensible that the lot I invite you to share, even if it be not unattended, as I trust it is not, with peculiar disadvantages of an outward kind, is one, I do not say unequal to your deserts, for that were saying little, but liable at best to changes and perplexities and pains, which for myself, I contemplate without apprehension, but to which it is perhaps selfishness in the main, with the sense of inward dependence counteracting an opposite sense of my too real unworthiness, which would make me contribute to expose another – and what other!

This was not the language of love, as anyone but Gladstone would have known, and almost anyone but Catherine would have been put off by it. That Catherine was not dismayed shows her discernment and the qualities of her mind. She was able to discount the diffuse and impenetrable verbiage and to perceive behind it a rare mind and a noble soul. And although she herself had the liveliest sense of humour she was able to take with a pinch of salt William's intense gravity. However, she was not as yet ready to accept his proposal and so she prevaricated, claiming to have been taken by surprise – hardly likely as William's protestations at the Colosseum, though opaque, must have given some intimation of his feelings – and, while refusing him for the present, sought to show that her mind might change. Soon afterwards William had to return to England, where he became depressed, agonizing endlessly as to whether he had been too precipitate and awkward and would have to face up to a third rebuff.

It was three months before the Glynne family returned, but by then Catherine was moving towards a decision and soon afterwards, when William proposed again, she accepted him. His joy at this knew no bounds but first, even before buying an engagement ring, he felt beholden to give to Catherine a copy of the letter he had written to another lady setting out his views on religious practices, and only when she had signified her agreement to them did he feel free to give rein to his happiness and share it with his family and friends.

Less than a week after Catherine's engagement her younger sister, Mary, became engaged to George, fourth Lord Lyttelton, a gifted if somewhat eccentric nobleman four years her junior whom she had refused not long before. But this came as no surprise: the sisters had always been so close that if one became engaged it was likely the other would follow suit. Their immediate thought was that they should have a joint wedding in Hawarden church. To this their future husbands readily agreed, and it took place on 25 July 1839. Defying superstition, the bridegrooms stayed at Hawarden Castle for the wedding and, no doubt at the instigation of Catherine, spent the day before distributing garments (some two hundred waistcoats and nightgowns) to the deserving poor. The wedding itself was a simple, somewhat bucolic occasion, the villagers of Hawarden turning out in force to show their affection towards the two sisters. Children strewed their path with flowers, and the long bridal procession contained no less than three local brass bands. Among the congregation were not only the great and the good but also the faithful retainers of the Glynne and Lyttelton families. To William this was an awe-inspiring occasion: 'such a gush of delight as I had not yet experienced. Such an outpouring of human affection on these beloved girls, combined with the so solemn mystery of religion'. Catherine's joy, too, was euphoric: like her husband she had been deeply in love with someone else less than a year before, but to both of them there was no question of the other being second best; they had no doubt that they had been destined for each other.

Certainly marriage greatly enriched the lives of both of them. For the first time, Catherine found herself under the domination of another and was completely happy that this should be so. Her life, too, became more focused: although not at heart a political creature, she was to dedicate herself devotedly to her husband's career. For William marriage brought even greater blessings. He had married, in the parlance of the age, 'above his station', and his wife's aristocratic connections would bring him, a rising young politician, great advantages. But much more important was the humanizing effect on him of marriage to Catherine. Unmarried, he was unbalanced and melancholic. With marriage came greater stability, self-confidence and, perhaps most important of all, the beginnings of a sense of humour. What he needed essentially was a wife who would enable him to embrace a family background different from the one in which he had been brought up, and who, while loving him dearly and supporting him completely, would occasionally tease him and deflate him and make him laugh at himself. Without this he would have been insufferably pompous and priggish and would not have developed into the affable, convivial figure of his later years.

Another powerful humanizing influence on Gladstone was the close relationship that developed between his family and the Lytteltons. Catherine and Mary could never be parted for long, and William soon formed a strong friendship with George Lyttelton. The two men had much in common: both were outstanding classical scholars with the same deeply held religious beliefs. In other ways they were less similar: George, who was nine years younger than William, was shy, inarticulate, somewhat uncouth, with no political skills and no business sense. His great achievement was the remarkable family he and Mary raised: four daughters, all strong and engaging personalities, and eight sons, including a future Cabinet minister, a general, a bishop and a headmaster of Eton (two of whom were also England cricketers). The atmosphere at Hagley Hall, the Lyttelton ancestral home in Worcestershire, was unique. Cricket was the ruling passion and this was played everywhere, including the Great Hall among valuable works of art. Spirits there were always high, often boisterous; at the dinner table when the meal was over grave and dignified visitors might find themselves in the middle of a bunfight, with rolled-up napkins flying in all directions – not what they expected in the house of the Lord Lieutenant.

The Gladstones settled down to married life in comfortable circumstances. John Gladstone saw to it that they were not short of money and provided them with an ample London residence in Carlton House Terrace. They also had an open invitation from Stephen Glynne to stay at Hawarden whenever they liked, and they were always welcome at Hagley.

It did not take Catherine long to discover, however, that marriage to an active politician involved sacrifices. The House of Commons made great demands on her husband's time. Catherine was no whinger, but she did dislike being left alone in the evenings and, even more, going out to dinner alone. In her letters she wrote that life was sometimes 'a little dreary' and of herself as being 'unduly vexed'. She did have some comfort from her rapidly increasing family; within a year of marriage a son was born and two years later a daughter and in time three more sons and three more daughters. These occupied much of her time. Unlike her own mother and most of her aristocratic relations care of her children was something she was not prepared to delegate; she became perhaps obsessively concerned with their health and upbringing, insisting on taking all decisions about them, even the most trivial, herself. And this led to further separation from William, as she was unwilling to bring young babies to what she regarded as the unhealthy air of London and felt that her place was with them in the country.

Marriage to William also involved adapting to his religious practices. Catherine had been brought up in the centre ground of the Church of England – going to church on Sundays, observing the outward forms of religion without thinking too deeply about their meaning and abhorring extremism. Of greater importance to her was living her religion in her life by works of charity and the example she set. Now this relaxed attitude had to be put aside. Attendance at church became more frequent, family prayers more prolonged and daily Bible readings more intense. To these she was ready to accede, but abstruse theological discussion, which was the staff of life for William, was not for her.

William, too, had to adapt to normal married life. He was willing and even eager to take on domestic responsibilities, and Catherine recorded how once, when they were engaging a cook, he cross-examined the woman closely, mainly on her religious proclivities. He was certainly a devoted and dutiful husband and tried to be tolerant of most of Catherine's idiosyncrasies; but he did have difficulty in coming to terms with her chronic vagueness and untidiness. To him, the most orderly and methodical of men, her overflowing drawers of assorted papers, her half-written and unposted letters and his letters to her left lying about for anyone to read were a sore trial. Many times she promised to mend her ways but seldom succeeded and when taken to task by William would tell him disarmingly: 'What a bore you would have been if you had married someone as tidy as yourself.'

In Parliament William's career soon gathered momentum. After a short time he was appointed Vice-President of the Board of Trade in the Conservative government of Sir Robert Peel, where he had outstanding success, so much so that he was soon promoted to President with a seat in the Cabinet. This was a remarkable achievement and he seemed to be heading even higher, but then, as was to happen again later in his life, he showed a lack of balance and sense of proportion when he felt it necessary to resign on an obscure matter of conscience concerning a government grant to a Roman Catholic college in Ireland. Peel was bewildered by this,[1] and it was generally expected that Gladstone would not be out of government for long, but then occurred the great split in the Conservative Party over the repeal of the Corn Laws (the duty on foreign corn), and it was to be nine years before he was again in office.

In 1846, seven years after their marriage, William found himself not only out of office but also for the time being out of Parliament. It might have been expected that then he and Catherine would have more time together, but this did not happen to any extent. Catherine was still unwilling to bring the children to London, and William always seemed to have calls on his time. Almost at once he took off for a prolonged visit to France and Germany, where he had conversations with a distinguished theologian as well as attending to the affairs of his sister Helen, who was having a *crise de nerfs* in the city of Ems. At the time Catherine had just given birth to her fourth child after a particularly difficult pregnancy and was in great need of support, but with typical unselfishness she agreed that William must go and bore her lot patiently.

Although it might seem that William was away from Catherine for longer than was necessary, he wrote to her every day, sometimes two or three times. Letter-writing for him was a relaxation, a means of releasing his tensions and clarifying his thoughts. His letters, although always affectionate, were never particularly intimate and were given an air of formality by his writing across the bottom 'Mrs W. E. Gladstone' as if they were business letters; and as always they tended to be long winded and diffuse. That Catherine cherished these letters is certain, although her description of them as 'pretty, happy and unstudied' seems curiously inappropriate. Her letters to him were totally different: spontaneous, haphazard and with little regard for spelling, punctuation or syntax. They were often written on odd scraps of paper (such as old envelopes or even sandwich wrappings) that happened to be at hand, and jumbled up together might be comments about the appointment of a bishop along with a description of the children's new clothes. Like his letters to her they were warm and loving and full of how much she was missing him and how incomplete she was without him but including little that was deeply personal.

It was not the case that William was a neglectful father; he loved his children dearly and when he was with them gave them a great deal of affection and attention, reading to them and playing their games as well as giving religious instruction. He was not a typical Victorian father: the children were encouraged to think for themselves and to argue and question, which they did at times with exuberance; and august visitors, who held William in great awe, were amazed to hear him contradicted and told he lied. But this family atmosphere – loving, informal, sometimes rumbustious – was just right for William. So much of his time was spent in solemn conclave and earnest discussion that light heartedness and badinage were just what he needed. No one was more aware of this than Catherine who, devoted as she was, was always ready with a little gentle mockery, once telling her husband after a long monologue that if he wasn't a great man he would be such a terrible bore. And he thrived under this treatment, ready to join in the fun and becoming on occasions playful, even skittish. One of his favourite turns was to sing with Catherine a music-hall song of which the chorus was:

A ragamuffin husband and a rantipoling wife,
We'll fiddle it and scrape it through the ups and downs of life.

Certainly William gave much to his family and received much back from them.

Soon after his return to England Gladstone found himself immersed in a major financial crisis of the Glynne family. Iron ore had been discovered on the family estate at Hawarden, and Sir Stephen Glynne, Catherine's younger brother, had formed a company to mine it. Sir Stephen was no businessman, his consuming interest being church architecture, and it was not long, owing to the machinations of an incompetent and dishonest agent, before the company was in deep trouble. Matters were allowed to slide, and in 1847 the company was declared bankrupt with debts of some £400,000 (around £26 million in present value). Sir Stephen was quite incapable of dealing with the situation, as was his younger brother, Henry, a retiring and unworldly clergyman. And so the problem passed to Catherine and William. At one time it looked as if the whole estate would have to be sold, but they were strongly opposed to this. Since their marriage, Hawarden, with the full compliance of Stephen, had become a second home. They were both deeply devoted to its meadows, streams, immemorial trees and remains of ancient buildings. Together they determined that it must be saved. It was fortunate that at the time William was out of office and was able to devote all his vibrant energy to the matter. In this he did not spare himself, attending a gruelling bankruptcy hearing and mastering all the details of the legal position in the course of which he wrote no less than 140 letters. He had been given a completely free hand by his brother-in-law, and eventually his determination and efforts bore fruit, and the castle was saved; but this was only made possible by a massive injection of William's own money, leading to an arrangement with the ever-amenable Stephen for a joint occupancy of Hawarden and an agreement that on the death of Stephen and Henry the estate would pass to a trust for the benefit of one or more of Catherine's and William's sons. These were all delicate matters and might have given rise to family discord, but, remarkably, relations remained entirely amicable throughout.

In spite of the great worry over the Hawarden estate the first ten years of the Gladstones' marriage had been on an even keel; there had been troubles but no tragedies. But 1850 was to be an *annus horribilis*. In April their second daughter, Jessy, a lively and engaging child of four, contracted meningitis and died a slow and painful death. This caused both parents agonies, and it seems that for a time even William's faith in an all-powerful and loving God was shaken. Six months later the Fates struck again when Catherine's sister-in-law Lavinia, the wife of Henry Glynne (and sister of George Lyttelton), died after giving birth to a fourth daughter.

It was not until 1853, when he was forty-four, that William again held office – in the coalition government under his close friend Lord Aberdeen, but when two years later the latter was replaced by Lord Palmerston Gladstone resigned. He had at first supported the Crimean War but then changed tack and urged that peace should be made at once. In recent years his general political stance had undergone a fundamental change: no longer was he the stern, unbending Tory speaking out on behalf of borough mongers and slave owners; more and more his sympathies were to be found with the weak and oppressed.

He was not yet ready to join the Whigs, the main stumbling block here being his distaste for the two Whig leaders, Lord Palmerston and Lord John Russell. For a time he was a loose cannon, floundering unpredictably; eagerly sought by both parties on account of his exceptional abilities but unable to make up his mind as to which direction he should take. At last, however, at the age of fifty, he came to a decision and joined the Whig government of Lord Palmerston as Chancellor of the Exchequer. In this office he was to have brilliant success, but, as always, he was a difficult and unpredictable colleague and his relations with Palmerston in particular were never easy.[2]

Amid all William's hesitations and tergiversations Catherine never lost faith in him. She had no doubt that whatever he did must be right. As she wrote, rather testily, to a friend who had questioned his course of action: 'To doubt William's sense and judgement seems to me altogether extraordinary.' Admirable as this total loyalty might seem, it must be doubtful if it always served William's best interests. There is a need sometimes for a politician's wife to speak candidly and bring her husband to his senses. And they still did not have too much time together. Catherine was finding it necessary to spend more time at Hawarden, where her responsibilities were forever increasing. She then had seven children of her own as well as the four motherless daughters of her brother Henry whom she had taken under her wing; and then there was the Lyttelton family, now numbering eight and still increasing, towards whom she always felt maternal.

Catherine did not, however, neglect entirely her duties as a political wife. She made a point of always being in the Ladies' Gallery whenever William made an important speech in the House of Commons. She also did her best as a political hostess, although this did not come easily to her. She and William never belonged to what Queen Victoria called 'the fast, fashionable set'. They were completely uninterested in such matters as cards, racing and clothes; they abhorred luxury and grandeur, and when they entertained it was on their terms. Splendid imposing dinner parties were not to their taste, and most often their hospitality took the form of breakfast parties – substantial meals held mid-morning and more nearly resembling early lunches. On these occasions good simple fare was the order of the day. Catherine, dressed plainly and practically, was always friendly and forthcoming, and William, too, was genial and attentive. But Catherine took little heed of social etiquette, not troubling much about such matters as placing her guests and remembering their names and faces. Even so, such was her natural grace and charm that most guests were delighted by her, but there were those who were put off, finding her inaccessible and her flow of talk, especially when interlarded with incomprehensible Glynnese, too arcane. Of all people Catherine was the least pretentious and arrogant, but her disregard of social niceties and lack of interest in society were seen by some as a form of snobbery.

Soon after the end of the Crimean War Catherine suffered perhaps the greatest loss of her life when her sister, Mary Lyttelton, died. Mary had had twelve children in eighteen years and it had worn her out. After the birth of her eleventh child the doctor had warned her that a further pregnancy would be fatal, but it seems that he did not, as he surely should have done, also warn her husband. George Lyttelton, like many Victorian husbands, seems to have had an unrealistic understanding of the matter of procreation. He is quoted as having once agreed with his wife that four was about the right number for a family but then did nothing to achieve this end, apparently thinking that this was a matter for his wife to attend to, while Mary seems to have thought that it was a matter for God. According to family legend she was asked shortly before her death whether she had not told her husband about the doctor's warning. 'Oh no,' she is said to have replied. 'Lord Lyttelton and I never talked about anything so nasty.' The result of this reticence was the birth of a twelfth child and Mary's death six months later. During her last days it was for Catherine that she repeatedly called, and it was in her arms that she died. For Catherine it was a crushing blow. No two sisters had ever been closer. They complemented each other perfectly: Catherine definite and authoritarian, Mary gentle and acquiescent. It is thought by some that Catherine never completely recovered from Mary's death. Certainly immediately afterwards her health gave cause for serious concern. At forty-five she herself had had eight children in fourteen years with one miscarriage. She was badly in need of rest and a change of scene in a warm climate, and an opportunity for this occurred when William agreed to go on a somewhat fantastic mission to the Ionian Isles, then a British protectorate, to report on the islanders' wish to be united with Greece. For this he was to be given the somewhat operatic title of Lord High Commissioner Extraordinary. Normally he would not have considered it, but partly because of Catherine's health and partly because of his passionate interest in everything Greek, especially Homer, on whom he was writing a book at the time, he agreed to go. The mission achieved nothing on the political front and no one on the islands could be found who had ever heard of Homer, but it was very beneficial to Catherine, and she returned home ready, in William's words, to go once more into perpetual motion.

During the later 1860s Catherine found herself with more time on her hands. Her elder children had grown up and the younger ones were at boarding-school; she still kept a watchful eye on them and was at their bedsides immediately at the first signs of illness, but they were less of a tie. She could then have begun to devote more time to the political scene, but she was not inclined to do so. As the wife of a senior Cabinet minister many charitable demands were made on her, and she was always ready to respond to these, especially in circumstances of the most acute suffering. For her, charity meant more than fundraising in drawing-rooms; she believed it was essential to be on the spot to see at first hand what needed to be done.

Thus, in 1861, when there was widespread unemployment in Lancashire following the outbreak of the American Civil War and the interception by the Northern states of supplies of raw cotton from the South to England Catherine was soon in the worst affected areas, organizing soup kitchens and refuges as well as arranging for young women to come to Hawarden to be given training for domestic service. The patient suffering of the mill operatives made a great impression on her, as did their idealism in boycotting cotton that had managed to get through the Northern blockade. Rather than work cotton grown by slave labour, they were ready to tighten their belts and remain unemployed.

Soon afterwards Catherine became aware of the increasing number of homeless people in London owing, in part, to the many houses demolished to make way for the railways. The problem was immense, and Catherine could do little to alleviate it, but, as always, she did not turn a blind eye and set about raising enough money to buy and renovate a disused slaughterhouse in Seven Dials, the poorest part of London. Conditions in the Newport Market Shelter were certainly rough, but many homeless people were glad of it.

In 1866 the East End of London was visited by a fearful cholera epidemic that claimed over eight thousand lives, and conditions in the hospitals became so horrific that nurses could not be found to go into them. But Catherine did and was soon in the worst wards, organizing such help as was available and comforting the dying. It was said of her by an associate that 'she faced all difficulties at a time when people outside seemed panic-stricken'. While she was in the hospitals she soon became aware of another heartrending problem – that of children made orphans by the plague. Here again she did what she could, raising funds for an orphanage in Clapton and bearing off a number of the children to Hawarden to be found homes there.

In all these works Catherine was strongly supported by William, who gave to them such time as he could, although at this time he was engaged in his own particular project, one that had come to obsess him, of rescuing London prostitutes from their fallen state and setting them up in a new life.[3] To this work he devoted large sums of his own money and a great deal of his time. Even when he was at his busiest, after long days in the office and in Parliament he would go out into the London streets in search of these women to persuade them to renounce their ways. Such activities inevitably exposed him to gossip and misunderstanding. To some people they were entirely charitable and honourable, but to others they were a flagrant example of Victorian hypocrisy – of an oversexed man allaying his urges under a cloak of philanthropy. With the publication of Gladstone's diaries it would seem that the truth lay somewhere between the two. There can be no doubt of his genuine wish to rescue and reform, and everything he did he did openly; there was no attempt at subterfuge. He seemed to be without fear or any sense that he was compromising himself. In a man of such sophistication it seems there was an innocent, unworldly streak that saw nothing wrong or dangerous in what he was doing.

Naively it did not occur to him that it could be misunderstood, nor did he appreciate the great emotional strain it would place on him. From his diaries it is clear that he indeed become emotionally involved with some of his 'cases' – one is described as being 'beautiful beyond measure' – and his behaviour was not always above reproach, and for these fallings from grace he would inflict on himself punishments which varied from self-flagellation to denying himself holy communion. Whether or not his association with these women was consummated is uncertain, but he should perhaps be believed when in old age he told his clergyman son Stephen that he had not been guilty of 'the act which is known as that of infidelity to the marriage bed'.

It was, of course, impossible to keep these nocturnal missions from becoming known. It was not long before rumours flew and tongues wagged. They were a constant source of anxiety to his friends, and on occasions they plucked up the courage to remonstrate with him and warn him of what might be the consequences. But he was not to be put off. He listened to them politely and admitted that they were 'not within the rules of worldly prudence', but they were essential to maintain his mental balance. The one person who was unperturbed was Catherine, who had always known what he was doing and approved of it and cooperated in it. Together they had founded the Reclamation of Fallen Women and had raised money for shelters where prostitutes could seek refuge. Far from warning her husband off such dangerous and dubious activities she encouraged him. It cannot always have been easy; it is not every wife who would have taken it calmly when her husband came home with a 'lady of the night', expecting her to be given comfort and sustenance and leaving it to his wife to explain to the domestic staff the presence of such an improbable visitor. But Catherine never complained. Good works had always been ingrained in her and she had never been unduly bound by convention and respectability.

Although in the 1860s Gladstone was a dominating figure in Parliament he was also a solitary one; there were few other members with whom he felt much rapport. Outside Parliament, however, he was forging new links and not with a group or sect but with the broad mass of the British working population, especially in the industrial north. In 1862 he and Catherine paid an official visit to Newcastle, where they were given a tumultuous reception. When they sailed up the Tyne every ship was bedecked with flags and pennants, and the crews swarmed up the mizzens to catch a view of the great man and his wife. At every stage of the tour working men – colliers, ironworkers, hauliers, bargees – turned out in their thousands to great them, and Gladstone was always ready with a spate of oratory which left them awe-struck. And Catherine was almost as much of a star. People loved her spontaneity and informality and the warm and genuine interest she showed in everyone's lives and problems. The visit was a milestone in Gladstone's career. Not only had he discovered a great affinity with the working classes but he had also become aware that he had the ability to address and to sway audiences of many thousands. It had been a thrilling experience, and it was heady stuff. In his diary he expressed the hope that it might not be intoxicating, but it surely was. For after Newcastle his language in public became ever more intemperate, alarming friend and foe alike.

When Gladstone joined forces with Palmerston in 1859 he might have expected that Palmerston, who was then seventy-four, might not last much longer, but he did, in the event, hold on to life and office for another six years. He was succeeded as Prime Minister by another elderly Whig, Earl Russell (formerly Lord John Russell), and it was not until 1868, by which time he was fifty-nine, that Gladstone at last became Prime Minister at the head of the newly named Liberal Party. By then Benjamin Disraeli had become leader of the Conservative Party, and the rivalry between the two men was at its height. Gladstone was victorious at the General Election of 1868, but Disraeli turned the tables on him in 1874.

While William was Prime Minister Catherine, as always, was supportive and provided him with the stable, loving family base that was essential to him, but, as before, she did not become closely involved in politics. William confided in her fully but did not seek her advice. Politics to her meant agreeing in principle with everything William said and did and not concerning herself with details, while at the same time maintaining, uncharacteristically, a strong personal animosity towards his political opponents whom she usually held to be not only incompetent but also nefarious. It is not difficult to find fault with Catherine as a Prime Minister's wife: she was not a competent organizer and tended to neglect duties she found uncongenial. At her instigation they did not move into 10 Downing Street, preferring to remain in Carlton House Terrace and using the former only as offices. At both establishments household arrangements tended to be, as a visitor once put it, 'incoherent'. Nor did she feel it necessary to reduce her charitable activities, which meant there were frequent separations from William – although these might have been to the advantage of both of them. William was left free to attend to government business (as well as his rescue operations), and his daily letters to Catherine, in which he poured out what was on his mind, acted as an essential safety valve. There was never any question of them drifting apart, indeed their marriage seems to have been strengthened rather than weakened by their separations.

After his defeat in the General Election of 1874 Gladstone was convinced that his political career was over. He was then sixty-five and he felt the time had come to devote himself to what he held most dear – his Christian faith and the great classical writers. But in this he was strongly opposed by Catherine, the first time in their marriage when she had disagreed with him on a major issue. She argued that, in spite of his age, he was as full of vigour as ever, that in stature and ability he far exceeded all other politicians and that the country and the Liberal Party could not do without him. At first, however, Gladstone was not to be moved, and in 1875 he announced his retirement from the leadership of the party.

The early 1870s had been another difficult and tragic period for Catherine. Her two brothers had died within two years of each other, and at the time of William's resignation she had been called to the deathbed of her niece Mary Lyttelton, who had been struck down by typhoid. And in the following year tragedy struck again when her brother-in-law George Lyttelton, after bouts of severe depression, took his life – a devastating blow to a family that Catherine had come to regard as her own.

One worry of which Catherine was soon to be relieved was that of William's retirement. There had always been signs that this might not be irrevocable; he refused a peerage, did not relinquish his seat in the Commons and let it be known that he might be ready to come out again 'upon the arrival of any worthy occasion'. In the event this was not long in coming. Stories of Turkish atrocities in Eastern Europe brought him thundering forth on the famous Midlothian Campaign. This was organized and orchestrated by the wealthy and influential Scottish peer Lord Rosebery, who wanted to see Gladstone once again leader of the Liberal Party and saw to it that everywhere he went he was greeted by bonfires, torchlight processions, fireworks and huge crowds. And Gladstone, at the age of seventy, with Catherine by his side, lived up to the occasion. Furiously he inveighed against the barbarity of the Turks and the wickedness of Disraeli (now Lord Beaconsfield) in supporting them. His audiences had probably never heard of Bulgaria and must have had difficulty in hearing, let alone understanding, the Gladstone oratory, but they were electrified by it. Lord Rosebery was delighted and said that Gladstone had 'set fire to the Scottish heather'. Lord Beaconsfield in response said that he had 'drenched it with rhetoric' and that Gladstone was 'worse than any Turkish atrocity'. But the rhetoric was to spread far and wide, and in the General Election of 1880 the Liberals were victorious and Gladstone was persuaded to become Prime Minister again.

Gladstone's second ministry was less successful than his first. He was beset by troubles abroad, but his greatest tribulation lay in Ireland, where the situation had become much more critical. When he first became Prime Minister in 1868 he had announced awesomely that his mission was to pacify Ireland, and during the following year he struggled heroically to grapple with the problems of that fated country. But all his efforts were plagued with misfortunes: the assassination of the Chief Secretary for Ireland, Lord Frederick Cavendish (husband of Catherine's niece Lucy Lyttelton), in Phoenix Park, Dublin; the end of his association with the leader of the Irish Nationalist Party, Charles Stuart Parnell, following his involvement in a divorce case; the split in the Liberal Party over the question of Home Rule; and finally his titanic achievement during his fourth ministry at the age of eighty-three in getting a Home Rule Bill through the House of Commons only for it to be rejected by the House of Lords.

In all these travails Gladstone was confronted with embittered hostility and not only from his political opponents; equally vitriolic were the breakaway Liberals, the Liberal Unionists, led by Joseph Chamberlain. And then there was Queen Victoria, who developed a deep-rooted dislike of him, which, as was her wont, she made no effort to conceal. In her dealings with him she found him awkward and pompous and complained that he addressed her as if she were a public meeting. The emergence of 'The People's William' also found no favour with her. She strongly disapproved of his oratorical outpourings to massed working-class audiences and the tumultuous receptions he was given, regarding these as the prerogative of royalty. Later the situation was exacerbated by his Irish policy, of which she disapproved. It seemed he could do nothing right in her eyes, and at one time she was quoted as saying that she would sooner abdicate than send for or have any communication with that 'half-mad firebrand', who would soon ruin everything and be dictator. While Gladstone said of the Queen that she was 'enough to kill any man', Catherine was greatly distressed by their bad relations. She knew her husband well enough to realize that shyness made him stiff and formal in the royal presence and urged him to 'pet' the Queen, to treat her as a woman rather than an icon. Her own relations with the Queen were always warm and friendly, and after an interview with her once she wrote: 'It is funny but we got on capitally and she chatted and talked comfortably.'

After his defeat at the General Election of 1874, William announced his retirement but was to remain active on the political scene for more than a quarter of a century. For most of the time his health was good and his vigour unimpaired. Until well into old age he continued with his rescue work in the streets of London, and he also found emotional relief in minor flirtations with notorious beauties. As always, Catherine was totally unbothered. In matters relating to sex she was as naive as her husband – in the words of Sir Philip Magnus, 'guileless, credulous and unsuspicious'. In her heart she never doubted that his association with other women in no way diminished his love for her.

It was this certainty that allowed Catherine to pursue her own interests and put up with frequent separations. Her charitable works were just as necessary to her as William's were to him. To the end of her life she gave tireless support to the orphanages, refuges and retirement homes she had founded, writing endless begging letters for money and maintaining constant personal contact. She was forever dropping in for a chat or some form of entertainment, and on these occasions formality was minimal. She might be the wife of the Prime Minister, but there was no trace of grandeur or pomposity in her manner, and in London her preferred method of transport was by tram, where she would engage in animated conversation with all around her. Although some people found this conduct startling, it was the way she liked to operate. In the 1880s Associations of Women Liberals were sprouting up all over the country, and in 1887 a National Association was formed, and Catherine, at the age of seventy-five, was persuaded to become its president. But this was not her *métier*; she was no committee woman; her absentmindedness, chatty informality and inherent lack of method did not make for smooth-running meetings. Besides she had little love for what she called 'political female meetings' and was not totally in agreement with all members of the association, some of whom were strident suffragettes. For the enfranchisement of women she felt little enthusiasm, considering it more important to 'preserve distinctive womanhood' and believing that women could achieve more by 'patience, kindness and charity and not quarrelling with their opponents'. After five years she was thankful to resign.

Catherine continued to be occupied with her family after they had grown up and gone out into the world, although in most cases it was not very far into the world, as she tended to be possessive and contrived to keep them at or near Hawarden. Her eldest son William (known as Willy to distinguish him from his father) was elected to Parliament at an early age but never showed any enthusiasm or aptitude for politics and was much more at ease managing the Hawarden estate and pursuing his interests in music and mountaineering. On the death of his uncle Stephen he became the legal owner of Hawarden, but it was never considered that his mother and father should move out of the castle, even when he married. Soon afterwards it was he and his wife who moved out, into a smaller house in the village, after his father-in-law suggested that his daughter might like an establishment of her own at a distance from what he, perhaps euphemistically, described as 'Mrs Gladstone's zeal and habits of management'. To the heartbreak of his parents Willy died of a brain tumour at the age of fifty-one, leaving a young son, who in time inherited Hawarden but was killed in the First World War.

Gladstone's second son, Stephen, was likewise unambitious. Since boyhood he had been set on going into the church, which, to his father's great satisfaction, he subsequently did and succeeded his uncle Henry as rector of Hawarden – financially rewarding but not unduly exacting. Stephen's son eventually inherited Hawarden. Of Gladstone's two younger sons Henry became a successful businessman while Herbert inherited some of his father's political skills, attaining several high offices of state including that of Home Secretary and first Governor-General of the Union of South Africa.

Like their brothers the Gladstone daughters were quiet, home-loving and in no hurry to get married. At the age of twenty-eight Agnes, the eldest, announced her wish to become a nurse, which it might have been expected that Catherine with her deep devotion to charitable works would have welcomed. But she was horrified, and took the same starchy view as Florence Nightingale's mother – that it was an unsuitable occupation for a lady and that she was too young to be working alongside male doctors and nursing male patients. Faced with this vehement opposition Agnes, unlike the steely Miss Nightingale, backed down and soon afterwards made a happy, if unworldly, marriage to a public school headmaster, Edward Wickham.

The second surviving daughter, Mary, inherited some of her mother's vivacity and willpower, interesting herself closely in her father's political career and taking over from her mother some of the domestic and family responsibilities at Hawarden. Her management skills were formidable, and she became known in the family as von Moltke (creator of the all-conquering Prussian Army). After a number of platonic friendships with famous men (including Tennyson, Ruskin and Arthur Balfour), she finally settled at the age of thirty-eight on marriage to the local curate, Harry Drew, a man of character but impecunious and some eight years younger than herself; among other blessings this enabled her to continue living at Hawarden Castle and to keep an eye on political and family matters.

To the youngest daughter, Helen, was bequeathed some of her father's intellectual gifts. For a time she lived at home, acting as an extra secretary to her father, but at the age of twenty-eight, in spite of some maternal opposition, she was allowed to go to Newnham Hall, Cambridge, a recently founded college for women, where in time she became vice-principal. But she was always firmly based at Hawarden and refused the higher academic appointments that would have meant a loosening of family ties.

As the Gladstones approached old age the nature of their relationship began to change. Ever since she had witnessed the stirring emotional scenes of the Midlothian Campaign Catherine had become convinced that William had a divine mission to bring peace and prosperity to England and more particularly to Ireland. She, therefore, held strongly that he must be sustained in office by every means. Until then, great as was their love and dependence on each other, they had been accustomed quite often to going their separate ways. In later years, however, Catherine was almost always by William's side – supporting him, cosseting him and, as far as possible, protecting him from life's irritations. She also gave him more advice and interfered more in political matters, and in this she was joined by her daughter Mary who felt that she, too, had a part to play. Although these attentions were well meant and involved much self-sacrifice and hard work, there were those who thought that they were misplaced. There were signs that they made William claustrophobic, and they certainly caused irritation in political circles, where there was grumbling about Gladstone's 'seraglio' and 'petticoat government'. Tact had never been Catherine's strong suit; her directness and candour endeared her to many but not to all, and in old age she became more insensitive and high-handed. Without realizing it she trod on several toes. An exasperated political colleague wrote that 'Mrs Gladstone was always waylaying everybody and scheming this and scheming that, intercepting letters and almost listening at keyholes.' And after one dinner party even the gentle Princess Mary of Teck (later Queen Mary) noted 'Mrs Gladstone is awfully fidgety and is always rushing after Mr Gladstone.'

Whatever the feelings in political circles, within the family Catherine remained, as ever, deeply loved and revered. She had always been unsparing in her love and care not only for her own family but also for the motherless Lytteltons and Glynnes, and for them 'Aunt Pussie' could do no wrong. Her excesses were readily forgiven, her idiosyncrasies treasured. They rejoiced in stories of how she filled William's hot-water bottle with soup, partly because she believed that soup retained heat longer than water and partly because he might like to take a draught of it in the watches of the night 'if he felt so disposed'. And it delighted them that when she attended grand dinner parties she bore off some of the choicest fruits so as to pass them on later to the objects of her charity. Above all, they marvelled at her vitality and hardihood. She was still perpetually on the move, attending sick-beds, visiting people she thought might be lonely and looking in on her charitable foundations to see that all was well. On these journeys she invariably took rigorous modes of transport, thinking nothing of travelling on the outside of coaches and on railways, always third class.

Well into her eighties her life was one of Spartan severity. She would rise early in the morning, take a cold bath in all weathers and then after somewhat hasty ablutions (some thought too hasty) she would set off with William on a walk of a mile or so to Hawarden church for early service. She had always been indifferent to personal discomfort. On her vigils by sick-beds she was quite prepared to sleep on the floor, and her own bedroom was uncompromisingly austere – arctically cold, with no carpets or curtains and the minimum of furniture, as such things, she believed, made a room stuffy and airless.

But in time old age was to take its toll even on her. In 1891, as she was approaching eighty, a friend noted that she was looking 'aged and haggard'. Then her mind became less clear and she developed obsessions on certain subjects, notably William's fulfilment of his 'divine mission'. It was largely due to pressure from her and her daughter Mary that in 1892 he became Prime Minister for the fourth time, and when his third Irish Home Rule Bill was rejected by the Lords she still urged him, at the age of eighty-four, to carry on the struggle.

After sixty years as a Member of Parliament, fifty-two as a privy councillor and fourteen as Prime Minister, it was to be hoped that Gladstone's political career would end becomingly and without rancour. 'God grant', wrote his Private Secretary, 'that it may come with decency, and the great Caesar fold his robes gracefully round him as he falls.' But it was not to be. Instead there was bitterness and discord. After the defeat of Home Rule he wanted to bring in a bill to limit the powers of the House of Lords, but his Cabinet and most of the Liberal Party were not ready for this, and there was a growing feeling that the time had come for him to step down. This came to a head when a deep-rooted disagreement arose between him and his Cabinet colleagues on the subject of naval expenditure. With the great powers of Europe forming themselves into alliances and building up armaments most people felt that at all costs Britain should maintain her naval supremacy. But Gladstone was inflexibly opposed to anything in the nature of an arms race, which, he maintained, would lead inevitably to war. With the whole Cabinet against him his resignation became unavoidable, but this did not occur gracefully. He said hard things about his colleagues and kept them guessing as to his intentions before finally agreeing to resign on the grounds of ill health and failing eyesight. When at last he announced his decision to the Cabinet there was an emotional scene. Warm tributes were paid and tears were shed, and all was forgiven when it was realized that the curtain was coming down on a career unique to that century, perhaps to any century. Sometimes brilliant, sometimes obtuse, but always high-minded and wholehearted, he had been the dominant force in Parliament for half a century.

Four years of life still remained to him, but the period of reflection and repose to which he had so looked forward was to have its tribulations. His driving energy did not desert him until the very end, but his eyesight was worn out and an operation for a cataract was only partially successful. Although this greatly restricted his reading, it did not so much affect his writing, and he completed several theological works as well as a translation of the Odes of Horace. During this time Catherine was as loving and devoted as ever, but all was not well with her. She could never rid herself of the idea that William ought still to be in office. With her husband no longer at the helm, she was no longer inside what she called 'the mainstream of history', and life lost much of its purpose. She struggled bravely, but much of her sparkle had gone and she was not always susceptible to reason.

In 1897 William was diagnosed as having cancer of the cheek, from which there was no recovery and which was to cause him such pain that he longed for the end. 'Thank God,' he murmured when he was told he was dying. His death on 19 May 1898 – Ascension Day – caused a wave of emotion and shock throughout the country and abroad. Hawarden was inundated with flowers, and trainloads of visitors, mainly from the industrial north, poured in to pay their last respects. There were so many messages of condolence that twenty extra postmen had to be drafted in to deliver them. At the centre of world attention Catherine, typically, took time to visit the widow of a young miner who had been killed in a pit accident on the Hawarden estate. In London people queued all night to file past Gladstone's coffin lying in state in Westminster Hall. At his funeral Westminster Abbey was filled with the great and the good from many countries, and the pallbearers included two future Kings and three Prime Ministers. The service was a deeply moving one, not least with the arrival of Catherine at the West Door, at which the whole congregation rose to its feet out of respect. Clouded as her mind had sometimes been of late, Catherine made a great effort for this supreme moment and carried out her part superbly, kneeling by the open grave with two sons, thanking the pallbearers and greeting everyone she recognized.

During her two years of widowhood Catherine lived more and more in a world of her own in the distant past. She had periods of lucidity, but on occasions, as her daughter recorded, there were scenes and she was difficult to manage. However, she was surrounded at all times by the care and love of her family and friends. She died peacefully and painlessly at Hawarden on 14 June 1900 and was buried by the side of her husband in Westminster Abbey. Many would agree with Mary Drew that with the death of her father and mother the world had become a much duller place.

Notes

1. Especially when the matter came to a vote in Parliament and Gladstone voted in favour of it.

2. He is quoted as saying later that he never attended a Cabinet meeting without a letter of resignation in his pocket.

3. In his survey *London Labour and the London Poor*, produced between 1849 and 1852 and published in book form in 1861–2, Henry Mayhew estimated that there were some 80,000 prostitutes in London and some 6,000 brothels.

8

FROM GEORGINA SALISBURY TO SARAH CAMPBELL-BANNERMAN

A rushing mighty wind. – Description of Lady Salisbury by her daughter-in-law

I have lost the best wife ever man had. – Lord Rosebery on the death of Hannah

GEORGINA SALISBURY

When Lord Robert Cecil, later third Marquess of Salisbury, became engaged to Georgina Alderson he met with strong paternal opposition. Although she came from a well-to-do and gifted family (her father was a judge) it was non-aristocratic and, more importantly, of no great wealth. His father felt strongly that if he did not marry money Robert could not live in the style required of the younger son of the Marquess of Salisbury. He did all he could to dissuade him, but Robert was not to be moved.

He had had a troubled and unhappy youth and had grown up solitary and introspective and subject to deep depressions, with no close friends and few interests. Although a gifted scholar he had no aesthetic tastes, no love for music or the arts and abhorred all games and sports and most social life. He was, however, no misogynist, and his great need was for feminine sympathy and understanding to draw him out and give him self-confidence. He had no doubt that Georgina was the only woman who could do this for him and he was not going to let her go. His father, however, was unrelenting, refusing to attend his wedding and making him only a small allowance, so that for the first eight years of marriage, until Robert became heir to the marquessate on the death of his elder brother, he and Georgina lived in straitened circumstances in an unfashionable house north of Oxford Street with five (later seven) children to provide for, which he managed by means of journalism.

None of this weighed too heavily on Georgina, who was a woman of great strength of character, which became manifest in 1868 when, on his father's death, Robert became third Marquess of Salisbury and she found herself the mistress of Hatfield, much of the management of whose 127 rooms and twenty thousand acres of land devolved on her. Robert concerned himself with the farming of the land, but everything else – domestic arrangements, maintenance of buildings, entertaining, care for the estate's sick and needy – was undertaken by Georgina. This awesome task she tackled with formidable energy and determination if not always with great tact and consideration for others (except her husband). Her grandson, Lord David Cecil, later described her as 'dominating, wilful and stormy', and one of her daughters-in-law wrote that she was like 'a rushing, mighty wind'. Another, who had suffered much from her, acknowledged none the less the magnitude of her achievement, above all that she sustained her husband, rescuing him from dark moods and putting his career before everything. Without her he would have achieved nothing.

Although sometimes withered by the blast of her personality, many also gained from it. She had a lively mind, was full of contentious ideas and was always stimulating company. And she was no tyrant: perhaps her greatest achievement was the bringing up of a remarkable family of seven attractive and, like her, mildly eccentric individualists. Her policy was always to give them as free a rein as possible. The Victorian precept that children should be seen and not heard was turned on its head: hers were to be seen at all hours and heard clamorously. Small importance was attached to such matters as punctuality, tidiness or even cleanliness, but they were expected to be perceptive, forthcoming and on the ball. Bad manners were not tolerated, and a look from their mother was enough to bring the children under control. In all of this she had the full support of her husband. Withdrawn and misanthropic though he might be, Lord Salisbury was totally devoted to his family and preferred their company to any other. He was prepared to sit for hours in the midst of a torrent of talk, putting his oar in occasionally and ready to question loose and undefined ideas. And always, like his wife, whatever the ages of his children he treated them as intelligent adults and was unwilling to impose on them his own ideas and beliefs, being more interested in helping them to develop their own. This even extended to their religious education, in which he took no part, leaving it entirely to Georgina; and this in spite of the fact that Christianity was the mainspring of his life.

In her multifarious activities at Hatfield Georgina came into contact with all kinds of people, and in her dealings with them she was no snob. She once said she was as much at home teaching in a ragged school as dining with a bench of judges and as happy at a theological lecture as at a ball – and that she had yet to find a person capable of boring her. But like her husband she had no love for large-scale entertaining, and this they could not avoid. In his position – he was Prime Minister three times between 1885 and 1902 – it was necessary for them to receive at Hatfield and in London important national and international figures. On these occasions Lord Salisbury put on as brave a face as he could, but it was left to Georgina to bear the brunt. This she did in her usual fashion, resolutely and bossily and with no pretensions to grandeur. Totally uninterested in clothes, she tended to dress down and took pride in it. When the Prince of Wales once remarked that he had seen the gown she was wearing before she replied bluntly that that could well be so and he was likely to see it often again.

In old age Georgina lost none of her vitality and authority. Always caring and benevolent she became an archetypal matriarch, requiring her family to be gathered round her and unwilling to let them go. She died in 1899, four years before her husband. Among the honours that had been bestowed on her was one from the Sultan of Turkey: that of the Order of Chastity – Third Class.

HANNAH ROSEBERY

No Prime Minister was ever so lavishly endowed by the gods as Archibald Philip Primrose, fifth Earl of Rosebery. Rich, charming, good-looking and with great gifts both as an orator and a writer, he should have had a dazzling career. And yet it did not come off as might have been expected.

He was fortunate in his marriage – to the richest heiress in England, who was also a devoted and supportive wife. Hannah Rothschild's grandfather, Nathan Rothschild, was born in a ghetto in Frankfurt but had moved to England at the beginning of the nineteenth century, where he made an immense fortune in banking and by acting as an agent for the British government during the Napoleonic Wars. Hannah Rothschild's father, Meyer, was Nathan's youngest son, a great sportsman and collector of art treasures with which he filled his magnificent mansion at Mentmore in the Chilterns.

The Rosebery and Rothschild families were drawn together by their common interest in racing, both owning outstanding strings of racehorses, and Archie first met Hannah at Newmarket where they were introduced by Mary Anne Disraeli. However, they did not become engaged until ten years later in 1878, by which time Archie had succeeded to the earldom and Hannah had lost both her parents and, as an only child, had inherited a fortune of some £2 million (worth at least fifty times as much today). At the time Archie, too, was well provided for, with the beautiful Dalmeny estate of 21,000 acres in the Scottish Lowlands as well as a large house near Epsom, from where he supervised his racing interests, and a London house in Berkeley Square. To this were now added Mentmore and a mansion in Piccadilly.

When their engagement was announced there was strong opposition not least from the Jewish community. Hannah was not the first Rothschild to marry a gentile, but it was always a matter of deep concern to Orthodox Jews, even when it was to someone of the highest rank, and the *Jewish Chronicle* wrote of its 'poignant distress'. Disapproval, too, came from the Rosebery family. Archie's mother, who since her second marriage had become the Duchess of Cleveland, wrote of her mortification that he had 'chosen as his wife and the mother of his children one who has not the faith and hope of Christ'. But Archie and Hannah were not put off; they were deeply in love.

Archie had assured his mother that his wedding would be a quiet affair, but this was not to be. There was never any question of Hannah giving up her Jewish faith, and so there were two ceremonies – one a civil marriage at a register office and another in an Anglican church. The first was relatively low key, but the second was attended by most of the *beau monde* headed by the Prince and Princess of Wales, and Hannah was given away by the Prime Minister Benjamin Disraeli (recently ennobled as Lord Beaconsfield).[1]

Predictably there were cynical mutterings about Rosebery having married for money and Hannah for high position and forebodings that the marriage would soon come to grief. These were to be proved wrong, although some credence was given to them by Archie's occasionally cavalier treatment of his wife. Like other noblemen he had a dread of showing his feelings and tended to treat emotional matters with a mask of flippancy. In his letters he sometimes addressed her as 'my dear little woman', which was presumably some kind of joke; and there were times when she became the butt of his sharp wit,[2] which she took quite calmly but which shocked others.

Certainly the marriage proved a perfect partnership. Four children were born to them and Hannah was a gracious hostess and active political wife, always ready to promote her husband's interests. Sadly the marriage was to last only twelve years, for in 1890 at the age of thirty-nine Hannah died of typhoid. It was then that Archie's deep devotion to her became evident and his emotions uncontrollable. He was devastated. 'I have lost the best wife ever man had,' he wrote. He was to live for a further thirty-nine years, but he never thought of marrying again. For him Hannah was irreplaceable.

Ever since he was a young man it had been generally expected that Rosebery would be a political high flyer. But this promise was only partially fulfilled, for his great gifts were matched by fatal flaws. He lacked commitment. He was prepared only to dabble in politics. He was the only Prime Minister never to have sat in the House of Commons and to have experienced the hurly-burly of the hustings. It is difficult to escape the conclusion that he was an aristocratic dilettante who was not prepared to take the rough with the smooth. Even so, he was twice Foreign Secretary and for sixteen months Prime Minister, but he was not a distinguished holder of these offices. Had Hannah lived she might have spurred his ambition. As it was, it seemed to die with her: he became disillusioned with politics and with the Liberal Party, fading from the political scene when he should have been at his prime, and for the last thirty years of his life he lived inconspicuously on the sidelines.

SARAH CAMPBELL-BANNERMAN

Sir Henry Campbell-Bannerman was Prime Minister at the head of a Liberal government from 1905 to 1908, and he would surely not have achieved this eminence but for his wife Sarah, who was the driving force behind him. He was a man of great charm and ability but inclined to be easy-going and conciliatory. Sarah, on the other hand, was always ready to put steel into him, and at every crisis in his career saw to it that he stuck to his guns.

Sarah was the daughter of a Scottish army officer and was herself of a military cast of mind. She was a relentless campaigner on her husband's behalf and took a vital interest in politics. There was never any question of her taking a back seat and leaving all important decisions to her husband. She was as ready to give advice as he was to receive it. Perhaps the most notable occasion on which her influence was felt was when Sir Henry became Prime Minister after the collapse of the Conservative government in 1905 and strong pressure was put on him by some leading Liberals to withdraw to the House of Lords and leave the leadership of the Commons to the more brilliant Henry Asquith. Left to himself, he was willing to consider this, but once Sarah brought her influence to bear he is said to have confronted his colleagues with the cry of 'No surrender!' Subsequently, in office he acquitted himself with much flair and ability.

Sadly, at the time of her husband's triumph Sarah was a dying woman. She had long been suffering from a mortal disease, believed to be neuritis, and died in the following year.

Notes

1. This in spite of the fact that he was a political opponent of Rosebery who was a strong supporter of Gladstone and was about to organize for him his Midlothian Campaign (see p. 90) in which the antagonism between the two party leaders reached its height.

2. One not altogether kindly quip was when he was about to leave and told the assembled company that he was going on ahead and leaving Hannah and the other heavy luggage to follow later.

9

MARGOT ASQUITH

I did not want to sign my own death warrant. – Margot Asquith on why she had not married before

I know nothing more important to the happiness of married life than the recognition of both husband and wife of their separate personal affections. – Margot Asquith

Charming, cassante, rude, dictatorial and magnificent. – Chips Channon on Margot

Among Prime Ministers' wives Margot Asquith was one of the more unconventional and controversial. Quick-witted, articulate and sometimes shocking, she was never long out of the public eye. Her natural place was centre stage, where she usually managed to impress and command attention. At first sight it might seem she achieved everything she sought in life: fame, riches, marriage to the foremost statesman of the age and being loved and courted by other great men. But there was also tragedy in her life: for long periods she was racked with ill health, three of her children died at birth and her marriage was not always on an even keel. Her husband was an entirely different human being to her and he, too, had his idiosyncrasies. He was a brilliant man with a proud record of achievement but, as with most politicians, his career ended with defeat and rejection, and Margot was deeply upset by this.

She came from a remarkable family. Her father, Charles Tennant, was a highly successful Scottish businessman. He was not, as Margot sometimes maintained, a self-made man, as his father had been reasonably prosperous and his forefathers had been small Scottish landowners ('bonnet lairds'). But to an exceptional degree Charles had the Midas touch and in his charge the family fortunes soared, so that he was able to acquire a 4,000-acre estate in Peebleshire where he built a massive mansion in Scottish baronial style, complete with turrets and battlements and twenty-nine bedrooms. It was here that Margot was born and brought up, and it always remained for her a place of enchantment. No joy could ever surpass that which she derived from its moorlands, hills, burns and dykes. And it was her great good fortune that as a child she and her brothers and sisters were given the freedom to roam over the country at will.

Both Margot's parents were special people in their different ways. At first sight her father might have appeared a hard-headed Scottish tycoon, but there was more to him than that: he believed that money was for spending. He acquired a large collection of books and pictures and endowed generously many charities. That he had a temper is certain. Margot once described him as 'a man whose vitality, irritability, energy and impressionability amounted to genius'. In the family circle, as Margot came to be aware, he needed careful handling, but he was never the severe, heavy-handed father and was too immersed in his business affairs to be concerned closely with the bringing up of his family. This he was content to leave to his wife, Emma (née Winslow), who was a very different person. The offshoot of an English country parsonage, she seemed reserved and undistinguished, but she had great inner strength and wisdom. She had to endure the death in childhood of her first four children; in due course she was to have eight more and the upbringing of these, especially the daughters, she oversaw with great good sense. Her instinct was to allow them as much freedom as possible and not to bind them by the conventions of the Victorian age. This suited all of them but in particular her two youngest daughters, Laura and Margot. Vital and independent, they thrived on the freedom they were given, so that each in her way became a unique personality. At that time it was rare for young ladies to go to school, and such formal education as they had was from an assortment of governesses who were not always sympathetic. Margot later described their lessons as 'superficial and scrappy: pianos with magenta pleating behind maple-wood fretwork were thumped; hard paints out of wooden boxes were used to copy flowers and fairies on weekdays and illuminate texts for school children on Sundays. English history was taught and retaught from Alfred the Great to Queen Elizabeth and we recited French fables in the presence of Swiss governesses to pained but interested parents after tea in the evening.' That the sisters did eventually learn much more was due to their initiative in making use of their father's library and their natural intelligence and curiosity. But for much of their childhood they were allowed to run wild in the countryside of the Scottish Lowlands. Margot claimed that this was the dominant force in her upbringing and had moulded her character. She became, she said, 'a child of the heather' and 'as untameable as the winds'. 'There was not a stone dyke, peat bog or patch of burnt or flowering heather with which I was not familiar, and I made friends with wandering tramps and every shepherd, farmer and fisherman on the Border.' But of all the joys of what she later called her 'glorious childhood' the greatest was that of riding; her love of horses became an obsession and her favourite occasions were those when she and Laura were let loose on horseback for a whole day. Dressed in a motley collection of warm clothes – jerseys, knickerbockers, scarves, skirts, boots – they were left to roam wherever the spirit moved them.

But Laura and Margot would not long be satisfied with the beauties of nature and the conversation of rustics. Soon they would discover the great world outside. Their father had become not only a rich man but a Liberal Member of Parliament and a considerable local figure, visited by some of the most significant figures of the age, whom the girls found fascinating. They loved to listen to them, question them and seek their guidance, while the visitors for their part were delighted by the freshness, intelligence and complete lack of shyness of the girls – so different from the prim Victorian misses prevalent at the time. When Lord Rosebery, the grandest political figure in Scotland, was a guest he loved to visit them in their sitting-room and described them as 'little quaint romping girls . . . turning up with bright demure faces in unexpected places'. And when the great Mr Gladstone came to their house in London he was led off, not at all unwillingly, for a private talk with Margot in her room.

At first Charles Tennant had been inclined to invite only older guests to the estate, but his wife persuaded him that if his daughters were not to elope with grooms or gamekeepers he must also ask younger men. These included some of the most eligible in the country, and the sisters were fascinated by them but unabashed; it did not occur to them to treat them with awe. Visitors had to accept that life at Glen was unconventional; they were allowed to go for long walks with the girls unchaperoned, and it was even permitted that after their elders had retired to bed they could adjourn to the girls' sitting-room for long talks into the night. It would have astonished them if it had been suggested that there was anything improper in this.

Many were the proposals of marriage that soon came their way (so many that Laura made it a condition before going on a walk with a young man that he would not propose to her). For at that time they had no thoughts of marriage; their lives were so rapturously happy that they could not think of a change. But then, sadly, they both succumbed at the same time to the same man. Alfred Lyttelton was certainly remarkable. He was an outstanding games player – an England footballer and cricketer as well as royal tennis champion.[1] But unlike most great games players he was also a man of considerable intellect and nobility of character. He came from a large, somewhat eccentric family (see p. 81), aristocratic but impecunious, and in due course would become a successful barrister and a Cabinet Minister.

It is likely that Alfred was aware of the feelings of both sisters towards him, but it was with Laura that he fell in love. She, too, was an exceptional person with fascinating charm and great vitality and warmth. Their marriage seemed to be of the gods, but after less than a year she died in childbirth. In a deeply emotional tribute Lord Curzon, who loved her dearly, described her as 'one of those ethereal emanations that sometimes flash for a moment from the unseen and then disappear again into it, leaving a wonder and enchantment that till the end of life creates a thrill in the heart of everyone who beheld the spectacle'.

This was a sad time for Margot. She was deeply disappointed that her love for Alfred was not requited and, devoted as she was to Laura, she could not but feel some pangs of jealousy. However, she was devastated by her death. She had been the closest companion Margot was ever to have, and life without her seemed unendurable. For some time afterwards she was haunted by nightmares and could hardly bring herself to go back to Glen, as everything there reminded her of Laura and their life together. However, courage and resilience were Margot's strong suits, and it was not long before she was creating a new life for herself; she now had greater freedom for this, as of the two Laura had always been the dominant partner and Margot had to a degree lived in her shadow.

One way in which Margot sought relief from her sorrow was in visits to the East End of London, where she befriended girls working in a box factory and took them on trips to the country. However, it is not clear how much of a solace Margot found this. At times she wrote that she derived more interest from visiting the poor than the rich and got on better with them, but at others she confided to her diary that she found it 'a penance'.

Another place, of a very different sort, where Margot found escape from her unhappiness was the hunting field. She had always been a passionate horsewoman, but it was not until she was sixteen that she was introduced to hunting, and she immediately became obsessed with the sport. To her there was no excitement like riding a strong, ungovernable horse, jumping dangerous fences and galloping over open country in the forefront of the chase. Later her exploits were described by Winston Churchill in typical Churchillian language:

> Few there were in the gay, hard-riding crowd which frequented Melton Mowbray or followed the Duke of Beaufort's hounds in the nineties able to surpass the featherweight daredevil, mounted upon enormous horses, who with faultless nerve and thrust and inexhaustible energy, spurred by love of chase and desire to excel, came sometimes to grief but always to the fore.

There were eight years between Laura's death and Margot's marriage, during which time she was to have many proposals and some love affairs, and a singular feature of her life was the happy and fruitful (and platonic) relationships she had with some much older men. It has already been seen how she captivated Mr Gladstone, who, uncharacteristically, broke into verse in her praises:

When Parliament ceases and comes the recess
And we seek in the country rest after distress
As a rule upon visitors place an embargo
But make an exception in favour of Margot.

For she brings such a treasure of movement and life
Fun, spirit and stir to folk weary of strife.
Though young and though fair, who can hold such a cargo
Of all the good qualities going as Margot.

Later Margot struck up a friendship with a famous scholar, initially in a rather bizarre fashion. She was staying in a house party and was performing a little dance when she took a tumble and found herself at the feet of an elderly clergyman, whom she first supposed to be the local vicar but who turned out to be the eminent Master of Balliol College, Oxford, Benjamin Jowett. It seemed unlikely that this would be the beginning of a close relationship, but Jowett was entranced by Margot's openness and spontaneity and perceived in her great talents, which he warned her not to waste 'before youth will have made itself wings and fled away and you find yourself fair, fat and forty-five'. Like all great teachers Jowett knew that he must not only instruct but listen, which he did with great attentiveness and sympathy. Their friendship was to be an entirely happy one, he expanding her perceptions and she bringing freshness into the last years of a lonely old man.

Yet another famous elderly man to fall under Margot's spell was the Poet Laureate, Lord Tennyson. He had been devoted to Laura, who had treated him with no great awe and not much respect, telling him on one occasion that he was untidy and that his personal hygiene was not all that it might be. This had amused him greatly, and he asked Margot if she agreed with her sister, and when she concurred he did her the special honour of changing for dinner. Later he gave her readings of his poetry and took her for long exhausting walks, discoursing freely all the way. From him, too, Margot received great intellectual stimulation.

It was not, of course, only with older men that Margot consorted. She had young male friends as well. There was at that time a distinguished group of gifted young people drawn from all political parties (but not all social classes), who used to meet regularly and talk deeply on great matters, as well as playing intellectual games and composing doggerel verse about each other. This not altogether self-effacing coterie claimed to be tolerant of everything except stupidity or silence and in the course of time acquired the sobriquet of 'The Souls' (almost certainly from an irreverent outsider, as they themselves abhorred it). To be a member, as Margot was, was considered a privilege and provided the opportunity to meet some of the most brilliant men and women of the time – men such as Lord Curzon, a future Viceroy of India and Foreign Secretary who loved Margot dearly but had no thoughts of marrying her, and Arthur Balfour, a future Prime Minister who also loved her but when asked if he might marry her said that he rather thought of having a career of his own.

There was, however, another brilliant and ambitious young man who did long to marry her. Alfred Milner, later Higher Commissioner of South Africa during the Boer War, was deeply in love with her and contrived to propose to her by moonlight in the shadows of the great pyramids; but to no avail. Margot was certainly fond of him and had great respect for his formidable intellect but could not see herself married to him and was not yet ready to give up what she most treasured in life: her independence. As she approached the age of thirty, however, she realized that this was a sacrifice she was going to have to make; the alternative of remaining for the rest of her life single and unattached was not to be contemplated. She nearly married a dashing young blade, magnificent on the hunting field and with great good looks and bravado but little else. She was certainly in love with Peter Flower but then came to the conclusion that after a diet of Jowett and Tennyson he would have been too much of a contrast. In the end she was to choose a husband of a very different sort.

Margot first met Henry Asquith in 1891 at a party in the House of Commons when she was twenty-seven and he was thirty-eight.[2] At the time he was the rising star in the Liberal Party and about to be appointed Home Secretary. Margot was immediately attracted by the power of his intellect and forceful but gentle personality, which put people at their ease and drew out the best in them. In her uninhibited way she poured out to him all that was on her mind and he listened with rapt attention, for the attraction was mutual, Asquith appreciating her wit and charm and riveted by her outgoing and unorthodox nature. He must also have been flattered by the eager attention paid to him by a woman younger than himself and a leading light in fashionable society.

Eminent as was his position on the political scene, Asquith at that time had had little contact with society. He came from a middle-class Nonconformist background in Yorkshire, where his father had been a prosperous cloth merchant. He died when Henry was eight and soon afterwards the family had moved south; his mother, who had bronchial ailments, went to live on the south coast, while Henry was put into lodgings in London and sent to the City of London School. While this hardly provided him with a warm family background it did afford him much greater freedom than if he had been at boarding-school, and he made full use of this to develop his outstanding intellectual gifts. In due course he won a classical scholarship at Balliol College, Oxford, where, without undue effort, he achieved the highest academic honours. There then followed a period when he strove to make a career for himself as a barrister, but in this, for once in his life, he had limited success; it seems that he was not an advocate of the top class. When he was elected to Parliament, however, he made his mark immediately and after only six years was appointed Home Secretary by Gladstone.

In the months that followed his first meeting with Margot their friendship deepened and they found opportunities to have long talks together. There was at this point no question of a love affair, let alone marriage, as Henry's first wife Helen was still alive. He had married her when he was a struggling barrister, and since then she had provided him with a stable, comfortable home and five children. But once he become famous and successful she had not been able, indeed she had not attempted, to keep pace with him. She had no interest in politics or society and preferred to live a quiet domestic life in Hampstead with her young family. Margot tried to get to know her and was respectful of her but not a little condescending, describing her as 'gentle, pretty and unambitious', saying that 'she lived in Hampstead and had no clothes'. Helen, for her part, kept her distance from Margot, telling her that she would never care for the sort of society she loved and was happier in the circle of her home and family. And when Margot told her that her husband was destined for the highest political distinction, she replied that this was not what she wished for him.

At the end of 1891 Margot's life became very complicated: she was just getting over her love affair with Peter Flower; Alfred Milner was yearning to marry her as also was a younger man, Evan Charteris. Towards all of these her feelings were ambivalent: she liked them and enjoyed their company (although in different ways) but did not want to be tied irrevocably to any of them. At the same time, however, she felt the need to be married and knew that at her age this could not be long delayed. And the situation became even more fraught, when, after the death from typhoid of Helen Asquith, Henry became a suitor. This was too much for Margot. The situation overwhelmed her. She was reduced to nervous exhaustion, unable to sleep or eat and perpetually on edge.

She had unbounded admiration for Henry; her association with him had been 'a great awakening', and there was no one to whom she looked more readily for companionship and advice; but love she did not feel, certainly not physical love. And their backgrounds were completely different: Henry's was urban and middle class and his life up to then had been narrow and domestic, with little experience of country life or society. On the hunting field and the dance floor, where Margot excelled, he was an incongruous, even ridiculous figure. They did have some interests in common, but their temperaments were poles apart: Margot impulsive, direct and excitable; Henry calm, straitlaced and aloof. But there was nothing aloof about his wooing of Margot. The floodgates opened as he poured out his heart to her. She was, he told her, 'all that is purest and highest in my life, my genius and my joy, the light of all my day and the hope of my life beyond politics'. 'Never', he declared, 'have I been so fully happy since I have loved you. You have made me a different man.' Margot could not but be moved by such protestations, but still she was confused and hesitant. Could she, the freest of the free, bear to lose her independence and make the sacrifices that marriage would entail? And would she be a suitable wife for a Cabinet Minister, she who had never known what it was to be tactful or discreet? In her distress she took refuge at Glen, but even there she found no solace and caused great anxiety to her family. The prospect of finally refusing Milner and accepting Asquith made her distraught, and for days she lay in a darkened room not wanting to see or talk to anyone. In time she recovered, to the extent of inviting Henry for a visit, and once again she was enchanted by his company and conversation but still held back from an acceptance, and he left Glen in a deeply gloomy frame of mind. But then, quite suddenly, she recovered some of her equilibrium, returned to London and wrote to Henry agreeing to marry him.

He was overjoyed. 'The thing has come which I have most longed for, prayed for, willed, as I never did with any other aim or object in my life,' he wrote. Two days after accepting him Margot broke her collar-bone while out hunting, and the announcement of their engagement was delayed for a month, and it was not for another two months after that that Margot made the acquaintance of her five stepchildren. Establishing a satisfactory relationship with them was to be Margot's greatest problem.

'Will I be able to love them?' she wrote to a friend. 'I cannot love to order.' She was to find that they were a remarkable and gifted family but cool and unapproachable. In her autobiography she wrote: 'I do not think that if you had ransacked the world you could have found natures so opposite in temper, temperament and outlook as myself and my step-children when I first knew them . . . Shy, self-engaged, critical and controversial, nothing surprised them and nothing upset them.' The eldest was Raymond, sixteen at the time, a scholar of Winchester, brilliantly academic, bookish and aloof. It has been said of Wykehamists that they can always be recognized by their powers of 'spontaneous aversion', and there can be little doubt that Raymond took a spontaneous aversion to Margot. The glittering fashionable figure was not to his taste, and to some extent this was passed on to the rest of the family. There was no open breach; they were too polite for that, but constraint and coolness were generally present.

In time the stepchild with whom Margot had greatest difficulty was not Raymond but his sister Violet. Margot's complaint that her stepchildren had 'hearts of stone' and were 'lacking in temperament' could not apply to her. Highly intelligent and already with a strong mind of her own, she was of all the children the closest to her father and would be likely to resent any intrusion into this special relationship. For the first twenty-one years of Margot's marriage Violet lived at home, and there were times when they found each other a sore trial. Not only was there a clash of temperaments but jealousy as to which was the closest to Henry. It says much for both women that during this time there was no open breach. Margot did not seek to impose too much advice and motherliness on Violet, while Violet regarded her stepmother with what she called a 'tolerant detachment'. She was ready to be guided by her in such minor matters as dress and deportment but not on anything more profound. Many years later she recorded her memories of Margot in mildly affectionate if patronizing terms: 'She filled us with admiration, amazement, amusement, affection, sometimes (as children) with a vague sense of uneasiness as to what she might, or might not, do next.'

Margot's behaviour after she had accepted Henry was hardly to her credit; there was little evidence of unselfishness. Although Henry in his joy was eager to let their engagement be known to the world she insisted at first on keeping it secret, and for a long time would not agree to the fixing of a wedding date. Henry's wish for a long honeymoon was also refused on the grounds that they might get bored with each other. Certainly there were no signs of excitement, let alone rapture. To the contrary, her letters were full of sadness and apprehension. Pathetically she wrote to a friend: 'Groping as I had been for years to find a character and intellect superior to my own, I did not feel equal to facing it when I found it.' And even more sadly: 'I often want help more than I dare own and there is loneliness in my life which few suspect.' Nor was there much comfort and joy when news of their engagement at last became public. Some of her friends openly bewailed it, impressing on her the differences between them and how much her lifestyle would have to change.[3] Others took the view that she should be 'groomed for the part' and loaded her with advice, which drove her to distraction. Years later she described the agonies of her engagement to her stepdaughter Violet, who was going through much the same ordeal: 'Nothing in the world makes one feel so ill. When I was engaged to your father I felt like death and lost two stone.'

While Margot fretted Henry remained confident and joyful; he found intoxicating the prospect of marriage to the brilliant Margot and the new life this would open up to him. But he sensed Margot's fears and unease and tried to reassure her. 'A wild horse is not tamed in a day,' he told her, and there were no promises he would not make: 'I will give you everything that is in me to give – shelter, devotion, unshakeable loyalty, timeless trust and homage, and I will take from you nothing but your love. The way of your life shall be as you determine and your choice shall be my law.'

Henry's friends, like Margot's, were uneasy about the marriage. It seemed to them Margot was too irresponsible and lacking in decorum, and they had worries, too (not unjustified as it proved), of the effect on Henry of too close an association with fashionable society.

However, in spite of much doubt and sorrow the engagement held,[4] and on 10 May 1894 Margot and Henry were married in style in St George's, Hanover Square, with no less than four past and present Prime Ministers signing the register.[5] But difficulties persisted. Their first year of marriage was hardly propitious. In the autumn Margot took Henry at his word that her way of life would be as she determined it and, despite the fact that she was pregnant, went off hunting as usual in Leicestershire, leaving Henry in a half-empty house in London. She was not to remain there for long, however, as after a few weeks she received an urgent summons to Glen, where her mother was dying of cancer.

She stayed in Glen until her mother died four months later, and during that time it did not seem to occur to her that she should be with her newly married husband or even take very much notice of him. When she did eventually rejoin him he was overjoyed to see her, but soon afterwards she was overcome by the agonies of a very difficult pregnancy and was convinced that she was going to die. In the event she did not, but the baby did, and this was something from which she never recovered. 'No true woman', she said later, 'ever gets over the loss of a child.' And in the following years she was to lose two more babies during childbirth. In the months after this she was racked with ill health – post-natal depression, phlebitis and, perhaps worst of all, constant insomnia. During this time Henry badly needed her by his side, as there was a General Election in which she might have played a vital part, but she was unable to leave her sick-bed and, although visited and comforted by the highest in the land, her spirits sank even lower. Not so low, however, that she was unable to hunt in the autumn, leaving Henry once again alone and in some discomfort without Margot to attend to his needs and organize his household. When her elder sister remonstrated with her about this she was defiant, saying that hunting was essential to her well-being and without it her nervous system would collapse.

Married life became less traumatic for Margot when at the beginning of 1897 she was safely delivered of a daughter, Elizabeth, and, rather to her surprise, found herself a doting mother. She spent many hours with the baby and formulated theories about her upbringing which may or may not have been beneficial to Elizabeth but which certainly benefited Margot, who became more relaxed and easy to live with; there was less talk of her nerves, and hunting became less of an obsession.

Following the Conservative victory in the General Election of 1895 the Liberals were to be out of office for the next eleven years. During this time it was necessary for Asquith to curtail his parliamentary activities. With a young family to educate, an extravagant wife and his own lifestyle becoming ever less simple he had to earn all the money he could at the Bar. He was widely recognized as the rising star of the Liberal Party and might have become its leader earlier than he did, but while it was in opposition this was something he could not afford.

Margot's father, Charles Tennant, had been wonderfully generous to her and Henry when they married, buying them a house in Cavendish Square and giving Margot an ample allowance, but this could not be relied upon to continue. In 1898 at the age of seventy-five the doughty old man married again and his new wife, thirty-five years younger than he, proceeded to bear him three more daughters, after which the number of his offspring amounted to nine.

Until then Margot had been well off and had spent freely. She was not good at economizing, besides which she was always impulsively generous, as, for example, when her stepson Raymond fell in love but felt he could not marry because of the inadequacy of his financial prospects; she immediately made him an allowance which she could ill afford (and he by his treatment of her did not, perhaps, deserve).

For a time, then, Margot's marriage was on a more even keel, but in 1900 disaster struck again when she became pregnant and lost another baby at birth and, as before, became devastated by post-natal depression and insomnia, which she described as 'akin to insanity'. Two years afterwards, to her great joy, she did manage to give birth safely to a son, Anthony, but then four years later in 1906 she lost a third baby at birth. Then at last her doctors laid down firmly that there should be no more pregnancies, and she and Henry felt bound to comply. This meant the end of the physical side of their marriage, which was no great loss to Margot, as sex had never been a great joy to her. But this was not the case with Henry, and such a development would, inevitably, put a strain on their marriage.

No one could have been a more indulgent husband than Henry. He had been infinitely loving and caring during Margot's illnesses and had borne with great forbearance her long absences and peccadilloes. It could be that what Margot needed was for him to be firmer and more dominant, but after 1906 there was a change in her attitude and lifestyle: she became less headstrong and independent; she spent more time with her family; and at last she got rid of her horses. At the same time she felt greater love and admiration for Henry and became more involved in his political career which was becoming much more active. In that year there was a General Election in which the Liberals were returned to power with a large majority, and there was a feeling among many party members that Asquith should head the incoming Liberal government. He, however, was not willing to displace the existing party leader, Henry Campbell-Bannerman, and, having been given by him free choice of any other post in the government, chose that of Chancellor of the Exchequer.

It was eleven years since Henry had been in office as Home Secretary, and it was a different man who took over the responsibilities of Chancellor. Marriage to Margot had wrought changes. The serious, hard-working, aloof figure had given way to a man of the world, more gregarious and pleasure-loving. He clearly found the social life, which came with marriage to Margot, captivating. He smartened up his appearance, took lessons in dancing and spent much time playing bridge. It was noticeable, also, that he now had a preference for feminine rather than masculine company. Whereas before his leisure hours were taken up mainly with serious intellectual conversation with other men, now he seemed to prefer light, even frivolous talk with society ladies. At first his work did not suffer, but this would not always be the case.

From the time that Henry took office again Margot became ever more embroiled in the political arena. Here her devotion to her husband was complete; he could do no wrong and his word was gospel. The slightest criticism or contretemps brought her out fighting. Certainly she was the most loyal of political wives, but loyalty requires more than adulation. There is also a time for candour (which Margot was only too ready to employ with others). Like other mortals Henry had his failings, and it should have been up to his wife to confront him with them. It was not in his best interests that the two women closest to him, Margot and his daughter Violet, should have blinded themselves to his faults and surrounded him only with praise and automatic accord.

Henry did not have to wait long for the premiership. In 1908 Campbell-Bannerman had a heart attack and resigned soon afterwards; Henry was his natural successor. Great as was Margot's excitement at Henry having attained the position that for so long she had proclaimed was his due, this delight did not extend to moving into 10 Downing Street. This was not then the national institution it has since become. In the past forty years it had been neglected and allowed to become run down; Prime Ministers had either not lived there or had not maintained it. Later Margot wrote that when she and Henry moved in it was 'liver-coloured and squalid on the outside and inconvenient and uncomfortable inside, and taxi drivers did not know the way there'.[6] But she set to work with a will and brought to bear her undeniable talent and good taste in transforming it. That done she entertained lavishly and heterogeneously – not just safe, solid citizens but what she called 'oddities', people from the byways as well as the highways, what her husband once called 'the usual menagerie'.

The government Asquith formed in 1908 was an exceptionally strong one; it contained men of outstanding ability and character, including two future Prime Ministers of great fame – David Lloyd George and Winston Churchill. It lasted for eight and a half years that included some of the most momentous times in the country's history and encountered many storms during which Henry needed all Margot's support. One of these was not long in breaking out.

The passing of the Parliament Act, restricting the powers of the House of Lords, engendered some of the bitterest political strife in the country's history. Family was divided against family, the best of friends could not bear to be in the same room together and in Parliament itself there was often bedlam. Throughout the two years it took for the bill to be passed the Asquith family was in the thick of the battle, the object of the most hysterical abuse, and at all times Margot stood by her husband and gave him strong and vociferous support, of which he had great need as he himself had an intense dislike for the infighting of politics. And further troubles lay ahead, for in 1912 the government took the decision to introduce another bill (the third) for Irish Home Rule. Until then these measures had always been blocked by the House of Lords. However, with the passing of the Parliament Act the Lords could no longer reject a Home Rule Bill, they could only delay it (for two years); this caused

frenzy in the Protestant provinces of Ulster. Here open rebellion was threatened, and it seemed that civil war was imminent. At the same time there was
the noisy and violent campaign of the suffragettes – mostly well-to-do ladies
– demanding the right to vote. Rather strangely for a Liberal Prime Minister
(and a great lover of ladies) Asquith was implacably opposed to this, as also
were his wife and daughter, which meant that he became the chief target of the
suffragettes' militancy and found himself not only being shrilly interrupted
at his political meetings, but being assailed with umbrellas and having his
windows broken. And looming over all these problems was the far more dreadful one of the threat of a European war.

The strain on Asquith at this time was indeed intense and he needed the
strongest support. This was always readily forthcoming from his wife and daughter, but he apparently required more. In order to preserve his mental stability
he felt the need to pour out his most intimate thoughts and feelings by letter
to a sympathetic correspondent, someone much younger than himself, feminine and outside of his marriage. This had always been the case: during his
first marriage Margot had been the main recipient of these outpourings, but
after his marriage to her she was replaced by others. Margot had always known
that her husband was highly susceptible and liked to be surrounded by eager,
attractive young women and at first had not particularly resented them, referring to them jocularly as 'Henry's little harem'.

In 1912 the situation assumed a different dimension when Henry became
infatuated with a much younger woman, Venetia Stanley, a close friend of
Violet's. She was a woman of no great beauty – a contemporary referred to
her 'dark-eyed, aquiline good looks' – but was cultivated, intelligent and a
good listener. As the strain on Asquith mounted so, too, did his need for a more
frequent and intense correspondence. In time he was writing to her as many
as four letters a day and these, which had at first been in the nature of chit-
chat, became more personal and passionate, containing also candid and detailed
comments on political affairs, including some state secrets.

It is extraordinary that Asquith did not realize how dangerous and irresponsible this was. It was almost inconceivable that Venetia would deliberately
betray his confidence, but she might be inadvertently indiscreet, and the letters
might fall into the hands of those who would make unscrupulous use of them,
including blackmail. And Henry's indiscretion was not confined to writing
letters. He went for frequent drives with Venetia in public view and stayed
frequently at her parents' home, where he went on long walks and played golf
with her. In those days there were not, as now, investigative journalists who
dogged ministers' footsteps and broadcast every detail in the popular press,
but such goings-on could not be concealed completely, especially not from
Asquith's family.

Since 1906, when Margot lost her third baby and she and Henry moved
into separate bedrooms, their marriage had been on a decline. Increasingly

they went their separate ways, notably on holidays, and sought the company of different friends. Most wounding of all to Margot, Henry ceased to consult her or confide in her on political matters. In the family circle politics were never discussed, and even on social occasions with government colleagues he was not to be drawn. Winston Churchill complained that, when entertaining him on the admiralty yacht, *Enchantress*, 'he maintained a reserve on all serious matters which was unbreakable'. But then this reserve came tumbling down in the avalanche of letters to Venetia. Margot must have known this and been deeply hurt by it. To a friend she described herself as being 'wounded, humiliated and bewildered'. As a result her health began to suffer: her insomnia returned, her nerves were always on edge and she smoked incessantly. Other troubles she had, too: she had never received much support from Violet, but now relations became even more strained. And Elizabeth was not always a comfort; she had as independent a mind as her mother and had no intention of being dominated by her. She became prone to tantrums and fretfulness and let it be known that she found the English social scene boring, showing no gratitude to her mother for all the trouble she took on her behalf. Outside the family, too, there were tensions: Margot's circle of friends was growing smaller. The uproar surrounding the Parliament and Irish Home Rule bills had led to broken friendships, and people were becoming less tolerant of her eccentric ways; the candour and sharp wit, so attractive in youth, were less becoming in middle age and were all too often causing offence.

Mortified as she was by Henry's infatuation with Venetia, Margot behaved as if it did not exist. She made no scenes and to most friends dismissed the matter as being of no importance. To her the essential thing was to 'keep up appearances'. Only a few people knew of her torment. Many years later in one of her several works of autobiography she wrote movingly of the strains a wife has to bear in marriage: 'No woman should expect to be the only woman in her husband's life . . . I not only encouraged his female friends but posted his letters to them if I found them in our front hall.' And in another work she wrote:

> I think that jealousy is the cause of half the unhappiness in the world. It is more of a punishment than a crime, but, worse than this, it distorts all sense of proportion, destroys the serenity of the soul and has marred some of the most promising married lives. If a woman has sufficient love for her husband she is selfish and vain to expect no other woman to care for him. She should welcome the friendships which give him pleasure, even if they are temporarily tinged by what is called 'physical attraction'. It is contrary to all wisdom to expostulate or enquire into every movement of the man you love. As his wife and the mother of his children, you will always be in the strongest position and if you are patient and keep him amused he will ultimately tire of his passing

passion. If you do not conquer your jealousy you will prompt him to deceive you and alienate the affection which is the foundation of your home and without which your married life must be a failure: you would be a rudderless ship which sails dangerously upon unknown seas.

Written in the comparative calm of old age, this advice must have been hard to take to heart at the time, when she saw her husband becoming more and more engrossed with a younger woman.

In August 1914 the country suddenly found itself engaged in the First World War, and from some of its other problems the government then had temporary relief. There was a surge of patriotism in the country, so that industrial strife subsided and the threat of civil war in Ireland receded; also the suffragettes laid down their weapons and threw themselves into the war effort. But it was not long before far graver problems emerged. Almost at once the war went badly. The German invasion of France through Belgium carried all before it, and the small British Expeditionary Force, which found itself directly in its way, had to make a long and rapid retreat to avoid being overwhelmed.

In the end the German advance was halted at the Battle of the Marne, and their forces driven back from Paris, but then British and French attacks were repelled, with heavy losses, and a deadlock was reached that would last for the next four years, the greatest offensives resulting in minuscule gains of territory at enormous cost. At the same time the Russian armies were driven out of Eastern Europe, and an attempt to knock Germany's ally Turkey out of the war by an attack on Gallipoli in the Dardanelles failed and had to be abandoned.[7]

Inevitably these disasters were laid at the door of the government, which came under vicious attack not only from the Conservative opposition but from the popular press of Lord Northcliffe. Asquith himself bore the brunt of this and was an easy target; he was not a natural war leader. Certainly he had great courage and judgement and infinite patience, but he was lacking in decisiveness and verve. More and more it was being said that a new government was needed if the war was to be won. With its majority in Parliament the Liberal government could not be displaced entirely, but there was a growing demand for a coalition with other parties, and to this, at the end of 1915, Asquith felt compelled to agree. Later he described the formation of the coalition government as the most uncongenial job he had ever had to carry through. It meant replacing close and loyal colleagues with men of a different kind, with many of whom he had little sympathy.

At the same time he was under great stress within his own family. Apart from the strained relations between Margot and Violet, three of his sons had gone to fight in the war. Of these Raymond was in the forefront of the battle in France (he was killed in 1916). Herbert (Beb) had been severely shell-shocked in Belgium, and Arthur (Oc) was in the midst of the gruelling and chaotic Gallipoli campaign in which he had been unpleasantly but not critically wounded. And then, with affairs at their worst, came a shattering blow when Venetia Stanley became engaged to be married and broke off her correspondence with him. This had become a lifeline to him and, more than anything else, so he believed, kept him sane and balanced amid overwhelming pressure. The situation was made worse by the fact that the man to whom Venetia had become engaged, Edwin Montagu, was a close friend and Cabinet colleague. Henry did, however, have a fall-back, and on the same day he heard of the engagement he embarked on an equally prolific correspondence with Venetia's sister, Sylvia Henley.

This was another bitter blow to Margot, who was teeming with advice and strong views and was longing to impart them and become once again Henry's main confidante; instead of which she saw her influence with him continue to wane. Never for a moment, though, did her loyalty to him falter. She stood by him stalwartly and fought his battles with gusto and, as always, was not backward in letting her views be known. Most people knew that she disliked and mistrusted the War Minister, Lord Kitchener, whom she described as 'a great poster' and 'a natural cad'. Also she was coming to distrust deeply Lloyd George who, she had no doubt, was jockeying behind the scenes to take Henry's place as Prime Minister. To all ideas of a coalition Margot had been vehemently opposed, regarding such a thing as 'un-English' as well as being an indication that Henry was failing in his job.

It was a great worry to her that Henry seemed to have little stomach for the fight or for standing up for himself; he seemed content to let the storms ride over him and wait for them to subside, which was certainly not her attitude. She believed passionately that Henry had the capacity to lead the country to victory and was the best man for the job. But it must sometimes have occurred to her that he was not the leader he had once been. Overwhelming stress combined with some over-indulgence, particularly in drink, had taken their toll. His mind was still clear and active but he often seemed aloof and indecisive. It was certainly not the case that he was neglecting his duties; his achievements in uniting the country and putting it on a war footing were inestimable. Sir Maurice Hankey, a civil servant who collaborated with him closely, later wrote of his 'masterly and courageous handling of one desperately difficult situation after another . . . I have often wondered how any man could find it physically possible to carry simultaneously so many heavy burdens.'

However, it seems that Asquith did not fully realize that his apparently calm and laid-back attitude could be misinterpreted, and it did not go unnoticed how much time he spent on the golf course and playing bridge with young women. People did not appreciate that for him to survive such intolerable strains relaxation was essential, and if this took the form of golf or bridge or writing endless letters to young female correspondents (sometimes even during Cabinet meetings), so be it. But as the war continued to take turns for the worse the press campaigns against him grew in intensity, and intrigues to replace him with someone younger and more dynamic gathered in strength. And such a man was at hand and all too ready to take over.

David Lloyd George, 'the little Welsh wizard', had had a meteoric rise to fame from humble origins and had now come to believe, like William Pitt before him, that only he could save England. He was therefore conspiring actively, and not all that secretly, with Conservative and Labour leaders as well as some disaffected Liberals to form a new government with himself at the head. It was not actually his intention to be rid of Asquith completely; he would have preferred to 'push him upstairs' into some harmless, honourable place; but on this Asquith was firm: he would not serve in a subordinate position. When it came to the crunch he played his cards with little adroitness; in the belief that no one else would be able to form a government he resigned so that this could be demonstrated, only to discover that a new administration was available and that he himself had been edged out and was no more than a leader of a small group of Liberals who had remained loyal to him but who counted for little. He was never to be in office again.

Margot would be for ever deeply embittered by this treatment of her husband. For her the battle was never over. She would not rest until he had been reinstated. But, sadly, at this moment of crisis she and Henry were at odds. Both of them were aware that there was constraint between them. Margot, usually the most forthright of counsellors, knew that there were subjects into which she could not venture, while Henry, desperately as he might need a confidante, could not bring himself to confide in her. She was too emotional and on edge. He needed someone calmer with less strong views of her own.

During the anti-Asquith press campaign it was always likely that Margot would come into the firing line; her idiosyncrasies and tactlessness made her a prominent target. At the beginning of the war the absurd notion had been put about that she was secretly pro-German. This seems to have derived from such petty matters as her refusal to dismiss the family's much-loved German (but long since Anglicized) governess and a warm friendship she had had with the departing German ambassador and his wife. All sorts of lunatic stories were spread abroad: she owned shares in Krupps steel works; her daughter was secretly engaged to the son of the German admiral von Tirpitz; she had taken expensive food to German prisoners of war and played tennis with them; even that she had been seen on the coast signalling to German submarines. Left to herself Margot would have ignored such rubbish and treated it with contempt, but she was fearful of how Henry would be affected, and so she brought a libel action against *The Globe* and was awarded £1,000 damages.

Cruel and unjust as these charges against Margot were, it was nevertheless thought by some at the time, including friends, that she did not do enough to bolster the war effort; in particular she did not give a lead in encouraging and helping all those women who were doing men's work. She visited hospitals frequently, and many were her acts of kindness to wounded soldiers of all ranks, but she did not become involved in any great organization or under-take hard, gruelling work. At the same time it was noted by her critics that she continued to entertain lavishly at Downing Street when others were leading lives of austerity. Certainly she did not deserve the hatred and malice directed against her in the press and elsewhere, and too little account was taken of the stressful life she lived and the example set by her family. Of her four stepsons, all of whom enlisted at an early stage, Raymond was killed in 1916 in the battle of the Somme and Arthur had a quite outstanding war, winning the DSO and two bars and being recommended for the Victoria Cross.[8] Herbert, too, endured all the horrors of trench warfare, being wounded and badly shell-shocked. All of them could, no doubt, have obtained safe staff jobs, but they opted to remain with their regiments in the front line. Cyril (Cys), the youngest, did not have this option owing to his ill health.

After Henry's loss of office his plight was dismal indeed. As well as being in the political wilderness he and Margot had at first no home to go to, as their house in Cavendish Square was let. They were also in financial straits. Henry had little money apart from his Prime Minister's salary and Margot's family money was drying up. As leader of the Liberal remnant which had not joined Lloyd George's coalition, he was the official leader of the Opposition, but he showed little stomach for the fight and, to Margot's despair, little interest in regaining his lost position; for the time being he relapsed into a quiet life of reading and letter-writing. Margot's efforts on his behalf were unremitting but without success and only caused bad blood and loss of friends. And she continued to be involved in controversy – even scandal.

In 1918, at a time of great crisis in the war, the nation was to be diverted by a major sex scandal – the so-called 'Black Book Trial'. This bizarre affair began when a maverick member of Parliament, N. Pemberton Billing, became obsessed with the idea that most of Britain's top people were indulging in sexual malpractices, and that the German secret service had compiled for blackmailing purposes a 'Black Book' said to contain the names of no less than 47,000 prominent men and women who were 'practitioners of vices all decent men thought had perished in Sodom and Lesbos'. Billing published an article on this matter in a magazine he owned, *The Vigilante*, and when this was not taken seriously followed it up with an explicitly defamatory article about an erotic dancer called Maud Allan who was about to play the part of Salome in Oscar Wilde's play, accusing her of being a lesbian. When she sued him for libel he produced in court a witness who claimed to have seen inside the 'Black Book', where were mentioned the names of numerous well-known people including Henry and Margot Asquith (as well as the judge who was presiding over the trial!). It was then revealed that some years earlier Maud Allan had been invited by Margot to 10 Downing Street, where she had performed a dance in bare feet which some people at the time considered shocking and which gave rise to the notion that Margot must have lesbian tendencies. Of course only few people took this nonsense seriously, but it added another absurd rumour about Margot to those already in circulation.

After his resignation Asquith's political life slowly and sadly petered out. As leader of the Opposition he made little impact. When he did criticize the government he was usually accused of jealousy and personal bitterness. In the 'Coupon Election'[9] of 1918 he suffered a major blow when, after thirty years representing East Fife, he was defeated. In a by-election at Paisley the following year he was elected but was deeply depressed on his return to the House of Commons. It seemed to him that a new breed of politician had taken over, one that gave him no welcome and, indeed, seemed to treat him with scorn. After the General Election of 1924 there was a hung Parliament in which the Liberals held the balance between Conservative and Labour, and Asquith took the critical decision to support Labour, thus letting in the first Labour government. In the following year he accepted a peerage to became the Earl of Oxford, and he went into partial retirement.

During Henry's last years in the political arena Margot did all she could to invigorate him and rekindle his ambition, but she must have known at heart that this was a losing battle. The zest had left him and his overwhelming wish was for peace and repose and time to brood over his memoirs. A quiet life, however, was never for Margot. She was not likely to relapse into a state of meditation and inactivity, and she began to find new interests. These came mainly through her son, Anthony (known as Puffin), who was artistic with many connections in literature and the theatre and was later to become a distinguished film director. Under his influence she became a regular theatregoer and delighted in meeting the leading actors and actresses of the day. During the war she and Henry had acquired a house near Oxford called the Wharf, a somewhat ramshackle ex-pub, and here she gave lively and unconventional parties for Anthony's friends from the university and the stage.

However, Margot's activities in the inter-war years were aimed primarily at restoring the family finances, and in 1919 she embarked on a volume of memoirs. When this became known there was, as might have been expected, considerable anxiety. With her reputation for directness and indiscretion friends and relatives shuddered to think what might be revealed; and when she said she intended to write just as she spoke their fears were enhanced. When the book appeared in 1920 there was a rush to buy it. People were expecting candour, and this they found, although the general tone of the book was milder than it might have been; there were no great sensations nor scandals.

Reviews were mixed: some were enthusiastic, some critical and that in *The Times*, owned then by her old enemy Lord Northcliffe, was blistering. 'A scandal that cannot be justified or excused,' it blazoned, 'prompted by a reckless desire for money or an inordinate craving for notoriety.' But this did no harm to the sales. The book was a sell-out and Margot immediately came under pressure to write a second volume. But first she had to endure what for her was the agony of a lecture tour in the United States. She loathed the idea of this and did her best to get out of it, but pressure from her publisher and her family was too great, and so in 1921, in a state of near panic, accompanied by a secretary, a maid and a vast amount of luggage, she found herself embarking on a sea voyage, which she particularly hated, across the Atlantic. In America she was the focus of attention. Pressmen besieged her everywhere she went. It soon became evident that she was not a natural lecturer (as she herself had been at pains to point out), and her lectures caused some disappointment, but people still thronged to them, longing to bombard her with questions about her life and loves and the way of life of the British upper classes.

On her return to England it was clear that Henry was not enjoying semi-retirement and his health was declining rapidly. He had a series of minor strokes, which left him listless and apathetic. To the end Margot remained completely loyal and devoted, and this in spite of the fact that his treatment of her was sometimes insensitive and offhand. He continued to maintain a correspondence with another woman (since 1920, Hilda Harrisson, a young war widow living in Oxford), and he seems to have been unappreciative of the fact that since his resignation Margot had been the principal family bread-winner. When he died in 1927 it was none too soon. By then his mind had almost completely gone and he had come to regard the Wharf as a prison and Margot his gaoler. In his will he had only £3,000 to bequeath; he left a number of legacies of which the largest was to Hilda Harrisson, with most of the remainder to his children; to Margot he left only a token. The sum total of these far exceeded his estate, but Margot, who might have felt embittered by such a distribution, regarded it as her sacred duty to find the money out of her own resources so that the legacies could be paid in full.

At the end of his life Henry's sufferings were such that Margot had prayed for his deliverance, but when this happened she was overcome with remorse and loneliness. Having always been the most gregarious of people she suddenly felt there was no one to whom she could turn. Her stepchildren were married and had lives of their own; her daughter, too, was married – to Prince Antoine Bibesco of Romania – and lived abroad, and her son Anthony was increasingly preoccupied with his career as a film director. Friends were becoming fewer partly because of death and partly because of her unrelenting outspokenness. As always, she did not mind what she said to anybody.[10] One of her weaknesses was that she did not know when she was causing offence. She was usually ready with copious apologies, but these did not always suffice. At the same time she was still as generous as ever – unstinting in hospitality and open-handed with money, whether she had it or not, so that people marvelled at the combination of such a kind heart and sharp tongue.

In old age Margot was an intimidating figure. The charm was still there, though now more startling than beguiling. The wit was as astringent as ever and her *bons mots*[11] were still eagerly sought after, but these, too, were different – intended to shock and to stun rather than to amuse. Her appearance, too, could be daunting: her dress was always striking and (for her age) she made extensive use of make-up. One person meeting her described her as 'looking like a death mask – an antique skeleton in black satin with bright red coat'. To others she seemed 'a witch' or 'a mad raven'. But she still had admirers. In the forefront of these was Chips Channon – American, socialite, Member of Parliament and keeper of a perceptive and candid diary. To him she was an endless source of fascination – 'charming, cassante, rude, dictatorial, magnificent', also 'a terrific character and the cleverest woman I know'. To Lord David Cecil, author and literary scholar, she was 'comic, disarming and winning'.

It might have been a merciful dispensation had Margot been spared the Second World War. The blackout, ration books, gas masks, to say nothing of the Blitz, were things she could not cope with. Throughout, she lived in London, the Wharf having been sold.

Bomb damage forced her out of her house in Bedford Square, and she took a strong dislike to the flat that was found for her in South Kensington. For a time she came to roost in the Savoy Hotel, where she was, at least, properly looked after and fed, but she soon tired of hotel life and moved into another flat, which she liked no better. She died in July 1945 at the age of eighty-one, but not before the Fates had dealt her another shattering blow. In March she had heard through the Red Cross that her daughter, Elizabeth, who had been marooned in Romania during the war, was alive and well, which caused her the greatest joy. But then a month later came another message that she was dead. After that the struggle to go on living became too much for her. At her memorial service in St Margaret's, Westminster, the church was half empty.

Notes

1. W.G. Grace said of his play that it was 'the champagne of cricket'.

2. His full name was Herbert Henry Asquith, and until he married Margot he was known as Herbert, but Margot did not care for the name and from then on he was called Henry.

3. Among these pessimists was Queen Victoria, whose consent to the marriage Asquith, as a Privy Councillor, felt he ought to obtain. This surprised the Queen, who remarked how curious it was that he should think her consent necessary, but that if it was required she would not give it, as she thought Miss Tennant most unfit for a Cabinet Minister's wife.

4. At her wedding Margot wore a chain given her by a previous lover and a locket containing the hair of another.

5. Besides Asquith himself, Gladstone, Rosebery and Balfour.

6. Violet Asquith also recalled later her amazement at the lack of facilities in Number Ten. In a BBC broadcast she said there were no bookcases and no baths. 'Did Prime Ministers',

she wondered, 'never read and never wash?'

7. The straits separating European from Asiatic Turkey between the Aegean Sea and the Sea of Marmora.

8. The New Zealand general (as he later became), Bernard Freyberg, the toughest of warhorses, said he was the bravest man he knew.

9. So called because candidates of any party with a proven record of loyalty to the Lloyd George coalition were given written backing.

10. A comic example of her outspokenness occurred when she was in Italy and visited the Fascist dictator Mussolini, who kept her waiting. This was not what she was accustomed to and after a few minutes she sent him a terse message: 'Would the Duce please hurry up as the Countess of Oxford and Asquith has some quite important shopping she wants to do' (family sources).

11. Some of these have become legendary, as, for example, when she said of Lord Birkenhead that he was very clever but his brains had gone to his head, and of Lloyd George that he never saw a belt without wanting to hit below it, and her description of an American general as 'an imitation rough diamond'.

10

MARGARET LLOYD GEORGE

Marriage is one of the very few institutions which carries one through the trouble, bother and worries of the world and enables people whose disposition and temperament are exactly the opposite to live in perfect harmony. – David Lloyd George

My supreme idea is to get on . . . To this idea I shall sacrifice everything – except, I trust, honesty. I am prepared to thrust even love itself under the wheels of my Juggernaut if it obstruct the way. – David Lloyd George on becoming engaged to be married

David Lloyd George and Margaret Owen were married for fifty-two years, for most of which time they lived apart. Their tastes and ways of life had always been different and, over the years, became unbridgeable. But their love for each other did not die, and there was never any question of divorce or legal separation, even when David was living with another woman, who eventually became his second wife.

Margaret Owen was born in a farmhouse (Mynydd Ednyfed Fawr) on the slopes overlooking the Bay of Criccieth,[1] a place of rare beauty and character with a splendid stretch of beach overlooked by a castle and the tradition of a submerged city out to sea. The lovely foothills of Eifionydd rose gently inland, and in the distance could be seen the mountains of Snowdonia. Today the area is largely given over to tourism, but in former times it included the shipyard and busy port of Portmadoc from where sailing ships with cargoes of Welsh slate travelled to all parts of the world. It was no wonder that such a unique place entered deeply into Margaret's soul. In the course of her life she was to visit many countries and to find herself in many different domiciles, but she could only ever look on Criccieth as home and became restless when she was away from it for too long.

Margaret – or Maggie as she was often called – came from farming stock. Her father, Richard Owen, a gentle giant of a man, was a tenant farmer with a fair-sized holding who worked very hard and made a reasonable living.[2] He was also a deacon of the Methodist Church and was widely respected both for his piety and good judgement as well as for his knowledge of Welsh history and legend. He claimed descent from the great prince Owen Gwynedd who had fought heroically against the English in the twelfth century.[3] His wife Mary was a lively woman of great determination and character who liked to have her own way and usually got it. Margaret was an only child and her parents doted on her; they wanted the best of everything for her, and as a child she attended a private boarding-school in Dolgelly where she was taught the manners and deportment of a fine lady. In due course, with her good looks and charm and prosperous background, she was to have many suitors, among whom was a rising young attorney of Criccieth, David Lloyd George.

David had an unusual upbringing. His father, William George, was from Pembrokeshire[4] and by profession a schoolmaster, but his career had been blighted by ill health, and as a result he never stayed long in one post. It was while he was teaching in a school in Manchester that David was born. When William's health took a further turn for the worse he decided to give up teaching and return to Pembrokeshire with the intention of earning a living as a smallholder; but soon afterwards he died, leaving his wife Elizabeth with two small children and another expected. In her extremity Elizabeth sent an appeal to her bachelor brother, Richard Lloyd, who was a shoemaker in the village of Llanystumdwy, a few miles from Criccieth. His response was immediate and positive. Leaving his business in the capable hands of his elderly mother, he set out for Pembrokeshire – a journey which, incredibly, took him more than two days[5] – gathered in his sister and her family and bore them back to Llanystumdwy. From then on he became a second father to the children – housing them, supporting them financially and, when necessary, disciplining them, which, as a strict Puritan, he did with some severity, not always sparing the rod.

Richard Lloyd, or Uncle Lloyd as he came to be called, was a remarkable character. At the age of six he had lost his father, and it had been necessary for him to go to work in the family shoemaking business when hardly more than a child. He had, however, been able to acquire some education and had become an unpaid minister in a Baptist sect known as the Disciples of Christ.

It did not take him long to realize that his nephew David had exceptional gifts and he started to groom him for an exceptional career.[6] He decided that his first objective should be a qualification in law, and as the village school could not teach him all the subjects needed for this he set about learning them himself so that he could pass them on to David. The efforts of this partially educated village shoemaker were not in vain. In time both David and his younger brother William passed their law examinations and soon after set up a partnership as Lloyd George and George. Inestimable as was David's debt to his uncle, it was not likely that he would remain for long under his aegis. He was too much of a free thinker, too strong an individualist and a natural rebel, and it was not long before this was attracting attention in his profession:

his championship of the underdog, his irreverence towards authority and his ruthless questioning of matters too easily taken for granted – all of these marked him out as a favourite lawyer among the Welsh Radicals, who were fast growing in strength and numbers at that time. In the political field, too, he was making a name for himself. In the Criccieth Debating Society he discovered debating skills and oratory which could keep an audience spellbound. He also became one of the brightest stars in the local Liberal Party, and in his early twenties was being approached as a possible parliamentary candidate. His ambitions were expanding all the time.

It is not known exactly when David Lloyd George and Margaret Owen first met. Probably they encountered one another in the street and David had passed the time of day with her. But it was certainly not love at first sight. The first mention of her in David's diary occurred in 1884, when he was twenty-one and she eighteen, where he described her, perhaps rather coolly, as 'a sensible girl without fuss or affectation about her'. It was two years before his feelings for her began to warm up and he conceded that 'there was a combination of good nature, humour and affection about her'. It was clear that by then he was in love, but the wheels continued to move slowly and it was to be another three years before they became engaged. Such delay is surprising. With his ardent, impetuous nature one would have expected David to act with more *élan*, more in the manner of Young Lochinvar,[7] but he seemed to be content to bide his time. There were, indeed, reasons for his reticence: in the first years of setting up on his own in business his financial position was, to say the least, precarious, and the engagement was strongly opposed both by Margaret's parents on the one hand and Uncle Lloyd on the other. Certainly David did not measure up to the expectations of Mr and Mrs Owen for their beloved daughter: with her gifts and background they were hoping for something more worthy than an impecunious attorney, the adopted son of a village shoemaker with a reputation for wildness and inconstancy. And there was an even deeper objection that accounted for Uncle Lloyd's opposition: David and Margaret belonged to different religious sects. The Owens were devout Calvinistic Methodists while the Lloyds and the Georges were zealous Baptists, and in Wales at that time this difference counted for much. So for a long time Margaret's father and mother did all they could to deter Maggie from such a match, pressing other suitors on her and refusing to allow David into the house, so that he had to resort to 'clandestine tactics', as he put it, 'lying in ambuscade like a footpad and smuggling in notes by means of servant girls'. Uncle Lloyd for his part paraded suitable young women of Baptist faith in front of David and even took to following him about at nights to keep a check on him.[8] But it was to no avail: David was in love and maintained his wooing, and in this he found an ally in Margaret's aunt Dorothy, a wise and worldly lady with a strong romantic streak, who acted as an intermediary and told her niece robustly that true love was more important than sectarian differences.

At first Margaret had had doubts about the sincerity of David's protestations, as he had only recently had a fling with a singer, Liza Jones, and she was not sure he had got her out of his system. For a time she held aloof and, as David put it, 'firmly chid all intimacy and a tendency thereto on my part'. But eventually David's vehement avowals overcame her doubts, and once she had made up her mind no parental pressure could move her. In time the Owens gave way with good grace, as also did Uncle Lloyd, and an ecumenical wedding was arranged in a Methodist chapel with Uncle Lloyd officiating. The ceremony was quiet and unpretentious with no other members of the bridegroom's family present. But the people of Criccieth were not to be done out of a celebration, and that night bonfires were lit and fireworks let off. For their honeymoon David and Margaret spent ten days in London, to which Margaret took an instant aversion. On their return they moved into her parents' farmhouse, which was to be their home for the next three years – an arrangement that might have proved irksome but does not seem to have given rise to undue stress.

In later years Margaret was to claim that at the time of her marriage she believed that David's ambitions did not stretch beyond North Wales and that he was aiming to be no more than a successful and prosperous country attorney. But this is scarcely credible. He was already deeply involved with the Liberal Party and had been offered a candidacy in a neighbouring constituency, which he had refused, but only because he had his eye on his home constituency of Caernarvon Boroughs. It may be that Margaret was deluding herself and perhaps looking for excuses not to spend more time with her husband in London. And full disillusionment must have come soon, as within less than a year of their marriage David was formally adopted as Liberal candidate for Caernarvon Boroughs. This may not have caused Margaret great concern at the time, as a General Election was not due for four years, and in any case Caernarvon was a Tory seat. But then came a thunderbolt. In the spring of 1890, as they were starting for a day out, a telegram arrived telling of the sudden death of the sitting Tory member. This cast a pall over their outing – it meant an immediate by-election – but there was still the hope for Margaret that the Conservatives might retain the seat. However, the movement for change in North Wales was gathering force, and in the hard-fought campaign all David's brilliant platform oratory was brought into play. In the end, after two recounts, he was declared the winner by eighteen votes.

Margaret had taken no part in the campaign, nor did she accompany her husband to London, so she was not present when he took his seat in the House of Commons. She was, it is true, nursing a baby at the time, with another on the way, but it was not until six months later that she managed a brief London visit. In the following years she usually found reasons for remaining at home, especially when a baby was expected, as she was insistent that all her children should be born in Wales.

The Hon.ble Lady Walpole.

Catherine, Lady Walpole, by John Simon after Michael Dahl, *c*. 1700

William Pitt the Elder's wife Lady Hester Grenville, Countess of Chatham, by Thomas Hudson, 1750

Mary, Countess of Bute, by Mrs Read, 1777

Lloyd George soon made his mark in Parliament. Defying tradition his maiden speech was not a bland and uncontroversial offering but sharp-witted and aggressive; however, it was well received and he wrote to Margaret that everyone, including the great Gladstone, had been delighted by it. During his first years he confined himself for the most part to Welsh affairs, making it known forcefully that Wales, like Ireland, had grievances which could not long be ignored. He also became much in demand as a speaker outside Parliament to orate on his favourite subjects, mainly Welsh nationalism but also on another matter near to his heart: that of temperance reform. He was no teetotaller himself but was appalled by the evil effects of drunkenness particularly among the poor; and for this he blamed the liquor trade, of which he once said: 'It reeks with human misery, vice and squalor, destitution, crime and death.'

Among the many successes Lloyd George had at this time there was always one sadness: Maggie's reluctance to spend any length of time in London. She could never adjust to city life and was convinced that the polluted air spelled death to her children. Left alone, David was bereft. Sometimes he lodged with friends, sometimes he took temporary flats, but he was hopeless at looking after himself: he could not manage his clothes or his food or the simplest household task. 'You can't leave me alone in town,' he wrote pitifully. 'That would be an act of desertion which I know you are too noble to contemplate'; adding rather ominously, 'Heaven knows what it might eventually lead to.' At the same time he was growing increasingly bored with Criccieth. 'I know of no place', he wrote, 'where it rains so incessantly. The air is too fresh, the water too pure and too much of it.' And in London he was developing new interests including golf (which he also played in Criccieth) and foreign travel, but these were not shared by Maggie, who took part in no sports and had even less love for foreign parts than she had for London. In view of their long separations and divergence of tastes it might seem their marriage was heading for the rocks, and yet their love remained intact. They wrote to each other constantly and affectionately, and David became very agitated if Margaret's letters to him were too infrequent or too short. They appeared to long for each other's company but, it would seem, were not prepared to put everything aside in order to come by it. David's devotion to politics overrode everything, as did Margaret's love for Criccieth.

There were, of course, dangers in such apartness. David was no natural monogamist and his libido was exceptionally strong; as even the unworldly Margaret must have known, he was bound to look for consolation and this could lead to scandal, which, as the Parnell case had recently shown, would mean the end of his political career.[9] The first time that scandal threatened was in 1896 when the wife of a Montgomeryshire doctor, one Catherine Edwards (a distant cousin of Margaret's), gave birth to a baby that, owing to the circumstances of her marriage, could not have been begotten by her husband.

Whereupon she made a written confession that she had committed adultery with Lloyd George and that he was the father of her child. This was strongly denied by him, and soon afterwards Catherine retracted her confession and said that it had been made under duress when her husband threatened her with a carving knife. In due course Dr Edwards sued for divorce, and when the case came to court it was proved beyond doubt and generally accepted that it was not possible for Lloyd George to be the father of the child. But what was not so clear was that his relationship with Catherine had been irreproachable. Inevitably there were murmurs of no smoke without fire, and years later Lloyd George's political enemies resurrected the case in an attempt to ruin him; they were quickly forced to withdraw, however, with an abject apology and damages.[10]

It seems that Margaret was not unduly upset by the Edwards affair, but to another of David's liaisons she took great exception. While he was lodging in Putney David had come into contact with a Mrs Timothy Davies (familiarly known as Mrs Tim), the wife of a prosperous Welsh draper.[11] They became intimate, which does not seem to have upset the husband unduly, but when Margaret came to hear of it she was furiously jealous and an acrimonious correspondence ensued between her and David. 'This business', Margaret wrote, 'comes between you and me more so than you can imagine and is growing. It pains me to the quick and I am very unhappy. If you must go on as at present I don't know where it will end.' To this David answered angrily: 'You threaten me with a public scandal. All right – expose me if that suits you. One scandal the more will but kill me the earlier . . . I have borne it for years and have suffered in health and character. I'll stand it no longer come what may.' And in a letter beginning 'My sweet but stupid Maggie,' he told her, 'to reflect whether you have not rather neglected your husband. I have more than once gone without breakfast. I have scores of times come home in the dead of night to a cold, dark and comfortless flat without a soul to greet me.' In time tempers cooled down, although David did not stop seeing Mrs Tim, and their relationship was to last for several years. One consequence was that Margaret began to spend more time in London in the house they had recently acquired in Wandsworth, then a comparatively rural area with reasonably pure air, although to Margaret it was never a substitute for Criccieth.

One of David's great delights at this time was foreign travel, and during the parliamentary recesses, including Christmas when he might have been expected to be at home with his family, he would make off abroad with a party of friends including sometimes unattached ladies, which usually aroused Maggie's jealousy. But David was aware of this and treated it in jocular fashion, addressing one letter to 'My dear suspicious old Maggie' and representing the ladies (not always accurately) as elderly and frumpish. It does not seem that otherwise Maggie resented these excursions abroad. She had no wish to be on them herself and they gave her an excuse to be at Criccieth with her family, which had lately increased rapidly (between 1889 and 1896: Richard, Mair, Olwen and Gwilym, and then eight years later, as an afterthought, Megan).

During his first ten years as Member of Parliament David's rise had been rapid and free from serious storms. He had had no great personal triumph, but he had been successful in numerous parliamentary skirmishes, and his skills as a debater and orator were acknowledged on all sides. At the end of that time an impartial observer (the Canadian government's agent in Wales) described him as 'the leading Welshman of today'. The first major crisis in his career came with the outbreak of the Boer War of which he disapproved strongly and spoke out against passionately.

The Boer War loosed a torrent of jingoism in Britain. Normally calm and rational people became overcome with fury, which they vented on all opponents of the war; and no one was subjected to more intense verbal and physical abuse than Lloyd George. To stick to his guns and make his viewpoint heard required great courage, and he showed this in full measure, as did Margaret, who supported him wholeheartedly and was constantly by his side. Despite being jeered and jostled and cut dead by friends, she was unflinching. At the same time the family finances took a battering, as people boycotted the law firm of David and his brother William, but Margaret maintained stoutly that she was ready to live on thirty shillings a week (about £20 at present-day valuation) in an attic rather than change course.

And yet, in spite of his unpopularity and gruelling experiences, Lloyd George emerged from the Boer War a politician of greater stature. Before he had been no more than a brilliant campaigner for Welsh causes; afterwards he became a statesman of national standing with ideas embracing the whole country. It was not long before his career was on an upwards spiral, and when in 1905 a Liberal administration was formed under Sir Henry Campbell-Bannerman he was given the post of President of the Board of Trade. Here he was to show great administrative ability and had outstanding success in settling seemingly intractable industrial disputes.

But then, suddenly, at the moment of triumph came tragedy. There was no one to whom Lloyd George was more deeply devoted than his eldest daughter Mair Eluned, a girl of beauty, charm and piety. In 1907, when she was eighteen, she suffered stomach pains which she disregarded as she was about to take school examinations to which she knew her parents attached importance. Too late appendicitis was diagnosed. An operation was carried out at home but it was not successful. When told she was going to die her last words were: 'God is wise and merciful.' The loss of Mair was the greatest blow Lloyd George ever had to bear, and for a time he was beside himself with grief and rage – rage against God for such cruelty and injustice. For Margaret, too, it was a dreadful tragedy, but she found comfort in her unshakeable religious faith – in the certainty of God's wisdom and love. It might have been expected that such a disaster would have drawn David and Margaret closer together, but this did not happen. David left their London house the day after Mair's death[12] and subsequently left Criccieth the day after her funeral; at Christmas a few weeks later he went off to France with the two boys, leaving Margaret and the two girls at home.

In later years David was recorded as saying that after Mair's death he and Margaret 'drifted apart', and there is much evidence for this. They had few interests in common, and although Margaret was mortified by David's infidelities he made little effort to mend his ways. In religion, too, differences between them were widening. Margaret's Christian faith was as strong as ever while David was inclining more and more to free thinking. 'I am more of a pagan,' he was to declare in later years.[13] Nevertheless the bond between them was not broken. It seems that Margaret alone could provide the security and stability necessary to his mercurial character. Without her, albeit at a distance, he felt adrift and inadequate. His need for her comes out clearly in his letters. After Mair's death he wrote to her: 'I would rather have you – jealous old Maggie as you sometimes are. I would rather see you near me in trouble than anybody else.' And later: 'And no one can cure me except you and your darling children and I think I alone can cure you.' In time he came to terms with Mair's death. In a letter to his brother, who had just lost one of his children, he wrote: 'I know now what it was for. It gave me a keener appreciation of the sufferings of others, it deepened my sympathy. Little Mair's death has been the inspiration of all my work to relieve human misery during recent years.'

A year after his daughter's death Lloyd George became Chancellor of the Exchequer and he and his family moved into 11 Downing Street. But although this was a historic residence and her husband was now the second most important man in the government Margaret refused to change her lifestyle or make any concessions to the world of fashion. Being incapable of artificiality or false bonhomie she was never at ease in society. And at 11 Downing Street (and later even less so at Number Ten) she did not feel at home and made little effort to make it comfortable or attractive. Her housekeeping had always been frugal to the point of parsimony, and it remained that way. After experiencing it a friend of the family wrote: 'It looked as if a small suburban household was picnicking in Downing Street – the same simple food, the same little domestic servant, the same mixture of tea and dinner . . . and yet with all that an air of simple dignity and distinction pervaded the room – no affectation, no pretension, nothing mean, nothing ignoble.'

Others were less kindly. Under the penetrating gaze of Violet Asquith she appeared at first 'homely and pathetic', although later she revised this judgement and wrote in her diary that 'she was a little darling with all her wits about her'. As in her other London residences Margaret insisted that all the domestic staff should be Welsh and Welsh speaking. She even brought decorators and maintenance men all the way from Wales. Nevertheless, Downing Street always seemed to her bleak and inhospitable. She entertained officia guests dutifully (if minimally) but visitors of her own hardly ever. It was as if she herself were a visitor there.

As Chancellor of the Exchequer Lloyd George's achievements were historic as he fulfilled his pledge to 'wage implacable warfare against poverty and squalidness'. It was then that the first steps were taken towards a welfare state with the introduction of old-age pensions and a National Insurance Act providing sickness and unemployment benefits. This led to the 'People's Budget' and the Parliament Act (see p. 114). In the furore that ensued he was in the thick of it, and when it came to a successful conclusion he was riding high.

But once again at a time of triumph Lloyd George was hit by disaster when he was embroiled in the Marconi Scandal, arising from his purchase of shares in an American company which doubled in value as a result of its English branch being awarded a substantial government contract. This led to a whispering campaign in the City and a Parliamentary Committee of Inquiry finally exonerating him of breaking the law. However, suspicion remained of insider trading and lack of integrity, and Lloyd George himself admitted that he had acted 'thoughtlessly and carelessly', which for a politician is almost as bad as dishonestly. The Marconi Scandal took a heavy toll on him, plunging him into a deep depression, so that he became at times vague and incoherent and brooded for hours alone in a darkened room. In such a state Margaret did all she could to comfort him. They may have drifted apart, but the sight of him in such misery aroused all her strong maternal instincts and drew him to her more closely than any of his triumphs.

But it was not only by Margaret that he was comforted at this time. There was another to whom he was to become even more closely drawn. Lloyd George first met Frances Stevenson when she was engaged as a holiday tutor for his youngest daughter Megan. At the time she was teaching in a girls' school in Wimbledon. When she accepted the post she had little idea of what was in store for her. Later she wrote: 'I left Downing Street under the impression I was a free independent person. In truth I was enslaved for the rest of my life.' It was not long before their relationship developed. Lloyd George was greatly taken by this attractive, intelligent, sprightly young woman.[14] Frances was of Scottish descent on her father's side and French-Italian on her mother's, but she had been brought up in suburban London, where her family's circumstances were modest. However, by dint of scholarships she had had a good education, including a degree at London University. She was also almost bilingual in English and French. At the same time she started to learn shorthand, and Lloyd George continued to find jobs for her, saw more and more of her and corresponded with her regularly. By July 1912, nearly a year after they first met, it became clear, as Frances later put it, that 'both of us realized for the first time that something serious was happening'. Lloyd George had had many transient affairs with young women, but this was different. They were both of them deeply in love.

At the end of 1912 Lloyd George proposed that Frances come to him as mistress with the duties of private secretary. Marriage, he told her, was impossible, as divorce would spell instant ruin, and, as always, his political career came first. At first Frances was inclined to hold back. Although she liked to think herself a woman of advanced views – she was a Fabian and a non-militant suffragette – she was at heart a Victorian, and the idea of 'living in sin' with a married man twenty-five years older than herself was abhorrent. But, like many another, she found Lloyd George's spell irresistible. 'He had', she later wrote, 'a magnetism which made my heart leap and swept aside my judgement.' It was not long before she capitulated; and on 21 January 1913 they made a compact that they looked on as an unofficial marriage. And so it came about that a young schoolmistress of twenty-three found herself suddenly catapulted from the obscurity of a Wimbledon girls' school into the centre of the nation's affairs. For Frances it was a dazzling situation – to become the closest companion and confidante of the country's leading politician. But it was not undefiled joy: her position was, to say the least, ambiguous. She was looked on neither as wife nor *maîtresse en titre*. Officially she was no more than his secretary and was usually treated as such, and it was a lonely position. When in time their relationship became known she was castigated, and even to some extent ostracized, by her own family, while at the same time being despised and rejected by Lloyd George's. But for him the situation was altogether more advantageous. His role as a bigamist (which in effect he was) suited him nicely. On the one hand, he had a gentle, wise, maternal figure, soothing and steadying. On the other, he had an attractive, totally devoted, compliant younger woman who was also a highly efficient secretary. And it was so convenient; there were good reasons for Frances always being at hand: no need, like other ageing politicians, to make clandestine assignments in suburban love nests.

Lloyd George's relationship with Frances was to cause no great public scandal. In time it became known within a limited circle, but there was no inclination, even among his political opponents, to dig it out into the light of day. So long as the affair was kept 'under the blanket' and the divorce courts avoided, it would not be stirred up.

It is probable that Margaret soon became aware of what was going on. At first she may have hoped that, like others, the affair would be impermanent, but by 1916, after three years, she had clearly given up this hope. 'I know very well', she told David, 'whom you would marry if anything happened to me.' And a year later David was writing to Frances: 'She is very tolerant, considering she knows everything that is going on. It is not right to try her too far.' And they did try to be discreet: they were seldom seen together in public, and David would not let Frances drive with him in the car from London down to his house in Walton Health in Surrey: she had to go by train lest it gave rise to talk. And of course she and Margaret were never in the house together. Frances would usually have departed long before Margaret's arrival, although there were times when she cut it rather fine and left behind unmistakable signs of her presence.

There is great irony that Lloyd George, the generally accepted spokesman of Welsh (and indeed English) Nonconformism should lead a double life: on the one hand, the devoted family man; on the other, the dissembler and sensualist. And it is all too easy for moralists to charge him with hypocrisy and self-indulgence. But this has to be put in the context of the ebbing of the physical side of his marriage to Margaret and his own strong need for an active sex life. It should be borne in mind, too, that during the First World War, in which he had a unique role and his responsibilities were awesome, he needed all the comfort and support he could get from whatever source. Although by then Frances had to a large extent supplanted Margaret in his affections, Margaret was still indispensable to him; only she could provide the family life and stable background he required. But he also had needs which she could not fulfil – and not only physical ones. He needed, too, someone who could share deeply and genuinely his political worries and on whom he could unburden himself, sure of a sympathetic and understanding response. Whatever the moral standpoint, it was surely in the interests of the country that during the war years Lloyd George was sustained by both women, otherwise his burden might have been insupportable.

At the outbreak of war Lloyd George was still Chancellor of the Exchequer, but a year later, in response to the 'shell crisis'[15] he agreed to be relegated to the most crucial post in the government, that of Minister of Munitions, a post created specifically for him. Then for a brief time he was the Minister for War before becoming Prime Minister of the coalition government in December 1916 (see p. 117). This is not the place to describe his prodigious efforts in overcoming the shell crisis, in the setting up of convoys to combat the U-boat menace and final victory gained in large measure by his fighting spirit and ability to achieve action. Nor is it the place to tell of his less successful struggle with British generals: first with the obstinate and arrogant Lord Kitchener, who as War Minister disdained Lloyd George's efforts to increase production of munitions; and later with Field-Marshal Haig,[16] commander of the British army in France, whose unimaginative conduct of operations and reckless extravagance with human lives appalled him. The first of these clashes came to an end when Kitchener was drowned on his way to Russia, but the second remained unresolved, for limited as were Haig's military abilities his skills in political intrigue were considerable, and Lloyd George found his position unassailable.[17]

But this is Margaret's story, and it is with her efforts during the war that we are concerned. She realized at once that vegetating in Criccieth was not an option, and she lost no time in asking her husband for the use of three rooms in 11 Downing Street as a depot for all kinds of woollen comforts for the British (and more particularly the Welsh) troops in the front line. Under her aegis these came pouring in, as also did large sums of money, amounting to some £1 million. The task of spending this appropriately as well as the sorting and dispatching of a mass of miscellaneous garments was an awesome one, but Margaret gathered round her a band of willing helpers (nearly all Welsh-speaking), and their achievement in relieving the intense hardships of soldiers in the trenches was considerable. It was for this work that after the war Margaret was made a Dame Grand Cross of the British Empire.

With the coming of peace it was open to Dame Margaret to lead a more public life if she had wanted it. According to her eldest son Richard, she had between 1910 and 1920 no fewer than ten invitations to stand for Parliament (and, remarkably, not for Welsh constituencies), but she had no hesitation in declining them. A political life was not for her. But she did become involved in local affairs in Criccieth – as a magistrate and chairman of the Urban District Council, where she is said to have displayed an unexpected toughness and incisiveness. She also took a strong interest in the Temperance Movement. Like her husband she knew what devastation could be caused in people's homes by drunkenness, but she was no fanatic. Although teetotal herself she did not expect it in others, and alcohol was not banned in the home. Otherwise she led an unpretentious life, enjoying simple pleasures – visiting friends, looking after her family and tending her garden. This was her solace and one in which she had great expertise; it was said of her there was nothing she could not make grow. She would arrive back from abroad with shrivelled twiglets taken from plants she had fancied and these were coaxed into life; any bouquets she received were gone over for anything which could be potted and made to take root.

There were some interruptions to this rural idyll, as for three years after the end of the war Lloyd George remained Prime Minister of the wartime coalition government, and although he and Margaret were leading increasingly separate lives they maintained an outward appearance of unity, and there were occasions when it was necessary for her to be by his side. In 1922, however, the coalition government came to an abrupt end and Lloyd George would not hold ministerial office again, although he was always to be a great and heroic national figure. Until Margaret died nearly twenty years later they continued to present to the world a show of concord.

The reality, however, was different. For most of the time Margaret was living alone at Criccieth while Lloyd George was at his newly built house in Churt, Surrey, in the company of Frances. And not only of her. Lloyd George's son, Richard, painted a lurid picture of his father's life at Churt. He tells how, as a result of the adulation lavished on him as 'the man who won the war', 'the Prime Minister of Europe' and other panegyrics he underwent a character change and became, in Richard's words, 'wayward, self-indulgent, spoiled and thoroughly reckless'. At the same time, nearly sixty though he might be, he was as attractive to women as ever and ever more susceptible to them. And so in his home in Churt, which included a farm of some seven hundred acres, he gathered round him a bevy of beautiful women – typists, filing clerks, land girls and general hangers-on (described by Richard as 'concubines, procurers and flatterers') who fawned on him and gratified his needs.

Presiding over this establishment like a Turkish pasha, he nevertheless reserved his greatest love for Frances, who still had to move out quickly whenever Dame Margaret appeared on the scene. One should, perhaps, take Richard's words with some reserve as he was a strong partisan of his mother and did not attempt to conceal the fact that he bitterly resented his father's treatment of her.[18] He also had a strong antipathy to Frances, wilfully blinding himself to her position and referring to her as no more than 'a particular friend of my father', 'the little schoolteacher' and 'a quiet, self-contained young person'. He was, however, under no illusions when she returned from France with 'an adopted daughter', probably fathered by Lloyd George.

It was a wonder that Lloyd George's lifestyle did not erupt in a blaze of scandal, but somehow his luck held and he managed (in his own words) not to 'commit the cardinal sin of being found out and dragged into public gaze'. He had come closest to this in 1909 when *The People* published a series of articles alleging an affair between Lloyd George and a married lady whose husband was about to sue for divorce, naming him as co-respondent, and adding that Lloyd George and friends of his were desperately trying to buy him off with a large sum of money. In the circumstances Lloyd George had no alternative but to sue for libel. This was a dangerous course as it would mean going to court and swearing under oath that the accusations made against him were without foundation – almost certainly an act of perjury. For him to be believed it was essential that Margaret should accompany him to court and give him open support by sitting beside him. This she had qualms about doing as she was shocked by the idea of perjury. But Lloyd George pleaded with her earnestly: 'You must stand by me, Maggie. Otherwise it's all over with me.' Eventually she did agree to go but, as she later told Richard, she did it not to save her husband's political career but because he was hurt and frightened and in great trouble and she could not deny him help. In the event Lloyd George won the case.

Although after the war Lloyd George's lifestyle drove them further apart, he and Margaret were never separated for long. Occasionally he visited her in Criccieth, but this was mainly to give a show of family solidarity, and he was always restless to be back in Churt. Dame Margaret paid periodical visits to London and accompanied him on trips abroad. She was with him in 1925 when he made a triumphant visit to America – ticker-tape flying and as many as fifteen speeches a day, including the largest-ever open-air meeting, where he addressed a crowd of some 400,000. In 1931 she came to London hurriedly when David had to undergo a serious prostate operation and displaced Frances by his bedside. And later in the year, when there was a General Election and

Lloyd George was not strong enough for electioneering, she stepped into the breach and saw to it that he retained his seat.

A month later, on doctor's orders, Lloyd George set out on a cruise to Ceylon. Ideally he would have liked to be accompanied by Frances, but Margaret insisted on coming with other members of the family. In consequence the atmosphere was at times strained, as Lloyd George did not always contain his eagerness to receive mail from Frances and had to be circumspect in posting letters to her and in buying gifts for her and her daughter. In 1936 he joined Winston Churchill for a holiday in Marrakech. On this occasion he was at first accompanied by Frances, but then Margaret sent word that she was coming and Frances had to go home (almost encountering Margaret on her way out). Later in the same year Lloyd George made his ill-fated visit to Germany, where he was mesmerized by Hitler and proclaimed that he was 'a very great man' and 'a born leader'. Unfortunately Dame Margaret did not accompany him on this trip. Perhaps if she had she might have kept his feet more firmly on the ground.

The Lloyd Georges celebrated their golden wedding in 1938 in Antibes, where David was working on his memoirs. His main concern seems to have been how soon the family could be induced to go home after the celebration, while Margaret is quoted as saying that but for the press it would never have taken place as David would have forgotten about it and she would not have mentioned it. Congratulations and messages of goodwill poured in from all over the world, but with David spending most of the year with another woman these must have had a hollow ring.

A year after the Lloyd George's golden wedding the Second World War broke out. When Winston Churchill became Prime Minister he made several attempts to find Lloyd George a suitable place in the government, but these came to nothing. For whatever reasons Lloyd George remained aloof. He did not want to join 'that gang', as he called Churchill's Cabinet, and perhaps in his heart he knew that his energy had been sapped and his judgement warped; also he would not have had the same ascendancy as before. But this does not excuse his subsequent conduct, which was scarcely creditable – curmudgeonly, self-centred and at times verging on the unpatriotic. In public he usually gave Churchill half-hearted support, but in private he was forever carping. From the beginning he was deeply defeatist and talked much of the need for a negotiated settlement (which he saw himself bringing about). It was a sad contrast to the lionheart of the previous war.

Dame Margaret's attitude to the Second World War was also unexpected. According to her eldest son Richard, she was detached and unconcerned. Unlike during the First World War, when she had worked so energetically to help the war effort, this time she remained in Criccieth and distanced herself from what was happening. As it was she did not survive it for long. At the end of 1940 she had a fall while visiting her brother-in-law William George and fractured a hip. This in itself was not serious, but it seems to have provoked a heart attack, and in January 1941 her condition became critical. When Lloyd George was informed he set off from Churt at once, but it was a winter of exceptional severity and in the Welsh mountains he was caught in a snowdrift. From this he was eventually rescued by willing hands from a nearby village, but he was too late and by the time he reached Criccieth Margaret had died. It was noted how pale and drawn he looked, and at the funeral he sobbed and trembled uncontrollably. No doubt his conscience was troubling him, but he had never lost his affection for her. 'She was a great old pal' was his somewhat inadequate tribute to her.

A quiet family funeral had been intended, but such was the love and respect felt for Dame Margaret that in spite of the deep snow people came from long distances to pay their respects and line the funeral route to watch her coffin being drawn to the church by a contingent of the local Home Guard.

Dame Margaret had borne the role of wronged wife with simple dignity. Deeply as she had been hurt by her husband's infidelities, she had never thought of severing the bond between them; she was always ready to receive him into her house in Criccieth and was willing to join him in London when the occasion demanded. The only thing she demanded was that she and Frances Stevenson should never be in the same house together.

At first sight one might be inclined to write Dame Margaret off as a 'homebody' with no outside interests such as music, painting (for which she did have some talent) or horse riding (in which her mother had been a star performer). But this is to underestimate her. If she had been no more than this her influence locally would not have been so broad. And she always retained the complete devotion of her family. Richard wrote of her that she was 'the best mother a boy ever had' and that 'her whole life was filled with countless instances of boundless charity and kindness and sympathy for the underdog'.[19] There may be an element of hyperbole here, but surely Dame Margaret's life bears out the precept that it is not what you do in life but what you are which is of the greater significance.

In September 1943, two and a half years after the death of Margaret, Lloyd George married Frances. It was no more than her due. For more than thirty years she had served him devotedly as secretary, nurse, hostess and lover. It had been an exciting life, but she had made great sacrifices. Lloyd George had not always been an easy person to live with: he had his moods and his tantrums and was always liable to trample on those around him. She also had to come to terms with a life of duplicity, being at one time hostess and mistress of the household and the next, when members of the family appeared on the scene, having to move out and become just one of the secretaries. She had to accept, too, that she was not the only woman in his life: he retained a strong affection for Dame Margaret (of whom Frances was inclined to be jealous), and there were as well numerous others of whom she was more tolerant as she knew they were only temporary. But the greatest sacrifice of all was that of a stable married life with a lawful husband and a family of her own; several offers of marriage were made to her but were refused so that she could continue to serve Lloyd George.

He was not unappreciative of what she had done for him, as the inscription in his war memoirs bears out,[20] and if, indeed, he could not have borne up without her the whole country is deeply indebted to her. The Lloyd George family, however, was greatly distressed by his second marriage and not one of them attended the ceremony at a register office in Guildford. Megan, the youngest of the family and the one closest to her father, was particularly outraged, regarding it as an insult to the memory of her mother. So strongly did she feel that she broke off all contact with him until the very end of his life.

A year after his marriage Lloyd George moved from Surrey back to his roots in Llanystumdwy, where he had acquired a small farm on which he hoped to create, as he had done at Churt, an orchard of fruit trees growing out of barren soil. But he did not regard this as a final retirement from the political arena. By then, September 1944, the end of the war was in sight and this necessitated a General Election. At eighty-one, in failing health, he could not face up to electioneering. But he still felt he had a message to the country and the world, and for this he required a platform. Ever since he had resigned as Prime Minister it had been open to him to accept a peerage, but he had always shied away from this. Now, with the prospect of losing his seat in the House of Commons, it seemed to have its advantages. And so his wishes were made known to Churchill, who responded immediately, and in December 1944 he was created Earl Lloyd George of Dwyfor. He was not, however, to enjoy his new station for long. His health continued to deteriorate and three months later, on 26 March, he died. At the time momentous events were occurring in Europe: British and American forces had crossed the Rhine, the Russians were closing in on Berlin, and VE Day was only six weeks away. But the world paused to take notice of his passing, and in Parliament Churchill paid tribute to him in characteristically sonorous language: 'When the English history of the first quarter of the twentieth century is written, it will seen that the greater part of our fortunes in peace and war were shaped by this one man.'

Notes

1. An inlet of Cardigan Bay.

2. A striking example of this was when he rode on horseback each year the three hundred miles to London, driving a large flock of sheep and cattle to take to a market there.

3. Presumably one of many as Owen is said to have fathered no less than twenty-five offspring.

4. Now part of Dyfed. Generally thought of as one of the more Anglicized parts of Wales.

5. It is an extraordinary fact that at the beginning of the twentieth century the quickest way from the far north of Wales to the far south was via London.

6. He marked his favour by insisting that David alone should have the surname of Lloyd George.

7. 'So faithful in love, and so dauntless in war. / There never was knight like the young Lochinvar' (from 'Marmion' by Sir Walter Scott).

8. David became aware of this and to prevent it resorted to the somewhat drastic measure of hiding his uncle's boots.

9. Charles Stewart Parnell was cited as co-respondent in a divorce case and was forced to give up the leadership of the Irish Party in Parliament.

10. Given by Lloyd George to a Welsh charity.

11. One of several who made good in London at that time including Peter Jones, D.H. Evans, John Lewis and Dickins and Jones.

12. Never to return to it. It was sold soon afterwards.

13. Although he was always to be a regular attender at a Welsh chapel in London, and at home one of his favourite occupations was the singing of emotional Welsh hymns round the piano.

14. Something which may have drawn Lloyd George even closer to her was that she had been a school friend of his beloved daughter Mair and reminded him of her.

15. The British forces in France were said to be desperately short of shells, and in this respect were at a great disadvantage with the Germans. On this issue there was a massive campaign in the popular press.

16. Described by Lloyd George as 'brilliant to the top of his army boots'.

17. Later he was to remark that if Haig and other generals had shown a tenth of the strategy in fighting the war as they did in fighting him and the French general staff millions of lives would have been saved.

18. He later paid the penalty for this when he was disinherited by his father, who left him nothing in his will and this, no doubt, increased his bitterness when he came to write Lloyd George's biography.

19. This in spite of the fact that she did not always spare the birch.

20. 'To Frances without whose sympathetic help and understanding I could not have carried through the burden of the terrible tasks whose story is related in these volumes.'

11

LUCY BALDWIN

He had no ambition, push or drive. My mother supplied them all. –
Lucy Baldwin's daughter Margaret

Mrs Baldwin is the dictator of England. – Emily Cunard, society hostess
between the wars

Few Prime Ministers in peacetime have had such a stormy passage as Stanley
Baldwin. During his fourteen years as leader of the Conservative Party and
eight as Prime Minister he was confronted with one crisis after another. At
times the odds against him seemed overwhelming, and he was tempted to
retire to what he imagined would be a quiet, idyllic life in the country, but from
this he was always prevented by his wife Lucy, apparently unremarkable and
even slightly comic but beneath the surface firm and resolute.

In his portrait gallery of British Prime Ministers Harold Macmillan wrote
that they all differed greatly from their public image, and none more so than
Baldwin.[1] He liked to present himself as a plain, stolid English countryman
with no great gifts of intelligence or imagination but straightforward, equable
and trustworthy. In reality he was very different. In the first place he was not
wholly English as his mother was half Welsh and half Highland Scots, nor was
he essentially a countryman, being the manager and part owner of an ironworks. His love of the English countryside on which he often dilated was, no
doubt, heartfelt, but it was the romanticized view of the townsman rather
than the down-to-earth view of a son of the soil. In a speech in 1924 he rhap-
sodized on 'The sounds of England, the tinkle of the hammer on the anvil in
the country smithy, the corncrake on a dewy morning, the sound of the scythe
against the whetstone, and the sight of a plough team coming over the brow
of a hill, the sight that has been seen in England since England was a land.'[2]

However, it was seen that he and Lucy did not take their holidays among
these delights but, rather, in the more solid comforts of the French watering
place of Aix-les-Bains. It was also noted by a political colleague, Neville
Chamberlain, that he could not name a single wild flower or tree and had no

country pursuits such as shooting, fishing or gardening. And he was by no means plain and unemotional. Beneath the mask he was highly strung, sensitive and artistic and not without guile.[3]

Lucy, known to her family as Cissie, was also not what she seemed. Underneath her ample, unfashionable clothes and large ornate hats few would have guessed that there was to be found not only a cheerful, outgoing personality but also an enthusiastic and skilful sportswoman. At cricket in particular she was no mean performer, and it is said that it was while scoring a half-century that she first attracted the attention of her future husband. Lucy's background was middle class, reasonably prosperous and happy. Her father, Edward Ridsdale, was a scientist and former Master of the Mint. The family, which consisted of two girls and three boys, lived in the village of Rottingdean outside Brighton where they were neighbours of the Burne-Jones family, and it was while on a visit there in 1891 that Stanley Baldwin first made Lucy's acquaintance. It seems they fell in love almost at once, and were married in the following year.

At the time Stanley was twenty-five and Lucy twenty-three. He was born and brought up in Bewdley in the county of Worcestershire, the only child of Alfred Baldwin, a wealthy ironmaster who provided him with a top-class education at Harrow and Trinity College, Cambridge, where, by his own admission, he led an idle life and left without any great academic distinction. At the age of twenty-one he joined the family iron foundry, starting at the bottom and working his way up. He is said to have hated the work cordially at first but stuck to it, and by 1892, the year of his marriage, he was promoted to a partnership.

Doubts have been cast as to how passionate was the love affair between Stanley and Lucy but, as was often the case with both of them, appearances could be deceptive. Certainly during their engagement Stanley seems to have cast off his usual taciturnity, bombarding Lucy with love letters and telegrams and writing to his mother that he was delighted with his bride and that what drew him to her was 'her innocence and unworldliness'. Their marriage, which was to last fifty-three years, was always perfectly happy, in spite of the fact that they were of differing personalities and had few interests in common. Lucy did not share Stanley's love of music and the arts nor his passion for the countryside and did not accompany him on the long country walks that were his great solace and delight. And their religious feelings were not the same: Lucy's were simple and Low Church, concerned little with doctrine or ritual but strongly with good works, while Stanley had High Church leanings with a vein of mysticism. He went regularly to Communion, but Lucy did not accompany him. However, they did join together each morning in prayer to dedicate themselves that day to the service of God.

For the first fourteen years of their marriage Stanley and Lucy led an affluent but unpretentious life in Worcestershire. During that time Lucy gave birth to six children – four boys and two girls – and it was she who saw to their upbringing. This was something which Stanley, who was a somewhat stern and distant father, was quite ready to delegate. He was also more than ready to delegate any entertaining they might do. This is recalled by their daughter Margaret:

> My mother was a most remarkable woman. Two people could not have been more unlike than she and my father, but I never heard them quarrel, or shout at one another. Should they ever differ, it was always done quietly and politely. She loved gaiety, entertaining and parties, and my father had to put a good face on it. He was terrified of big receptions and always tried to keep near the wall in case the floor gave way.

While Lucy coped with life at home Stanley was preoccupied with the family ironworks, which was a model of its sort – profitable, smooth running and with excellent labour relations. He also took on various local responsibilities which he felt incumbent on someone in his position – magistracy, membership of the county council and governorship of schools. This steady, unspectacular life suited him well, and he might never have forsaken it. According to Margaret it was Lucy who provided the spur: 'If it hadn't been for my mother my father would have remained quite happily where he was in Worcestershire, going daily to the office and back. He had no ambition, push or drive. My mother supplied them all.'

Stanley's emergence from Worcestershire on to the national Conservative scene began in 1908 when at the age of forty-one he succeeded his father as Member of Parliament. During his first eight years in the House of Commons there were few signs of activity or ambition. However, in 1917 he was appointed Financial Secretary to the Treasury, and in the coalition government after the war he was President of the Board of Trade. He soon developed feelings of profound mistrust towards Lloyd George and took a leading part in breaking up the coalition and bringing in a Conservative government under Bonar Law, in which he was Chancellor of the Exchequer. But after only five months Bonar Law had to resign because of ill health, and to everyone's surprise Baldwin was chosen as his successor. And so at the age of fifty-five, after only three years of Cabinet experience, the backwoodsman from Worcestershire – plain, morose, seemingly honest and pedestrian – had reached the top position, and without any great gifts of oratory or debating skills had out-manoeuvred the political giants of the time. Of these Lloyd George never held office again while Churchill, Birkenhead and Austen Chamberlain were glad later to take office under him.

His first spell as Prime Minister did not last long, for his first action was to call a General Election in which the Conservatives lost ground to the Labour Party, which with Liberal backing took office under J. Ramsay MacDonald.

This only lasted ten months, however, and there was then another General Election, in which Baldwin gained a large overall majority.

During all these upheavals in her husband's career Lucy had provided the quiet undemanding support he needed. She was no intellectual, nor was she politically minded, but she was soothing and sympathetic and, when needed, bracing. With her Stanley could relax as with no one else. When roused he was capable of great efforts, but these exhausted him and afterwards he needed, and seldom failed to take, a long period of rest away from the political arena, talking with Lucy on matters of no consequence, reading light literature, solving crossword puzzles, playing patience and ruminating on long country walks. This might seem strange for a man of his sophistication, but it was what was necessary to restore his equilibrium. On Stanley becoming Prime Minister Lucy lost no time in taking advantage of her position to further her various works of charity.

She had always been ready to undertake these, and at the end of the First World War had been awarded the OBE for her work on behalf of Belgian refugees and the Red Cross. After the war she had focused her attention on the care and welfare of expectant mothers. The agonies that some of these endured and the high death rate among them appalled her, and she was in a position to know about such matters as she herself had had altogether seven difficult pregnancies with one baby stillborn. She had always been a strong supporter of women's rights, including the right to vote, but she abhorred militancy and would vigorously have denied that she was a feminist. She was just convinced that as long as the right to vote was confined to men women's affairs would be neglected, and nowhere was this more evident than in the matter of easing the pains of childbirth. There had been possibilities for this since the discovery of ether in 1846 and chloroform a few years later. However, these had been used sparingly, partly because of the dangers involved but partly, too, because of an ingrained quasi-religious belief that the pains of childbirth were something a woman had to put up with and were her punishment for her natural sinfulness. Was it not stated in the book of Genesis 'In sorrow shalt thou bring forth children'?

For these notions Lucy had nothing but contempt, especially when they were propounded by men, and she lost no opportunity to stress the pain and suffering endured by expectant mothers, pointing out that the death rate among them was one in two hundred, almost as great, she said, as that of men in the trenches going 'over the top'.

Some progress in the use of pain relief had been made, especially since 1853 when Queen Victoria had availed herself of chloroform in the delivery of Prince Leopold. But in the 1920s it was still regarded with some misgivings even among strong feminists who thought it improper to talk about such matters in public. The British Medical Association, too, had reservations and refused to countenance it being used by midwives delivering babies at home. As it was not cheap it was still confined to the use of wealthier mothers; it was beyond the reach of the poor. Lucy's objective, then, was clear: to dispel old notions and superstitions about pain relief, to bring the subject out in the open and to provide painless, or relatively painless, relief to mothers of all classes. And to this end she devoted her efforts, addressing public meetings, broadcasting from Chequers and raising funds by 'at homes' in Downing Street, in all of which she had the full support of her husband.

Lucy was engaged in other good works besides maternity welfare, most of which were concerned with improving the lot of women. She was on the board of management of the YWCA Central Club and she also espoused the cause of single mothers.[4] She was one of the first to realize how much could be achieved for women by their newly gained right to vote. She was also a prime exemplar of the effectiveness of patient and dedicated efforts with the minimum of aggressiveness and stridency.

Ensconced in power with a large majority it was open to Baldwin to undertake great works, but instead he did little and waited on events. What the country needed, he said, after so much frenetic activity was a period of peace and prosperity. But this was not to be. Unemployment remained fearsomely high, and in 1926 came the General Strike. This lasted just over a week before being called off unconditionally by the unions – owing in large measure to Baldwin's calm, placatory yet firm attitude. In the General Election of 1929 the Conservatives lost 150 seats, and a second minority Labour government took office. But in 1930 the Great Depression reached England from America with a massive run on the pound as foreigners unloaded their English currency, and the threat loomed of national bankruptcy.

This was a situation with which the Labour government was incapable of dealing, and at the strong urging of King George V a coalition government was formed consisting of Conservatives, a minority of the Labour Party and some Liberals. Ramsay MacDonald remained as Prime Minister even after the General Election of 1931, which brought a large Conservative majority, but in 1935 his health broke down and he had to resign, and Baldwin became Prime Minister for the third time.

Once again it was not to be plain sailing. Almost at once a crisis arose. In October 1935 the Italian dictator Mussolini invaded Abyssinia. This was an act of flagrant aggression, but the League of Nations could do nothing to prevent it. In the following year Hitler sent troops to reoccupy the Rhineland. Baldwin was not the best man to face up to the Fascist dictators: he was not basically interested in foreign affairs, he was too slow in rearming Britain and too ready to accept a policy of appeasement (although in this he was supported by a majority of the country). In May 1937 he resigned, but not before confronting a crisis of a different sort at home when the new King Edward VIII announced his intention of marrying the American divorcée Wallis Simpson. Baldwin's adept and tactful handling of the situation, which led the King into abdication of his own accord, was widely admired. His own retirement, unforced and at the height of his powers, came amid a glow of warmth and appreciation. 'No one', wrote Harold Nicolson at the time, 'has ever left office in such a blaze of affection.' Sadly, this was a situation that was not to last.

During the last years of her husband's political career the pattern of Lucy's life did not change greatly. While still fully engaged in her charitable works she continued to provide the comfort and support which were essential to Stanley and without which he could not have kept going.

It had not all been easy. There had been family troubles. Her eldest son Oliver, whom as a child she had spoiled terribly, was to prove something of a black sheep. After an unhappy time at Eton he had joined the army under age at the end of the First World War and had subsequently become a prisoner of both the Turks and the Armenians. After this gruesome experience he became on his return to England a somewhat bitter rebel against his background and class. He joined the Labour Party and said and wrote acrimonious things about his father, and when in 1929 he was elected to Parliament he confronted him across the floor of the House of Commons. In later years they became to some extent reconciled, but for a long time there was strong antagonism.

There were also financial problems. For the first forty years of their married life the Baldwins' circumstances had been affluent, but at the time of the Great Depression the family ironworks struck hard times – no dividends were paid and the value of their shares sank to less than one-fifth of their previous value. And so when in 1929 Stanley lost his Prime Minister's salary as well as the use of 10 Downing Street and Chequers finances became tight.

In good times and bad Lucy never lost her vitality and affability. Contrary to appearances she was not starchy or buttoned up, and at social occasions she was as forthcoming and friendly as Stanley was morose and aloof. And she never lost the 'innocence and unworldliness' Stanley had noticed when they first met. On occasions her naivety was to give rise to some hilarity, as, for example, when she said of a senior Conservative that he was becoming troublesome and in danger of becoming another Nancy (meaning Nancy Astor); and when she greeted Robert Boothby, whom she had last met on a slimming course at Aix-les-Bains, with 'Still a fairy then?' And once when someone was commiserating with her about the strain under which she was living she replied that she was all right, as, at times of stress, 'I lie down, prop my head against the pillows and relieve myself.' A remark also attributed to her, although not fully authenticated, are the words to her daughter on her wedding night: 'Shut your eyes and think of England.'

In spite of these solecisms and the essential simplicity of her character Lucy was always greatly loved and respected by her husband and had a powerful influence on him. It was she who kept him going and saw him through the periods of acute fatigue and depression which at times overcame him. To her mother-in-law she wrote: 'I feel that I am Stan's "trainer" for the Arena and I have to see that he husbands his strength for the fighting times.'

In later life Stanley used to say that he had become Prime Minister by accident, which no one believed, regarding it as part of the image he had created for himself; but it must be doubtful if he would have stirred himself to achieve high office without Lucy behind him and once there to have stayed the course without her to make him, like Lady Macbeth, 'screw his courage to the sticking place'.[5]

In taking the strain off her husband Lucy spared herself no pains, but there were those who thought she was too protective and withheld from him matters he ought to have known about. Lord Derby once said of her: 'No doubt she means well but the worst thing for a man like that is to be allowed to live in a fool's paradise.' There is perhaps some substance in this, but in giving her husband indiscriminate support and shielding him from harsh realities Lucy was like most other Prime Ministers' wives. Only a few knew that there are times when criticism and candour are the best service a wife can render.[6] Lucy was also like most other Prime Ministers' wives in that she did not aspire to be a public figure in her own right and was content to remain in the background.[7] She was never tempted to tread the corridors of power or dabble in political intrigue. A leading society hostess of the time, Emerald Cunard, noticing the hold she had over her husband, said once that she was 'the dictator of England', but this was not the case. Stanley did sometimes confide in her on political matters, but she did not encourage him and was not affronted if he did not. On one occasion she was deeply shocked when, somewhat brazenly, the wife of a political colleague (Lady Diana Duff Cooper) started questioning him about the political situation. 'I would never have dared to ask such questions,' she said.

Lucy might well have expected that when Stanley resigned the premiership they could look forward to a peaceful and honoured old age, free of controversy and strife, with plenty of repose and doing those things they most enjoyed in their beloved Worcestershire. But this was not to be their lot. She had yet to see him through the saddest period of his life. All was well at first, but then after war broke out and the country was in desperate danger people looked for a scapegoat, and on no one was their anger vented more bitterly than on Baldwin. During the inter-war years he had been in high office longer than anyone else during that period and so, some thought, must be most responsible for the country's unpreparedness and for allowing Britain to be outstripped by Germany in rearming.

On the outbreak of the Second World War the Baldwins had just returned from a successful speaking tour of the United States. Back in their Worcestershire home at Astley Hall Stanley soon began to feel restless and longed for some worthwhile work he could do to help the war effort. This was not forthcoming, and it was borne in on him that he had been shelved, and this feeling was strengthened by his refusal of all invitations to speak or write – either newspaper articles or his memoirs. At first although there was neglect there was no bitterness, but in June 1940 after the fall of France and the imminent prospect of a German invasion of Britain the situation changed drastically for the worse. Angry and abusive letters started appearing in the press focusing on Baldwin as the man mainly responsible for the country's desperate plight. The gist of these was that during his thirteen years in office ('the locust years' as they came to be called) he had achieved nothing, had deceived the electorate about rearmament and had put his own interests before those of the country. And then came the hate mail, pouring in on him at home, and without any secretarial help he had no protection from it. Some letters were vicious and personal, calling him a traitor and a trickster who had 'inflicted untold misery on the world'.

During the war life at Astley became very bleak. The house, half full of evacuees from the industrial Midlands, was in a run-down condition, and with wartime shortages and restrictions nothing much could be done about it. Domestic staff was minimal and the garden was untended and overgrown. A friend visiting wrote that there was a general atmosphere of decay about the place. For years Stanley had been looking forward to a life of leisure and repose, and now that he had it he did not like it. His great joy of long country walks was now denied him by arthritis, and he had no other country pursuits to take its place. He still did much reading, but here, too, old age was taking its toll with failing eyesight. But worst of all was the loneliness and the feeling of being despised and excluded from the mainstream when he longed to be occupied and to be of use. A few faithful friends still visited him and he made occasional journeys to London, on one of which he was greatly gratified to be invited to Downing Street by Churchill, who was relenting towards him and with whom he had a long and friendly talk, but this was a one-off and generally he was aware of lapsing into obscurity.

This lonely, downbeat life was a sore trial to Lucy. She had always been gregarious and it did not suit her at all to be buried away in the depths of the country with few people to talk to and little to do, and it affected her spirits. She who before had dealt so efficiently and cheerfully with the running of a household was now finding it oppressive. Wartime controls – rationing, the black-out, inadequate transport – weighed heavily on her, and much of the burden devolved to Stanley. And there were other troubles: she had had to bear the odious experience of a burglary in which she lost most of her jewellery. But although somewhat down she was by no means out. One visitor reported that she was 'vigorous and voluble' and another that she was 'formidable and overwhelming in laying down the law'. Certainly she was still the mainstay of Stanley's life, and when she died in 1945, soon after VE Day, he was desolate without her.

Lucy Baldwin's life was one on which she could look back with pride. Without any great gifts of intellect or a particularly strong personality she had not only made possible the unique career of her husband but she had also, in a quiet way, achieved much on behalf of women. Because of her efforts an increasing number had relief from the pains of childbirth, which in some cases saved their lives – an achievement matched by few women of that time.

Notes

1. *The Pastmasters*, Macmillan, London, 1975.

2. Stanley Baldwin, *On England*, 1926.

3. He was first cousin of the poet Rudyard Kipling and the painter Edward Burne-Jones.

4. One of Lucy's famous gaffes occurred when she was addressing a largely male audience and said she wanted 'each one of you here to be responsible for at least one unmarried mother'.

5. *Macbeth* (Act 3, Scene 7).

6. Notably Emily Palmerston and Clementine Churchill.

7. The main exception, perhaps, is Margot Asquith.

12

FROM ANNIE BONAR LAW
TO ANNE CHAMBERLAIN

No drudgery was too great or too unpleasant for her. – James Ramsay MacDonald on his wife Margaret

I have the good fortune to be able to count upon the assistance of a lady whose affection and understanding have for many years made all my troubles seem light. – Neville Chamberlain on his wife Anne

ANNIE BONAR LAW

Andrew Bonar Law, sometimes called 'the Unknown Prime Minister', was born in 1858, the youngest of four brothers, and raised in Canada where his father was a Presbyterian minister of Northern Irish descent. At the age of twelve Andrew was brought to Scotland, where in time he became an ironmaster, Member of Parliament, leader of the Conservative Party and Prime Minister for seven months, in 1922–3, before having to resign owing to the onset of cancer.

His character and lifestyle were sombre. Steeped in the doctrines of Puritanism, he had few pleasures: he was a teetotaller, an abstemious eater and had a strong aversion to music and the arts. Into this austere existence his wife, Annie Pitcairn Robley, a charming and vivacious Glaswegian, born in 1866, brought light. They were married for only nineteen years from 1891, during which time as well as bearing him six sons and two daughters (a first child was stillborn) she prevailed on him to take a more relaxed view of life and even to partake of some of its joys.

When she died in 1909, following an operation for the removal of gallstones, he was plunged into grief, compounded by the death of his two eldest sons during the First World War. From this personal tragedy, until his death in 1923, he was never fully to recover.

MARGARET MACDONALD

Mrs James Ramsay MacDonald (née Margaret Gladstone but no relation to the Prime Minister) came from a prosperous middle-class family resident in Bayswater. Her father, Dr John Gladstone, was a distinguished scientist, and her mother, who was the doctor's second wife, had died soon after Margaret was born, so that she was brought up and to some extent educated by four elder stepsisters. It was a happy family and a deeply pious one, and at an early age Margaret had declared her resolve to live the Sermon on the Mount in her life. When still young she was taking part in good works: teaching in Sunday School, helping out in boys' clubs and attending to the welfare of girls training to be domestic servants. However, greatly as she cherished her religion, which was Nonconformist, Margaret became convinced that it was not enough; it did not provide her with the opportunities she sought for improving the lot of mankind.

More and more she found herself being drawn towards socialism. In the early part of the nineteenth century socialism was anathema to most people – it was associated with atheism and the Paris Communards, but later on it became more respectable when it found adherents among Church of England clergymen, including the novelist Charles Kingsley. The Christian Socialists made a great impression on Margaret, and when she was twenty-six she joined the Independent Labour Party, a popular socialist party founded three years earlier. Already by then she had met one of the leading lights of the party, James Ramsay MacDonald, and in the same year they became engaged and then married.

Ramsay MacDonald came from a very different background to that of his wife. He was born out of wedlock in the small Scottish fishing village of Lossiemouth in Morayshire. He never knew his father, a local farm worker, and had been brought up by his mother in the tiny cottage of his grandmother and three aunts. Although his childhood had been one of great poverty he somehow acquired a rudimentary education and at the age of eighteen sought his fortune in London. Here he found the going extremely hard but managed to make some sort of a living, first as a clerk and then as a journalist. He also became involved in radical politics, including the recently founded Fabian Society, and discovered that he had a natural gift for oratory – impassioned, sentimental and discursive – as well as the ability to hold the attention and sway the emotions of a massed audience. In 1900 he was one of the founder members of the Labour Party and its first Secretary.

His marriage to Margaret was to be an entirely happy one but of brief duration – no more than fifteen years. During that time Ramsay was elected Labour Member of Parliament for Leicester and was a dominant influence in the rapid rise of the new party. In this he had great support from Margaret, but she also had work of her own to which she devoted herself unstintingly.

By then she had decided that her mission in life was to improve the working conditions of women and children in employment. In many cases these were ghastly – hard, long hours in cramped, unhealthy conditions at minimal pay. To bring about improvements Margaret saw it as her task to investigate these conditions, to make them public and then set about improving them, and she became deeply involved in this work. She was a member of numerous committees – among others the National Union of Women's Workers, the Women's Industrial Council and the Anti-Sweating League – and she produced a large number of pamphlets and reports bringing to light the most scandalous cases, not least those of women and children working at home. Certainly she never spared herself, toiling endlessly and laboriously. As her husband wrote later: 'No drudgery was too great or too unpleasant for her.'

At the same time she had to run a home. She and Ramsay set up in a modest establishment in Lincoln's Inn Fields, where six children were born to them. Domestic duties did not come easily to Margaret, but she strove to cope. Every week she and Ramsay had an 'at home' for Labour activists, radical intellectuals and trade unionists – the catering for which was somewhat *ad hoc* but the bandying of ideas and argument vivid. Ramsay's marriage to Margaret removed from him the threat of poverty, as she had a private income, providing them with a reasonable standard of living including foreign travel on which they embarked extensively, visiting socialist organizations in Europe, America and India.

In all her works Margaret was a dearly loved figure – good-humoured, simple and warm-hearted; and she was not loved the less for her idiosyncrasies. Like many intellectual women she was careless about her personal appearance and made very little effort with her dress. Fashion was something she could not be bothered with – any clothes would do; the older the better.

The end of her life came tragically and suddenly. In 1911, when she was only forty-one, she contracted blood poisoning from a burst internal ulcer and died after a prolonged and painful illness. It then became apparent how loved and venerated she had been. Tributes poured in testifying to her selflessness and dedication. There were those who thought she was a saint. Her death devastated Ramsay, leaving him numbed and inward-looking. He was to live a further twenty-six years, but he never thought of marrying again, and when it was suggested to him he answered that 'I buried my heart in 1911'.

And so Margaret did not live to witness the most tempestuous years of Ramsay's career: his bitter unpopularity during the First World War for his pacifist stance; his re-election as leader of the Labour Party after the war and his becoming Prime Minister of a minority Labour government for ten months in 1924; his fatal attraction to high society and infatuation with the Marchioness of Londonderry, the leading Conservative hostess of the time; his second term in office in 1929, when his government was over-whelmed by the Great Depression; and his decision to form a coalition with the Conservatives and Liberals in the so-called National Government – a decision for which he was never to be forgiven by most Labour Party members and which has blighted his memory, overshadowing his great achievements for the party and undoubted gifts as a statesman. During these years he was in desperate need of the support and advice of Margaret. If he had had it, it may have been that the history of Britain would have been different.

ANNE CHAMBERLAIN

Mrs Neville Chamberlain (née Ann de Vere Cole) was the daughter of an army officer; her mother was of Irish aristocratic descent. When she married Neville in 1911 he was a successful Birmingham businessman who had just been elected to the City Council. He was then forty-two and, left to himself, might not have become involved in national politics; but Anne persuaded him that he should, and in 1918 he was elected to Parliament. By then he was rising fifty, a greater age than that of any other English Prime Minister entering Parliament for the first time.

Anne was the perfect wife for Neville. Devoted and competent, she provided him with exactly the home life he needed, one where he could relax and enjoy the simple pleasures of life. Each morning they would take a walk in St James's Park where they would sometimes feed the ducks. In the evening Neville was never so happy as when he was alone with Anne, who might play the piano or read aloud to him or they might talk on any subject other than politics, for Anne was no political sophisticate and never sought to influence her husband on the issues of the day. This did not mean that there were not times when Neville unburdened himself and confided in her as, like most Prime Ministers, he needed a confidante to whom he could pour out his woes. Like Henry Asquith before him he found comfort in writing long letters about the people and prob-lems that beset him, although in his case these were not to much younger women but to his two maiden sisters.

It must not be imagined, however, that Anne was no more than a home-body providing domestic bliss. She took her share of public responsibilities. Entertaining did not come easily to her, partly because she was subject at times to agonizing bouts of depression and at the best of times she was not an easy conversationalist. Chips Channon, a perspicacious American married to a Guinness heiress and a strong Chamberlain supporter, said of her that she had a quick mind but was lacking in humour.[1] But however great the strain, she always made brave efforts to do what was expected of her, and Neville was appreciative of these. 'I have the good fortune', he once said, 'to be able to count upon the assistance of a lady whose affection and understanding have for many years made all my troubles seem light. She has shared all my plans, she has been privy to all my secrets; she has never divulged one.'[2] From one not noted for his warmth and effusiveness this was high praise indeed.

Neville's career in government started admirably. As Minister of Health and then Chancellor of the Exchequer he achieved a number of vital if unspectacular reforms in such matters as housing, health and Poor Law reform. A later Prime Minister, Harold Macmillan, wrote of him that he was 'one of the most progressive and effective social reformers of his own and almost any time'. But his career was to end in tragedy. When he became Prime Minister in 1937 it was the time of Nazi aggression, and he took upon himself the task of dealing with Hitler personally. No one could have been more unsuited for such a task. At Munich in 1938 he was completely deceived by Hitler, thinking he had achieved the peace of Europe for ever. Only six months later he was disillusioned and forced to recognize that his policy of appeasement had failed. For the first six months of the war he remained as Prime Minister. He then served under Churchill but died five months later of cancer.

In these last bitter months Anne was the greatest possible comfort to him. Without her he would indeed have been a soul in torment: She died twenty-seven years later at the age of eighty-four.

Notes

1. He also found fault with her taste in the furnishings she brought into 10 Downing Street, which he described as 'elementary'.

2. It is not without interest that the brother of this gracious, highly respected woman was a notorious prankster. At Cambridge Horace de Vere Cole had once passed himself off as the Sultan of Zanzibar and been received with great ceremony by the senior fellows of his college. Later he pulled off an even more spectacular coup when with collaborators in attendance (including, improbably, the novelist Virginia Woolf) he masqueraded as the Emperor of Abyssinia and was royally entertained on board the battleship HMS *Dreadnought*. On another occasion he took charge of a group of somewhat bemused workmen and got them to start digging up Piccadilly while a policeman was induced to redirect the traffic.

13

CLEMENTINE CHURCHILL

There in the doorway was a vision so radiant that even now, after 61 years, my always roving, always fastidious eye has never seen another vision to beat it. – Sir Alan Lascelles on his first glimpse of Clementine

Your triumph is that you have been and are everything to Papa. – Mary Soames to her mother

The guardian angel of our country's guardian. – Public Orator of Oxford University

Winston Churchill and Clementine Hozier were married for fifty-seven years, during which time there were two world wars, a deeply troubled peace and great vicissitudes in Winston's political fortunes. But through all this in spite of differing tastes and temperaments and occasional squalls they remained devoted and dependent on each other with no looking aside.

Clementine on her mother's side was descended from an historic Scottish family. The Ogilvys, later the Earls of Airlie, had played a prominent part in Scottish history and been much embattled, sometimes on the winning side and sometimes facing disaster. The nadir of their fortunes occurred in 1746 after the battle of Culloden when as staunch Jacobites and supporters of the Young Pretender they had been stripped of their lands and titles, which were not restored until 1826.[1] Then, as before, the Ogilvys were brave and honourable people but uncouth and much given to hard drinking, hunting and gambling. However, the tenth Earl of Airlie (who had been educated at Eton) had wider interests and broke with tradition by marrying a woman from England, the Honourable Blanche Stanley, daughter of Baron Stanley of Alderley. She was a lady of intellectual leanings and a formidable personality who saw it as her mission in life to bring culture and civilization into the backwoods of Scotland. She was held in great awe by her family, not least by her granddaughter Clementine. Her eldest daughter, who was also called Blanche, was a young woman of charm and beauty but was not married until she was twenty-six and then to a man who could hardly be considered an ideal match for the daughter of an earl. Henry Hozier was fourteen years older than Blanche, a divorcé (who had also been cited as co-respondent in another divorce case) and of no great fortune. He was sprung from a line of prosperous brewers by the name of McLehose,[2] who in time had acquired a country estate as well as the title of Baron Newland.

Henry was certainly a man of great ability: he had had a brilliant army career, passing first in and out of the Staff College, and had established a reputation as a military correspondent and historian. But it was in business that he excelled, being one of the principal creators of Lloyds of London. He was not, however, a kindly or agreeable man. It seems that before marrying Blanche he had not told her of his murky matrimonial past, also that he had a strong aversion to children and did not want any of his own.

It was never likely that their marriage would be happy. Their temperaments were far apart. Blanche was warm-hearted and wayward and quite unsuited to being the wife of a dour, unfeeling insurance executive. She also had a great desire for children, and when these were not forthcoming from her husband she decided to have them by someone else. There has been some speculation as to who this might have been, but it has been revealed recently by Clementine's daughter, Mary Soames, that following the discovery of secret letters it is certain that is was a dashing cavalry officer, Bay Middleton, who died young.

Between 1883 and 1888 four children were born to Blanche Hozier – a daughter Katharine (known as Kitty), Clementine and twins Bill and Nellie. Then in 1891, after twelve years of unhappy marriage, she and Henry separated. The terms imposed by Henry were severe, but they had to be accepted as he threatened that otherwise he would reveal all Blanche's infidelities. The financial provisions made were minimal and, although he can have had no illusions about the paternity of the children (in his entry in *Who's Who* he made no mention of them), he insisted on having custody of the two elder daughters. This was presumably an act of revenge, as he saw little of them and soon packed them off to a grim boarding-school in Edinburgh where they were miserably unhappy and pleaded with him to take them away, which he did not do. However, word of their plight came to their mother, who acted with typical eccentricity. On being refused permission to take the children out for the day she proceeded to install herself in the school, attending classes and generally making her presence felt. In the end Henry was persuaded to allow the girls to leave and return to the care of their mother.

For the reunited family life with their mother during the next fifteen years was to be at times enjoyable, at times upsetting and always unpredictable but seldom dull. Blanche was a loving and understanding mother but flighty and extravagant. Looming over everything was shortage of money: so much so that Blanche could not afford – or thought she could not afford – a permanent home, but moved around from one furnished lodging to another – at one time in Bayswater, then in Seaford and then, on a whim, in Dieppe. Tight though finances might have been, however, money was always found for governesses so that the education of the children was not neglected. In these circumstances the two elder girls became very close. Their characters were different, but they complemented each other perfectly: Kitty dominant and mischievous, Clementine gentle, passive and inclined to be tearful. It seems she did not resent Kitty's dominance over her nor the fact that she was the favourite child of her mother.

The family's sojourn in Dieppe was colourful and agreeable – apart from the occasion when Henry Hozier arrived on the scene in a clumsy and unsuccessful attempt to entice the elder daughters to come back to him. But then came a dreadful tragedy when Kitty at the age of seventeen contracted typhoid from which she died – a devastating blow both to Clementine and her mother.

Back in England Blanche's next choice of lodgings was, for some reason, in Berkhamsted in Hertfordshire, where Clementine and her younger sister Nellie attended the local grammar school. This proved a happy interlude. Clementine enjoyed herself and did well there, passing Higher School Certificate in French, German and Biology. There was talk of her going on to a university, but here Blanche put her foot down; she did not want a blue-stocking for a daughter. Far more important that she should come out, do a season and meet eligible husbands. As usual Clementine fell in with her mother's wishes, but there were difficulties. A season for a débutante was an expensive business, and Blanche did not have the money for it. There was also the matter of Blanche's divorce, which in those days carried a social stigma. But help was forthcoming from an aunt of Blanche's, Lady St Helier, who took Clementine under her wing and financed her. This proved to be money well spent, as in her late teens Clementine had grown into an outstanding beauty and, no longer overshadowed by Kitty, was developing a strong and engaging personality.

Almost at once she was much sought after – for the most part by men much older than herself. At the age of eighteen she was ardently wooed by a man who had much to offer – wealth, charm, intellectual gifts and great kindness – as well as being the son of a viscount. Sir Sidney Peel, however, was fifteen years older than Clementine and, although she admired him, she was not in love with him. Lady St Helier and her mother did not think this was of overriding importance; it would be such a splendid match for a young girl whose position in society was insecure. Twice Clementine entered into secret engagements, but each time she was overwhelmed with doubts and broke them off. Two years later she was again being courted, this time by a man twice her age. Lionel Earle was a civil servant of good repute and considerable wealth. He also had winning ways and Clementine did become formally engaged to him but once again was beset with doubts, and the engagement was broken off and wedding presents returned.

Clementine first met Winston Churchill when she was introduced to him at a ball in her first season, but the meeting was not a success. Winston was struck by her beauty but seemed abstracted and (for once) speechless and did not ask her to dance, which Clementine found gauche and unappealing in such a famous man. They did not meet again for four years, by which time Clementine was twenty-three and Winston thirty-four. The occasion was unpropitious – a dinner party given by Lady St Helier which neither of them wanted to attend and for which Winston arrived surly and late, while Clementine was peeved that the place next to her was empty for so long. But their moods soon changed. Once again Winston was stirred by Clementine's beauty, and this time he started to talk, and continued talking in a way that only he could, and Clementine was overcome. For the first time she knew she was in love. Winston, too, was in love but not for the first time. For months he had been proposing to Pamela Plowden (later Countess of Lytton), a woman of great beauty and charm who had returned his love but who had come to the conclusion that his total dedication to politics as well as his lack of any significant fortune made him an impossible marriage prospect. Winston had also proposed to the daughter of a wealthy Hull shipowner and was said to have had flings with the actress Ethel Barrymore and musical comedy star Mabel Love, all of whom had shied away when they realized that they would always be a sideline to his political career.

After their second meeting Winston was determined that he would marry Clementine, but he was a dilatory suitor and it was nearly five months before they became engaged. Admittedly he did have much on his hands during that time. He had been promoted from junior minister to Cabinet minister (President of the Board of Trade); he had fought and lost a by-election in Manchester and fought and won another in Dundee. Also for much of the time Clementine was away with her mother on a visit to Germany. It was not until August of 1908 that the scene was set for a proposal at Blenheim Palace. Clementine was asked to stay, and Winston arranged to meet her in the rose garden the next morning – and then, characteristically, overslept and kept her waiting. When he finally appeared it started to rain and they had to take refuge in a Grecian temple, where he proposed and she accepted.

Then at last Winston showed some signs of haste, and the wedding was arranged to take place a month later during a lull in the parliamentary timetable. Predictably for one of his fame, it aroused widespread interest. St Margaret's, Westminster, was full to overflowing, and there was a large crowd of well-wishers outside. By common consent Clementine looked superb, and her bridal gown was deemed perfect. By contrast Winston's wedding ensemble was described by *The Tailor and Cutter* as resembling that of a glorified coachman.

At the time of his marriage Winston, at the age of thirty-four, was already a celebrity – one of the most prominent and controversial politicians in the country. His career had been adventurous and eye-catching. After an undistinguished time at school he had joined the army, not in order to make it his career but as a stepping stone into politics, his idea being that if he made a name for himself as a gallant and enterprising soldier it would open the gates into the political arena. Entry into Sandhurst, however, proved difficult, and he only scraped through the entrance examination on his second attempt, passing out with only moderate distinction. However, with his social standing he was accepted into a famous cavalry regiment, the 4th Hussars.

Winston was to be in the army for seven years, seeing service in far-flung parts of the world – the north-west frontier of India, the Sudan (at the battle of Omdurman) and Cuba (fighting for Spain against rebels). He left the army in 1900 but soon afterwards was engaged by the *Daily Telegraph* as its correspondent in the Boer War. In South Africa he had an exciting escape after being taken prisoner, and several times he came close to being killed.

Back in England he stood for Parliament and was elected Conservative member for Oldham. He soon made his mark but found increasingly that he was out of place in the ranks of the Conservatives, and in 1904 he took the bold step of crossing the floor and joining the Liberals. The following year, when a Liberal government took office, he was appointed Under-Secretary at the Colonial Office.

This then was the man that Clementine had married: vital, ambitious and – some felt – brash and loud-mouthed. And if his career had been embattled before it was as nothing to what lay ahead. In the year after their marriage there began the fight for the Parliament Act, which was to prove one of the most vicious of all parliamentary crises (see p. 114), and Winston was in the thick of it; as an ex-Tory and the grandson of a duke he was regarded with special venom by the opponents of the bill. Clementine, too, came in for her share of malignity; but she was unperturbed and stood four-square behind her husband. She had been brought up as a staunch Liberal, and her views on most issues were to the left of Winston's – and she, too, was a fighter. When in later years she was asked if she had hated this period she replied: 'I didn't mind it a bit. It was so exciting. It made me feel heroic and proud.'

In the first years of her marriage Clementine had other worries than political combat. There were also problems at home, financial in particular. Winston had no private fortune and as a cavalry officer he had depended partly on the proceeds of his books and articles but mainly on an allowance from his mother, the American heiress Jennie Jerome. By this time Jennie, who had little sense of economy, had got through most of her inheritance; Winston as a Cabinet Minister had little time for writing, and his ministerial salary was barely enough to live on. At the same time he made little attempt to curtail his lifestyle. He had been used to running up large debts and he continued to do so, which was anathema to Clementine. She had been accustomed to financial straits all her life but had always attached great importance to living within her means. She hated being in debt and even more receiving hand-outs from wealthy friends and relations, and Winston's extravagances, especially gambling to which he was quite strongly addicted, appalled her.

She had other worries, too. Relations with her mother-in-law were not easy. Jennie had been the great prop and support of Winston's early life, acting as confidante, financier, string-puller and literary agent. She had, however, welcomed warmly his engagement to Clementine and had tried hard to be helpful, but she and her daughter-in-law were very different in character and there was little rapport between them. Besides, at the age of forty she had contracted a second marriage to a man half her age and an almost exact contemporary of Winston. Winston had adapted easily to this situation, but Clementine found it bizarre – as did others. She also felt an aversion to some of Winston's friends, notably to one of the closest, the brilliant politician and barrister F.E. Smith (later Lord Birkenhead) whom she blamed for Winston's heavy drinking and gambling. She and Winston had few enough close friends and even fewer in common.

Certainly Clementine had much to put up with during her first years of marriage. Winston never concealed that politics came first and family second. He was away for long periods of time and then would arrive home at all hours often with political cronies and expecting dinner; and at meals he tended to read newspapers or talk shop. Most of this Clementine took stoically as part of the price of being married to a political frontliner. She was without self-pity and seldom complained. One thing, however, which did grate was Winston's continued intimacy and, as she saw it, flirtatiousness with former female friends. This aroused jealousy, and Winston had to be very soothing and conciliatory. Her fears were unfounded, however: Winston was not a natural philanderer, and his deepest love was only for her. This was demonstrated vividly in the frequent letters he wrote to her when they were apart, which invariably contained protestations of his undying devotion. In one he wrote: 'Your sweetness and beauty have cast a glory upon my life.' And in another: 'My sweet cat,[3] my heart goes out to you tonight and I feel a vivid realisation of all you are to me and of the good and comforting influence you have brought into my life. It is a much better life now.' Friction and misunderstandings there may have been, but these were quickly resolved, and on her first wedding anniversary Clementine could write: 'The year I have lived with you has been far the happiest in my life and even if it had not been it would have been well worth living.'

As the newly wed wife of a leading politician it was to be expected that Clementine would come under close scrutiny by fashionable society. Most impressions were favourable, and all were agreed as to her striking classical beauty, but there were those who wondered if there was anything much more to her. With strangers she tended to be shy and reserved and tried to cover this up with a flow of small talk. The Asquith family, which was not without a vein of intellectual snobbery, took a dim view of her. Surprisingly for one with such a keen eye for feminine beauty, the Prime Minister found her 'a thundering bore', but then he liked women to be forthcoming and of not too strict virtue and would have been put off by the puritanical side of Clementine's character. His keen-witted and sharp-tongued daughter Violet,[4] who was a close friend of Winston, was even more critical, indeed catty. To a friend she wrote:

> The news of the clinching of Winston's engagement to the Hozier has just reached me from him. I must say I am much gladder for her sake than I am sorry for his. His wife could never be more to him than an ornamental sideboard as I have often said and she is unexacting enough not to mind not being more. Whether he will ultimately mind her being as stupid as an owl I don't know – it is a danger no doubt – but for the moment she will have rest at least from making her own clothes and I think he must be a little in love.

It seems that Winston sensed those penetrating critical eyes, for he told Violet that there was much more in Clemmie than met the eye, to which Violet with her usual quickness replied: 'But there is so much that meets the eye.' In spite of this scornful attitude, however, the Asquiths and Churchills were to be on good terms and spent much time in each other's company.[5]

After the passing of the Parliament Act there was no remission in the pressures on the Liberal government and on Churchill in particular. In 1910 he was appointed Home Secretary, responsible for the maintenance of law and order, and perhaps no holder of that office has inherited such a turbulent situation. For in that year industrial unrest, which had been fomenting for some time, came to the boil. There were strikes in all the main industries, often accompanied by violence and lawlessness. At that time, too, violence broke out among the suffragettes (see p. 115). This movement had been growing in strength for some years and their methods had at first been peaceful and lawful, and Winston and especially Clementine had felt some sympathy for them. But the women turned to violence and pursued vendettas against leading government ministers, notably Churchill, who on one occasion was belaboured with a horsewhip on Bristol railway station and was in considerable danger when he was nearly jostled in front of an oncoming train. These methods lost the suffragettes much support, and Clementine in particular was disgusted by them. 'All women', she declared, 'must feel a sense of humiliation and degradation at the scenes we have just witnessed.'

But far the greatest threat to law and order at that time – as so many times before and since – lay in Ireland (see p. 112). When the situation was at its most tense Winston decided that he must go to Belfast to address a massed rally in favour of Home Rule. In spite of unequivocal advice to the contrary Clementine insisted that she would go with him, as she thought that her presence would have a restraining influence on the angry crowds, but in the event they were angrier than ever in the Protestant area, screaming and raging and threatening to overturn their car. However, both Winston and Clementine kept their nerve superbly until they reached the Catholic part of the city, where the mood was different and Winston addressed a large crowd for over an hour.

In 1911 Winston was transferred from the Home Office to the Admiralty with the brief of putting the Royal Navy into readiness for war with Germany. This was a task he greatly relished, and he devoted himself to it with all his usual energy and flair; but it did mean frequent and prolonged absences from home while on board the Admiralty yacht *Enchantress*. At this time he visited ships and dockyards all over the country and abroad. Clementine missed him terribly but accepted the situation and found much to occupy herself, taking up golf and tennis as well as hunting where, under the tutelage of her cousin by marriage, the Duke of Marlborough, she proved an intrepid horse-woman. She also had a growing family to care for.

In 1909 she had given birth to a daughter, Diana, and then two years later to a son, Randolph. But in 1912 she had a miscarriage, which laid her very low. To speed her recovery Winston organized a cruise to the Mediterranean on *Enchantress* with visits to naval establishments and classical sites. This should have been a splendid occasion – on a beautiful yacht, in the greatest luxury and with guests who included the Asquith family, Admirals Fisher and Beatty and other eminent people. But it seems it did not come up to expectations. Winston talked at inordinate length on naval matters, while the Prime Minister buried himself in guidebooks, which he often insisted on reading aloud, and his wife, Margot, as always was demanding of attention. After dinner they were made to play bridge; it was doubtful who was the worse player – the Prime Minister or the First Lord. Admiral Beatty, for one, was bored stiff and Clementine was ill at ease. She felt out of her element in such company and had little interest in either naval dockyards or classical sites. Besides, she was dogged with ill health, the aftermath of her miscarriage, and was greatly relieved to return home.

The outbreak of war, when it came, took most people by surprise. It had long been expected, but few thought it would arise from the assassination of an Austrian archduke. At the time Clementine was on a seaside holiday with her family on the coast of Norfolk and, rather surprisingly, she lingered on there for a few weeks; Winston did not urge her to return home, although he must have known that the east coast would be a likely target for raiding German warships and possibly even a German invasion. However, she arrived back in London safely and soon afterwards gave birth to her second daughter, Sarah.

War and the prospect of battle had an electric effect on Winston. As minister responsible for the war at sea he had a vitally important role and every aspect of it thrilled him. But then came disaster. Following the failure of the Dardanelles campaign, for which, unfairly, he was held to be mainly responsible, he came under heavy fire from the Conservatives, who made it one of the conditions of joining a coalition government (see p. 117) that he should be excluded from any post of major responsibility. Herbert Asquith, the Prime Minister, was a friend and admirer of Churchill, but, under pressure, he felt he had to comply.

Suddenly, then, at a crisis point in the war Churchill found himself ousted from the Admiralty and fobbed off with the post of Chancellor of the Duchy of Lancaster (described by Violet Asquith as 'the waste paper basket of the Cabinet'), but he did not remain there long. 'Well-paid inactivity', as he called it, was not for him. Other fields beckoned. He still had his commission in the army, and he could join his regiment on the front line in France. And so from the comforts and privileges of a high office of state he found himself in the midst of war in the trenches. The squalor and danger of this he described vividly in a letter to Clementine, but in spite of them he could still write: 'Amid these surroundings, aided by wet and cold and every minor discomfort, I have found happiness and content such as I have not known for many months.'

This happiness and content, however, were not shared by Clementine. For her this was a period of great anguish. With Winston's removal from office it was necessary for her to leave Admiralty House, which was no great sorrow to her, but she had nowhere ready into which to move, as their family home in Eccleston Square was let. For a time she had to make do with borrowed accommodation before settling into a large house in the Cromwell Road with her sister-in-law Lady Gwendeline Churchill and her family.[6] She also had to face up to a halving of the family income. This had never been lavish but was now meagre indeed.

Clementine's greatest worry, of course, was about Winston. She had shared fully the agony he had endured at the time of his dismissal, feeling keenly the scathing things that were said about him and, almost as bad, the cloying sympathy from Job's comforters. And then with Winston's departure for France came gnawing anxiety about his safety; when he was in the front line she expected to hear at any moment of his death or disablement. She knew only too well how rash he was liable to be and in her daily letters urged him not to go prowling about no-man's land in the moonlight.

It was perhaps some relief that she had at this time much to occupy her. Some mothers might have found the upbringing of three young children enough, but Clementine, although caring and affectionate, was not an obsessive parent; she was ready to delegate. Certainly she had many other claims on her time. From Winston in the trenches came a stream of requirements, and she was kept busy providing him with such items as brandy, cigars, chocolate, sardines, towels, socks and a sleeping bag. But more important by far were the letters she wrote to him. It is impossible to overestimate the role she had at this time in sustaining his morale and keeping afloat his political career. There can be little doubt that this was then in the balance and but for her might have foundered. She lost no opportunity of telling him that his fortunes were only temporarily in decline and the day would come when his achievements at the Admiralty would be justly appreciated. She also took it upon herself to maintain contact with leading political figures and see to it that he was not forgotten and that the sacrifice he had made in giving up a soft government job for the rigours of the trenches was fully recognized. This was not a task she found agreeable, as she was inclined to be shy and unsociable and had scant regard for most politicians, notably Asquith ('the old block') whom, she felt, had let Winston down badly and more particularly for Lloyd George whom she mistrusted profoundly, describing him as 'a direct descendant of Judas Iscariot' and telling Winston that 'if he doesn't do you in he will let you down'.

As if all these cares were not enough Clementine had also embarked on some challenging and arduous war work. In response to the urgent need for more munitions a number of new factories had been established in north London, but the catering arrangements for these had been found to be entirely inadequate, and the thousands of workers employed were going hungry. Clementine set to work with a will to remedy this and was to take a leading role in improving the existing canteens and setting up new ones. The work was hard and time-consuming (not least the journey by public transport to and from such places as Ponders End), but her heart was in it and she showed considerable management skills in organizing nine canteens with staff (mostly voluntary) of some five hundred.

On the Western Front Churchill won golden opinions from many quarters. He showed exemplary qualities of leadership and, after a somewhat chilly initial reception, succeeded in winning the confidence of the men under him who marvelled not only at his coolness and courage but also his cheerfulness. 'War is a game', he told his junior officers, 'to be played with a smiling face.'

It was not long, however, before he began harbouring thoughts of returning to the political arena. The command of a battalion provided inadequate scope for his towering abilities. But the timing of such a return was difficult. If he went too soon he might fall flat. If he went too late the opportunity might be missed. On this Clementine had decided views. Much as she longed for him to be back in England and out of danger, she was convinced that if he came too soon he would be a lone figure with little support and strong opposition. 'Bide your time,' she wrote to him. 'Don't pluck the fruit before it is ripe. Everything will come to you if you don't snatch at it.' Also the great kudos he had gained by taking himself off to the front line might be lost with an early return. Some of the letters that passed between them were couched in strong terms, but it soon became clear to Clementine that Winston had made up his mind and was not to be deflected.

In March 1916 Winston came home on leave, and this should have been a wholly enjoyable occasion, but it was marred by an excess of politics – Clementine had to do a lot of uncongenial political entertaining when she wanted her husband to herself. Also they did not agree as to when Winston should return to politics. After his return to France he wrote to Clementine: 'I cannot tell you how much I love and honour you and how sweet and steadfast you have been through all my hesitations and perplexity.' Nevertheless two months later he resigned from the army and came back to England. At first it was as Clementine had predicted: he was a lone figure. Six months later Lloyd George replaced Asquith as Prime Minister and Winston had great hopes of a post in the new government, but he was disappointed. Lloyd George regarded him as being still blighted by the Dardanelles, and Conservative opposition to him was as strong as ever. It was not until March 1917 that he felt able to offer him the post of Minister of Munitions which Winston gladly accepted.

During the final years of the war Clementine's life was as full as ever. She continued with her work in the canteens (for which she was appointed Commander of the British Empire) as well as taking on board ever-increasing family responsibilities. In 1918 she was again expecting a baby. After a few months the family moved out of the house in Cromwell Road and for a time was without a settled home in London, relying on temporary accommodation borrowed from friends and relations. In 1919, however, following an unexpected inheritance from a distant cousin of Winston's, they were able to purchase a house in Bayswater.

After the war Churchill served in the Lloyd George coalition of Liberals and Conservatives, which was not at all to the liking of Clementine who was a stronger Liberal than he and who had a profound mistrust of Lloyd George. She was not therefore all that sorry when in 1922 the coalition was broken up. However, she could not but regret that in the ensuing General Election Winston, standing as a Liberal Free Trader, lost his seat.

Once again, then, Winston was in the political wilderness. Clementine was glad of the break, as it meant he was able to spend more time with her and the family. She was in need of comfort at that time, as 1921 had been a dreadful year. After an idyllic holiday at the beginning of the year in Egypt with Winston, accompanied by Lawrence of Arabia and the famous explorer Gertrude Bell, she arrived home to hear of the suicide of her brother Bill Hozier, an inveterate gambler. Then a few weeks later came the death of her mother-in-law, Lady Randolph. Jennie by then had become a legendary figure. After the failure of her marriage to George Cornwallis West she had married another man more than twenty years younger than herself, a Mr Montagu Porch, once of the Northern Nigerian Civil Service, with whom she lived happily until her death.

Of his mother Winston wrote: 'The wine of life was in her veins. Sorrows and storms were conquered by her nature and on the whole it was a life of sunshine.' If Clementine was able to sustain the death of her mother-in-law relatively calmly, there then came a disaster which shattered her. Her youngest child Marigold died of septicaemia. For Clementine this was the most terrible blow of her life, and for once her iron self-control broke down.

Winston's period in the wilderness came to an end in 1924 when he rejoined the Conservative Party and was adopted for the safe seat of Epping, which he represented for over forty years. He had hesitated before taking this step, and Clementine had been forthright in her views: 'Do not let the Tories get you too cheap,' she wrote to him. 'They have treated you so badly in the past and they ought to be made to feel it.' In the event the price was not small, as after the General Election of 1924, in which the Conservatives gained an overall majority, the new Prime Minister Stanley Baldwin, to Winston's amazement, offered him the post of Chancellor of the Exchequer, one that he was to occupy for nearly five years with grace and distinction although not without controversy.

Clementine was naturally delighted by Winston's accession to such an exalted post, but it was unfortunate that at the same time there occurred a major difference between them. They were both agreed that with a growing family (another daughter, Mary, was born in 1922) they needed a place in the country, although Clementine's views on this were not so extravagant as Winston's. In 1921 he discovered an old manor house in Kent called Chartwell and fell in love with it at first sight.

It stood on a hill with marvellous views, a lake, and land and gardens with great possibilities for development. But it also had flaws. The house, which was not beautiful, had been unoccupied for several years and was in a state of decay, riddled with damp and dry rot. The garden, too, was chaotic – totally overgrown and with a right of way going through the middle of it. But to these drawbacks Winston was impervious. He saw only the beauty of the surrounding country, the opportunities for painting ('paintatious' as he called it) and the scope for improvements. Clementine, however, had no illusions. She realized at once the tremendous expenditure of money and effort that would be needed to make the place habitable and then to keep it in running order; and she knew it was beyond their means. She was therefore strongly opposed to acquiring it, and made her views plain. But Winston was not to be put off. He loved the place and was sure that in time Clementine could be won round. And so, rashly and perhaps not quite straightforwardly, he proceeded to buy it behind her back and presented her with a *fait accompli*, something to which she took great exception and found difficult to forgive.

Unlike the rest of the family she did not come to love Chartwell; it was a constant source of anxiety to her, and her forecasts as to costs proved an under-estimate. More and more needed doing to the house, and when finally finished it could only be managed with a large domestic staff. The garden, too, proved a great expense, as also did Winston's landscaping projects and his efforts at amateur farming. But it did not occur to Clementine to turn her back on the place. She accepted that it was her duty to make out of it as attractive and comfortable a home as possible, and in this she had considerable success: the house was at all times run elegantly and efficiently. But her heart was not in it; it is perhaps significant that in 1924 when the family finally moved in she was away on a holiday abroad.

The purchase and restoration of Chartwell meant a return of financial worries for the Churchills. The inheritance from Winston's cousin had been entirely absorbed and Winston's salary as a minister was not adequate for their new lifestyle. This meant that it was necessary for Winston to do more and more writing – both books and newspaper articles. Fortunately these were exceptionally well paid, but in order to make ends meet he had to work very hard, usually well into the night.

It became noticeable to some friends and members of her family that during the Chartwell years (some forty in all) Clementine became more aloof and imperious, not aggressively so but enough to fill people with awe. There were those to whom she showed marked hostility, and there were occasions when dinner guests were angrily contradicted and even times when she left the table in a fury. And it was one of the tragedies of her life that she did not find relations with her children easy. She was loving and caring but was not, seemingly, warm-hearted, and there was a barrier between them; there was no intimacy or jollity. Her youngest daughter Mary has recorded that in her childhood her mother treated them with a mixture of tenderness and severity and that her main feelings towards her were ones of admiration and respect.

It was sad, too, that she disapproved of nearly all her children's marriages. She thought, rightly as it turned out, that Diana's marriage to John Bailey, the son of a South African millionaire, would not last and had doubts about her second husband, the politician Duncan Sandys, her marriage to whom also failed. She had little sympathy for her second daughter Sarah's wish to go on the stage, but she had the good sense not to stand in her way and was proud of her when she became successful and was taken on by the well-known impresario C.B. Cochrane as one of his celebrated 'young ladies'. However, she was appalled by Sarah's marriage to a popular comedian of American-Austrian-Jewish origins known as Vic Oliver. Here, too, though, she and Winston tried to accept the situation and bring Oliver into the family, and when the marriage collapsed their relationship with Sarah was intact.

It was with her son Randolph that Clementine had the most unsatisfactory relationship, however. At an early age it became clear that Randolph was gifted but flawed. With great good looks and plenty of charm, when he chose to exert it, he was also quarrelsome and wilful. Clementine was constantly at odds with him, so much so that he became convinced that she hated him, which perhaps made him all the more obstreperous. In coping with him Clementine had little help from Winston, who doted on him, indulged him and thought him brilliant. When Randolph was still a boy Winston would bring a dinner party of eminent people to silence so that Randolph's adolescent views could be heeded. On leaving university Randolph made some sort of living as a journalist and lecturer; he also made occasional forays into the political scene, but these were ill-judged and intemperate and caused his father great embarrassment, notably when he stood as an Independent Conservative in a by-election, thereby splitting the Conservative vote and letting the Labour candidate in.

When two strong personalities live together in close contact it is almost always necessary that from time to time they should have a break from each other. Both Winston and Clementine were aware of this and accepted that occasionally their ways should diverge. This was often the case when they went on holiday, for here their tastes differed. For Winston the South of France provided all the things he loved most – splendid food and wines, lovely 'paintatious' country and opulent houses where he was entertained with such diversions as polo (he continued to play until he was fifty), boar-hunting and the insidious pleasures of the casino. But Clementine had no love for the South of France. It brought out all her puritanical instincts. Basically shy and unsocial, she tended to be bored by the rich and pretentious, and too much luxury made her claustrophobic. Besides, she thought that that way of life had a pernicious effect on Winston, especially the opportunities for gambling. Much later she told one of his private secretaries: 'It epitomized for me the shallowest side of his character.' Her own taste for holidays was much simpler – staying with family and old friends in a comparatively modest hotel where she could go walking and sightseeing[7] and indulging her favourite pastime of playing tennis, at which she was no mean performer, having considerable success in local handicap tournaments. There was a strong sporting element in Clementine: at the age of fifty she developed a taste for skiing, and at Chartwell into old age she was a highly competitive croquet player. She and Winston did have some very good holidays together, but more often than not they went separately.

One particularly memorable holiday for Clementine occurred in 1934. She and Winston had been invited by Lord Moyne (Walter Guinness) to join him on his yacht on an expedition to the South Seas in search of dragon-like lizards for the London Zoo. Winston was unable to accept the invitation, but Clementine longed to go, and Winston, realizing how much she needed a break, gave his consent. The voyage was to last four months, during which time the yacht sailed the South Pacific, often in uncharted seas, and visited unexplored islands which Clementine found enchanting: 'the loveliest, wildest, strangest spots in the world', she wrote, 'with innumerable paradise beaches and wild rocks with coral gardens'. In her letters to Winston she wrote vivid descriptions of these as well as of their efforts (only partially successful) to capture the lizards. In return Winston, who wrote regularly, kept her up to date with events at Chartwell – the progress of the wall he was building, the mating of the black swans, the children's dogs and their lack of house-training and (in some detail) the creation of an island on the lake with the help of a somewhat temperamental mechanical digger. And in all their letters there were always declarations of deep devotion and of how much they were missing each other.

In one of his letters Winston wrote movingly: 'Is it not joyous to see how great and growing is the treasure we have gathered together amid the storms and stresses of so many eventful and to millions tragic and terrible years?' Clementine arrived home to a rapturous reception from her family. She was overjoyed to be back, but not long afterwards she was writing to a friend that she was longing to start out again. But not many opportunities remained to her. All too soon ominous and crushing events would close in, requiring her greatest efforts yet.

Churchill remained as Chancellor of the Exchequer until 1929, when the second Labour government under James Ramsay MacDonald took office. Soon afterwards he found himself in strong disagreement with the Conservative leadership on the question of self-rule for India, which, he considered, was being granted too soon and under undue pressure mainly from the Indian spiritual leader Mahatma Gandhi.[8] This meant that for the next ten years he was in the political wilderness, not included in MacDonald's National Government nor in the subsequent Conservative governments of Stanley Baldwin and Neville Chamberlain. During this time he was still a member of the Conservative Party but a loose cannon and generally regarded with disfavour and mistrust. This was disastrous, as it meant that his voice was not heeded on a more momentous subject about which he was proved to be right: the rise of Hitler and the rearmament of Germany.

For the most part his warnings about these dangers fell on deaf ears, and the policy of appeasement was accepted by most of the country. This was to survive Hitler's occupation of the Rhineland in 1936, Austria in 1938, the German-speaking parts of Czechoslovakia a few months later and of the rest of Czechoslovakia six months after that. But when on 1 September 1939 German troops invaded Poland there were few appeasers left, and Britain declared war. Then at last Churchill was brought into the government as First Lord of the Admiralty, a post from which he had been sacked twenty-four years earlier. Eight months later, following the disastrous Norwegian campaign, he became Prime Minister. At the time he later recalled: 'I felt as if I were walking with destiny and that all my past life had been but a preparation for this hour and for this trial.' This was 10 May, the same day as German armoured forces invaded Holland, Belgium and France and once again carried all before them. Ten days later the British Expeditionary Force was cut off and faced annihilation, but by a miracle most of the men (but not their equipment) were evacuated from the beaches of Dunkirk. Two weeks later the French were compelled to sue for peace and Britain stood alone.

This is not the place to record all the events of the Second World War, only Clementine's part in them. At first she was concerned with moving into 10 Downing Street and the Prime Minister's official country house at Chequers in Buckinghamshire. Here the domestic arrangements were to a large extent in the hands of the Civil Service, which left her with time for other activities;

these soon crowded in on her. As the wife of the Prime Minister and a great popular hero letters poured in from all over the country – some from well-wishers, some from those in trouble, some from cranks and charlatans – but Clementine read them all and saw to it that they were answered. She attached importance to this, as she felt it kept her in touch with popular feeling, which she could pass on to Winston.

Inevitably, too, she became associated with a number of charities, something of which she had not previously had much experience. Family and political responsibilities had occupied nearly all her time, besides which she had always had an aversion to committees; she preferred individual direct action. Now this was to change. She became involved in the management of a maternity home for officers' wives and in 1941 became President of the Young Women's Christian Association Wartime Fund, charged with the raising of funds and the providing of hostels for women in the services. Here she proved a mighty force, insisting not only on high standards of comfort and cleanliness but also a friendly and homely atmosphere. In order to achieve her aims she could be very demanding, and there is evidence that hostels were sometimes transformed after a visit from her.

Clementine's greatest undertaking came at the end of 1941 when she became chairman of the Red Cross Aid to Russia Fund. This was immensely successful. The British public had been deeply stirred by the heroism and suffering of the Russian people in the face of the most brutal and barbarous invasion and longed to give help. With Clementine as chief fund-raiser money poured in from all over the country. Within three months £1 million had been raised and within a year £2 million. In two years this had been doubled and in three trebled. The responsibility for spending these huge sums was considerable: finding out what medical supplies were most needed by the Russians (who were never reticent in their demands) and then getting them produced, packed and transported past the enemy required formidable organization; in the first fourteen months some 300,000 tons were safely delivered – a notable feat in which Clementine played a leading role.

Other activities, too, demanded Clementine's attention. A typical day in her life was described in a letter to her daughter Mary: 'Today for three hours I have been trudging round the Borough of St Pancras looking at ARP[9] canteens and decontamination centres till I thought I should drop. I had to make three speeches and grin and look gracious the whole time! Both my stockings laddered and a heel nearly came off my shoe!'

A task she found arduous and heartrending, but which she never shirked, was accompanying Winston on his tours of bombed cities. Dressed in sensible, practical clothes, her hair usually tied up in a scarf, but always contriving to look well turned out, she was a tower of strength on these occasions. People warmed to her immediately and felt she really cared for them and would do all she could to help them. She also took it upon herself to visit air-raid shelters during the Blitz so that she could see at first hand how dreadful were the conditions in some of them – damp, lice-ridden and insanitary. In order to achieve improvements she used the full force of her position and personality and was invariably successful in overcoming obstruction and delays.

One great anxiety of Clementine's was that Winston might be caused embarrassment by a careless action on the part of a member of his family. This was not likely to come from his daughters, whose behaviour throughout the war was exemplary. Diana had been commissioned into the Women's Royal Naval Service (WRENS) but had had to resign to look after a young family and care for her second husband, Duncan Sandys, after he was badly injured in a car accident. After the break-up of her marriage to Vic Oliver Sarah had gone through a period of unhappiness and instability but had then joined the Women's Auxiliary Air Force and after a period in the ranks had been commissioned and trained for skilled work in photographic intelligence. She also acted at times as an additional aide to her father, a job she performed with great tact and aptitude. In 1943 the youngest daughter, Mary, joined the Auxiliary Territorial Service (later the Women's Royal Army Corps) and was assigned to a Heavy Mixed Anti-Aircraft Battery where she was in the front line against the Luftwaffe and where her main concern otherwise was to be treated in the same way as all other rankers.

The member of the family who, as before, caused his parents the most concern was Randolph. He had not mended his ways. His drinking was as uncontrolled as ever, his gambling debts, although often paid off by his father, continued to mount, and his general behaviour was no less aggressive. Even Winston, in whose eyes he could do little wrong, felt constrained to remonstrate with him for the 'ever increasing lavish folly of your ways'. At the same time the panache and charm were no less potent and he was never lacking in courage. Before war broke out he had joined his father's old regiment and, expecting to see early action and possible death, was concerned about a Churchill heir and successor. He accordingly began to propose marriage to most women of his acquaintance, who had the prudence to refuse him; but then he was accepted by Pamela Digby, daughter of Lord Digby and at that time a comparatively unworldly nineteen-year-old.[10]

Most of Pamela's family was opposed to the marriage, as was Clementine, who nevertheless did all she could to support her and welcome her into the family, well knowing what turbulence lay ahead of her. This was not long in coming. Pamela was later to describe life with Randolph during the first winter of the war as 'ghastly'. When he was on leave he neglected her for much of the time, was often drunk and made little effort to control his rages. And his debts grew ever larger while she was expected to live on a shoestring. In her misery she sought comfort from Clementine, who was sympathetic but adamant, telling her in effect that she must grin and bear it, as she herself had often had to do in the course of her marriage to Winston. She had had to make many sacrifices and on occasions had been under such stress that she had taken herself off for a few days to cool down, but she had always known that her place was by Winston's side and that her life must be devoted to him; she could only advise Pamela to do the same for Randolph. Stoical advice but scarcely feasible.

Soon afterwards Clementine persuaded Pamela to make her home at Downing Street and Chequers, where she established a happy relationship with Winston who was delighted by her, especially when at the end of 1940 she gave birth to a son named, inevitably, Winston. Four months later Randolph was at last sent abroad and any chances that the marriage might survive were dashed when on the troopship going out to the Middle East he ran up further enormous gambling debts, which he expected Pamela to pay off. She knew then that marriage to Randolph was impossible. They were not divorced until 1945, but in the meantime Pamela consoled herself with a number of lovers including the eminent and all-powerful American Lend-Lease coordinator Averell Harriman, who was a frequent guest at Chequers and who continued to be invited there by Clementine (for whatever motives) when she must have known what was going on.

During the war it might have been possible for Clementine to become a great public figure in her own right, but this she did not aspire to be. She never lost sight of the fact that her main function was to prop up Winston – to provide for his needs, humour his idiosyncrasies (most of them) and protect him from spongers and bores. She also felt bound on occasions to protect him from himself. In the summer of 1940, when his power and popularity were at their height, she became aware that he was becoming unduly autocratic and bad-tempered and considered it her duty to point this out to him. As always, when she had something important to say to him she did it by letter:

My Darling,

I hope you will forgive me if I tell you something I feel you ought to know.

One of the men in your entourage (a devoted friend) has been to me and told me that there is a danger of your being generally disliked by your colleagues and subordinates because of your rough, sarcastic and overbearing manner. It seems your Private Secretaries have agreed to behave like schoolboys and 'take what's coming to them' and then escape out of your presence shrugging their shoulders. Higher up, if an idea is suggested (say at a conference) you are supposed to be so contemptuous that presently no ideas, good or bad, will be forthcoming. I was astonished and upset because in all these years I have been accustomed to all those who have worked with and under you, loving you. I said this, and I was told 'No doubt it's the strain.'

My Darling Winston I must confess that I have noticed deterioration in your manner, and you are not as kind as you used to be.

It is for you to give the Orders and if they are bungled – except for the King, the Archbishop of Canterbury and the Speaker, you can sack anyone and everyone. Therefore with this terrific power you must combine urbanity, kindness and if possible Olympic calm. You used to quote: 'On ne regne sur les âmes que par le calme.' I cannot bear that those who serve the Country and yourself should not love you as well as admire and respect you.

Beside you won't get the best results by irascibility and rudeness. They will breed either dislike or a slave mentality. (Rebellion in war time being out of the question!)

Please forgive your loving devoted and watchful Clemmie

The text was concluded by a drawing of a cat.

This was a courageous and remarkable letter. Winston's immediate reactions to it are not known. Years later, however, many people who served under him at this time recorded in glowing terms their admiration and love for him, and this may have been due in part to Clementine's letter.

At the same time as Clementine was taking Winston to task for being too dictatorial there were those who found her manner somewhat arbitrary. Jack Colville, Winston's devoted private secretary, had a great admiration and love for her but often found her overbearing. 'Mrs Churchill', he later wrote, 'considers it one of her missions in life to put people in their place and prides herself on being outspoken.' And: 'She can never resist the opportunity of taking a contrary view . . . and her views on politics are as ill-judged as they are decisive.'

It seems the strain was telling on her, too, as well it might have done, for she was becoming an increasingly lonely figure. It was Winston's custom to confide in her completely and tell her the most confidential information about the war, and she found this a heavy responsibility. In casual conversation she could so easily have let slip some crucial secret. As a result she became more and more reserved, hardly ever letting herself go, and falling back on the platitudinous. This was noted by Eleanor Roosevelt on a visit to England: 'One feels she has had to assume a role because of being in public life and the role is now part of her, but one wonders what she is like underneath.' The only people with whom she could have felt completely at ease were her family, but her daughters were away on active service and Winston was so busy that she only ever saw him at meals, when there was usually a bevy of official guests.

When her daughter-in-law came to live *en famille* she was struck by how often Clementine had dinner alone on a tray in her room. This was due partly, no doubt, to exhaustion but in part also to her distaste for some of Winston's cronies whom he gathered round him. As a result she was not present on some historic occasions, notably the night when the news came through of the Japanese attack on Pearl Harbor and America's entry into the war. Of that night Churchill later wrote: 'Saturated and satiated with emotion and sensation I went to bed and slept the sleep of the saved and the thankful.' But Clementine was not with him. As on many evenings she was keeping herself to herself.

With the USA in the war it became necessary for Churchill to do much travelling abroad. Confidence between Britain and America had to be established and long-term plans made. Only a week after Pearl Harbor he was on his way to Washington for a five-week visit to confer with President Roosevelt and the Chiefs of Staff and to make a stirring address to both Houses of Congress. Until the end of the war trips abroad were to become a regular feature of his life, not only to America but to many other places including Russia, North Africa, Greece and Turkey. Clementine did not accompany him on most of these tours as she found them tiring and uncongenial and she had plenty to occupy her at home; but she did see to it that Winston's personal doctor always went with him; and this was just as well as the strain of long and often very uncomfortable journeys began to tell. On his first visit to Washington he had a minor heart attack and in Tunis in 1943 he had a serious bout of pneumonia, serious enough for Clementine to make an emergency flight out to his bedside and to cause the South African Prime Minister General Smuts, who was with him, to remark that he 'doubted whether Winston would stay the course'. But stay the course he did, although by the end of the war the strain had become overwhelming.

Clementine herself came close to a nervous breakdown at times, but in the last weeks of the war in Europe she found the energy and resolution to go on a long and exacting tour of the Soviet Union. This was at the invitation of the Russian Red Cross, whose members wanted to express their thanks for the medical supplies that had been sent to them. The red carpet was laid down for her in a big way, and she was received graciously by all the Russian leaders, including Marshal Stalin, who awarded her the Order of Red Banner of Labour. She visited hospitals and schools all over the country, including Leningrad (now St Petersburg), which was just recovering from a two-and-a-half-year siege, and which she said was the most beautiful city she had ever seen. She also went to Stalingrad (now Volgograd), beginning to rise from its ruins after six months of the fiercest and most destructive (and most decisive) battle of the war.

Everywhere she went she was fêted and welcomed with rapture. On the political front relations between Russia and the Western powers were declining ominously as Stalin failed to honour the pledges he had made, particularly in regard to Poland. But on her travels Clementine saw no signs of this wall of mistrust that was being built up. Everywhere were smiles and good feeling. While she was in Russia momentous events were occurring in the rest of the world – the war in Italy came to an end, President Roosevelt died, the Russian and American armies met up, Hitler committed suicide and then, on 8 May, the Germans capitulated. Clementine's tour came to an end three days later. It had been a triumphant success. She had generated goodwill wherever she went – almost the last instance of this before the onset of the Cold War. The only sadness was that she was not at Winston's side at the moment of his greatest triumph.

And a triumph it was. On all sides it was acclaimed that he more than any other had brought about the downfall of Hitler and Nazism, and praise and honours were lavished on him. But after triumph came disaster. It was found that the British people no longer wanted him as their leader. Much as they loved him and revered him and loudly as they cheered him whenever he appeared in public, they nevertheless did not trust him and the Conservative Party to set up the new post-war Britain they were looking for. In the General Election a few months after the defeat of Germany the Labour Party won a landslide victory.

And so it came about that Winston, with fresh honours ever being bestowed on him, suddenly found himself out in the cold – no momentous decisions to be made, no Cabinet meetings to dominate, no dispatch boxes with the latest developments and no longer a seat in the Council of Nations. At the Potsdam Conference of world leaders, then in session, where Marshal Stalin and President Truman confidently expected his return, he was replaced by the self-effacing, worthy but lacklustre Labour leader Clement Attlee.

For Clementine as for Winston this was a bleak and stressful time. Her great hope had been that when the war was over Winston would rest on his laurels and withdraw, a great national figure above the fray of party politics. But this was expecting too much. Having tasted power at the highest level he was loath to give it up. He was not ready, as he told her, to be put on a pedestal, and when she tried to comfort him about the election results, saying that they might be a blessing in disguise, he could only remark laconically that in that case they were very well disguised.

The most pressing problem that had to be faced was that of domicile. It was necessary to move out of Downing Street and Chequers at once, and the only other house available to them then was Chartwell, which had been shut up during the war and was not immediately habitable. From the prospect of being homeless they were rescued by their daughter Diana and her husband Duncan Sandys, who gave up to them for the time being their flat in Westminster. Clementine was deeply grateful for this unselfish act but was dismayed at their new lifestyle. During the war at their official residences all domestic matters regarding catering, staff and heating had been taken care of by the Civil Service. Now suddenly all these matters were landed on her and she had to cope with minuscule food rations (even more rigorous than during the war), fuel crises and the ever-increasing difficulty of finding suitable domestic staff. It was tragic that this period, which should have been one of great exaltation, was marked by edginess and stress. In a sad letter to her daughter Mary, Clementine wrote:

> I am very unhappy and need your help with Papa. I cannot explain how it is but in our misery we seem, instead of clinging to each other, to be always having scenes. I'm sure it's all my fault, but I'm finding life more than I can bear. He is so unhappy and that makes him very difficult.

Relief came when in September 1945 (two months after the election) Winston went off for a month's holiday to Italy where he had been lent a luxurious villa by one of his wartime commanders, Field-Marshal Alexander. He wanted Clementine to go with him, and certainly she was in need of a break, but she was too agitated and felt she must stay in England to cope with the London house they had just bought in Hyde Park Gate as well as making Chartwell habitable once more. This was a sadness to Winston, for in spite of any differences they may have had he missed her greatly. He wrote to her almost every day and in one letter said movingly: 'I feel so tenderly towards you, my darling, and the more pleasant and agreeable the scenes and days, the more I wish you were here to share them and give me a kiss.'

It is evident that at this time Clementine's family became seriously worried about her. In a wonderfully compassionate and understanding letter Mary sought to comfort her:

> I hate to see you hedged round with so many tedious vexations and I grieve that you feel so low and exhausted in spirit . . . It is difficult to put down on paper all I want to say. But I do understand that these days for you are not smiling ones. That in addition to the depressing scenes around and before us all, you have many sadnesses and disappointments and mortifications which are made harder to bear by physical fatigue . . . Turn your eyes from the intricate, tiring, vexing piece you have got to now and rest them by dwelling on all you have accomplished already. I gaze on it with so much love and, admiration.
>
> It seems to me such a triumph that after so many events – which have all of them left their marks on your own private life and experience you and Papa should have come through still loving each other and still together. For despite all his difficulties – his overbearing – exhausting temperament – he does love you and needs you so much.
>
> I know you often feel you would gladly exchange the splendours and miseries of a meteor's train for the quieter more banal happiness of being married to an ordinary man . . .

But one of the ingredients of your long life with Papa is the equality of your temperaments. You are both 'noble beasts'.

Your triumph is that you really have been – and are – everything to Papa. Many, many great men have had wives who ran their houses beautifully and lavished care and attention on them – but they looked for love and repose elsewhere. And vice versa. You have supplied him with all these things – without surrendering your own soul or mind.

One worry that was lifted from Clementine's shoulders was that of money, which until the end of their lives was to be plentiful. This was mainly due to Winston's *War Memoirs* and *History of the English Speaking Peoples* but also to a generous act by a group of his friends (they chose to remain anonymous) who purchased Chartwell and presented it to the National Trust on condition that Winston and Clementine could live there for the rest of their lives. Clementine had hoped that after the war the big house would become a Churchill museum, while she and Winston lived quietly and unpretentiously in a smaller house near by; but this was not at all Winston's idea. He envisaged expansion.

As has been seen, his farming operations pre-war had not been financially successful, but this did not stop him buying up surrounding land and farming on a larger scale – altogether some five hundred acres. Although Clementine was deeply disquieted by these plans she felt obliged to go along with them and, as always, did not spare herself in the task of refurbishing the house. And this was no light task. During the war all the curtains and soft furnishings had been packed away and when brought out were found to have been attacked by mice, and they could not easily be replaced as such material was on ration for several years after the war. Also, the inside of the house had to be adapted to take account of the fact that only a limited number of domestic staff was going to be available; this, too, was made difficult by severe restrictions on building works imposed by the government at that time. The garden had also been let go and a major operation was needed to restore it – one which was constantly impeded by Winston's habit of taking gardeners off for his pet projects of farming and landscaping. But Clementine persevered, so that in the end Chartwell became a much more attractive and manageable proposition, and even she became fond of it.

In London, too, Clementine contrived a comfortable and well-run house at 28 Hyde Park Gate, although it soon became evident that it was not going to be large enough to accommodate Winston's rapidly increasing secretariat. Providentially, however, the house next door came on the market, and although Clementine thought it grossly extravagant to buy a whole house for the sake of one or two extra offices she was prevailed on to agree on condition that the rest of the building was sublet.

After the trauma of the 1945 election Winston had quite soon adapted to his new way of life. He had always been resilient. Once again painting came to the rescue and for this he had plenty of opportunities, especially in the South of France where he had open invitations to stay in great luxury in the houses of rich friends. Back in England, too, he found much to occupy him. He was an active and vociferous leader of the Opposition, and his *War Memoirs* and developments at Chartwell took up much of his time. He also discovered an entirely new interest when his latest son-in-law, Christopher Soames, who had married Mary in 1947, introduced him to horse-racing and persuaded him to buy a horse that was to have considerable success. Sadly, Clementine shared few of these interests. She could never work up any enthusiasm for racing and her antipathy to the South of France remained as strong as ever. 'God, the Riviera is ghastly,' she wrote to Mary. 'One is suffocated with luxury and *ennui*.' The company of such people as Somerset Maugham, Noël Coward and Greta Garbo was not for her. She longed to stay quietly with family and close friends where she would be unencumbered and free to go her own way.

It was unfortunate that at this time of stress Clementine did not have more things she enjoyed doing. She still liked sightseeing and the theatre, but she had few relaxing pastimes such as needlework, bridge or even gardening, although for the latter there was plenty of scope. Tennis and skiing had once been great pleasures, but these had faded as she grew older, although she still played a keen game of croquet.[11] It was work of one sort or another which took up so much of her time. Apart from running two houses to a very high standard and seeing that Winston was cared for and humoured, there were any number of public duties which crowded in on her, especially in Winston's constituency. She did not enjoy these at all but felt she had to undertake them, especially now that Winston could do so little.

In her late sixties Clementine was to have further calls made on her. By 1951 the British people, wearying of socialist austerity, had voted the Conservatives back in, and Winston became Prime Minister for the second time. The strain of this on Clementine was crushing. At the time she was just recovering from a hysterectomy and the prospect of moving back into Downing Street and Chequers just as she had organized her life round Chartwell and Hyde Park Gate filled her with gloom. For a time her nervous system was on the verge of collapse, but she snapped out of it and faced up to a heavy programme of official entertaining, particularly at the time of the Coronation in 1953. But her health remained uncertain, and her nerves and temper were always under pressure.

In 1953, three weeks after the Coronation, Winston's health took a sudden turn for the worse. He had a stroke during an official dinner at Downing Street and for a time was seriously incapacitated. The question then arose urgently as to whether at the age of seventy-nine, with impaired speech and blurred mental faculties, he should resign and hand over to his heir apparent, Anthony Eden, who had been waiting in the wings for nearly ten years.

At times he was manifestly incapable of carrying out the duties of Prime Minister, but at others his mind cleared and he was almost his old self again. For Clementine this was an agonizing situation; her own feelings were strongly that he should resign, but she could not bring herself to urge him to do so. He felt passionately that he should stay, as he believed that he and only he could establish an understanding with the Soviet Union. Clementine appreciated the strength of his feelings but at the same time dreaded that he was not up to the job and might have a humiliating public breakdown. Lady Violet Bonham Carter, who visited Winston at this time, saw with acute insight the position she was in:

> I must tell you, darling, what intense admiration I felt for your courage, wisdom and dispassionate judgement, when your emotions must have been so deeply involved. I cannot imagine anything more difficult and agonizing than these last weeks must have been for you – with all their conflicts of hope, fear, anxiety and decisions for the future.

In the event Winston was to battle on for another two years, still believing fervently that he had a vital contribution to make towards world peace (as well as having growing doubts about the suitability of his successor). When he did eventually resign he insisted on keeping his seat in Parliament, although he hardly ever spoke there and visited his constituency only on rare occasions. The Woodford Conservatives were very understanding and were unwilling to raise with him the matter of his relinquishing the seat. Clementine, too, held back: she seemed to sense that it was a matter on which Winston felt so deeply that if she took a strong line he would become alienated from her.

Winston's last years were a tragic story of deteriorating health and intensifying depression. As he lapsed into lethargy and incomprehension he became more and more remote. His interest in public affairs grew less and his pleasures in life fewer. He could no longer paint or write and had little joy from smoking or drinking. 'I'm so bored with it all,' he said on one occasion when he was offered a glass of champagne.

During his long decline Winston became more and more dependent on Clementine. It seemed that only she could get through to him and give him comfort and amusement. She was never away from him for long, although the strain of this was intense as her own health was always precarious. She suffered much from neuritis, a nagging and painful affliction, and when this cleared up came an attack of shingles. She also tended to be accident-prone, suffering several falls resulting in broken bones.[12] But her courage and willpower did not fail her and were a wonder to family and friends.

There were also family troubles at this time. In 1963 her daughter Diana committed suicide after a long period of instability following the break-up of her marriage to Duncan Sandys. Clementine had never been close to Diana, but at that moment, with Winston in final decline and she herself in hospital for a nervous condition, it came as a shattering blow. The affairs of her daughter Sarah were also troubled. Her second marriage, to Anthony Beauchamp, a society photographer, had not lasted long, and in the year following their separation he had committed suicide. By then Sarah had a drink problem, but in 1962 she married Lord Audley. This promised to be a happy and tranquil union, but after only one year Lord Audley died from a heart attack. For her youngest daughter, Mary, Clementine had no worries. Her marriage to Christopher Soames was happy and lasting. For a time they lived in a house on the Chartwell estate and both gave invaluable support in propping up her morale and looking after Winston.

In 1962 (when he was eighty-eight) Winston had a bad fall in the Hotel de Paris in Monte Carlo, breaking a hip, which caused him to be in hospital for two months. After this the deterioration in his condition gathered pace: he became very deaf and almost speechless and any kind of communication with him became ever more difficult. But he lingered on until being carried off finally by a stroke in 1965. At his magnificent funeral Clementine was unfaltering and at the end of the day told her daughter: 'You know, Mary, it wasn't a funeral. It was a Triumph.'

In her widowhood of twelve years Clementine at last achieved a measure of tranquillity and relaxation. Her life was now her own, free of worrying responsibilities and no longer under the shadow of a titanic husband. She lost no time in selling the houses in Hyde Park Gate and moving into a convenient flat, where she managed her life along practical, unpretentious lines – the sort of life she had often longed for. And in her new freedom she rediscovered enjoyment. Taking her grandchildren out for treats, mingling with the crowd on open days at Chartwell, theatre-going – all of these gave her pleasure. And honours continued to pour in on her. Before the death of Winston she was already a Dame Grand Cross of the Order of the British Empire (although she never wished to be known as Dame Clementine) and had been given honorary degrees from Oxford and other universities. Soon after her widowhood, on the recommendation of Labour Prime Minister Harold Wilson, the Queen conferred on her a life peerage and she took the title of Baroness Spencer-Churchill of Chartwell.

Until the end of her life Clementine was a deeply revered figure. Within the circle of family and friends she mellowed considerably: there was more humour and less temper, although she did still have it in her to be imperious and intemperate. This was notably evident in the matter of Graham Sutherland's portrait of Winston, which had been commissioned by Members of Parliament as a gift to him on his eightieth birthday. At first all had gone well; Winston had struck up a friendship with Sutherland, and both he and Clementine seemed to approve of the first drafts of the portrait. But when the final work was presented to them they were appalled. In their eyes Winston was portrayed coarse-featured and scowling, a picture of aggression and ruthlessness. At the formal presentation he managed to be tactful, describing it as 'a remarkable example of modern art which certainly combined force and candour', but in private he said it was 'filthy and malignant' and made him look like 'a down-and-out drunk who has been picked out of the gutter in the Strand'. The more he saw of it the more he detested it and so did Clementine, who vowed that it would never see the light of day; at some point she saw to it that it was destroyed. This was a ruthless way to treat a work of art by an eminent artist and exposed her to strong criticism after her death. In defence of her action, it should be said that family and friends were agreed that the portrait was not the true Winston: it was the populist image of him, one of the façades he had thought fit to project; the true Winston was a nobler, gentler, more human character. It is understandable that Clementine should not have wanted such a portrayal of her husband to pass down to posterity, but he was surely a great enough man to have survived it.

Three years after Winston's death tragedy came to Clementine again when Randolph died at the age of fifty-seven. His had been a tumultuous life, almost always at odds with someone, as often as not his mother or father. But at the end he and Clementine had been drawn closer together, and in a moving letter he had expressed his deep appreciation of 'the terrible time you have had in the last fifteen years'. At the time of his death he was engaged in the writing of his father's official biography, a task he was undertaking with great devotion, to be left unfinished after the publication of two volumes.

Clementine died suddenly and peacefully in 1977 at the age of ninety-two. The service of thanksgiving for her life at Westminster Abbey was full and included representatives from sixty foreign countries.[13] Everyone sensed the passing of a noble and vital individual, a personality in her own right but also 'the guardian angel of our country's guardian'.[14]

Notes

1. Their sympathy with the Jacobite cause did not lapse. Clementine Hozier was named after Princess Maria Clementina, wife of the Old Pretender (son of James II).

2. One of whose kin was Nancy McLehose, the great love of the poet Robert Burns.

3. A little surprisingly, the letters of both of them contained some baby talk (accompanied by drawings); Winston was Clemmie's 'beloved pug' (or even 'my little puggy woo'), while Clemmie was Winston's 'sweet cat' and their children 'puppy kittens'.

4. Later Lady Violet Bonham Carter and later still Baroness Asquith of Yarnbury. Brilliant and incisive, she was known in the Churchill family as Ultra Violet.

5. Much later Lady Violet changed her tune completely. In *Winston Churchill As I Knew Him* (Collins, 1965) she recalled her first meeting with Clemmie at her coming-out party: 'She

had come out a few years before me, and as I gazed upon her finished, flawless beauty and reflected on her wide experience of the world I was just stumbling into, I felt an awe-struck admiration. Awe vanished, admiration stayed, and with it began a friendship which no vicissitude has ever shaken.'

6. The wife of Winston's brother Jack. Known for some reason as 'Goonie', she was one of the people closest to Clementine.

7. Something Winston actively disliked. 'How bloody! How absolutely bloody!' he once exclaimed when confronted with some ancient remains.

8. Described by Churchill as 'a naked fakir'.

9. Air Raid Precautions.

10. Later among various liaisons she was to be married to Leland Hayward, a Broadway producer and Averell Harriman, a millionaire diplomat. She also in the course of time became American ambassador to France.

11. She particularly enjoyed outmanoeuvring Field-Marshal Montgomery.

12. In one bizarre incident she needed hospital treatment after being struck on the head by a football while walking in Hyde Park.

13. But regrettably not from the one most deeply indebted to her – the Soviet Union.

14. The words of the Public Orator at the Oxford Encaenia when Clementine was made an Honorary Doctor of Civil Law.

14

DOROTHY MACMILLAN

I'm a perfectly useless person. We shall be a pretty comic couple. – Dorothy Macmillan on becoming engaged

Perhaps there will be storms of wind and rain, and high waves may threaten us sometimes, but we'll always sail on together, won't we? – Harold at the same time

To the casual observer she is just a typical upper-class cup of tea; but on closer inspection he would find that it is laced with liquid of a more stimulating kind. – John Grigg on Lady Dorothy

The marriage of Harold Macmillan and Dorothy Cavendish lasted for forty-five years. For most of that time Dorothy was deeply in love with another man and openly consorted with him, and the marriage would have ended in divorce if Harold had agreed to it. But they continued to live together and to keep up appearances, and Dorothy was always to give Harold unstinting support in his political career.

Dorothy was descended from the highest ranks of the Whig aristocracy. Her father was the ninth Duke of Devonshire and her mother was the daughter of the fifth Marquis of Lansdowne, both families with a long record of distinguished public service. The fourth Duke of Devonshire had been Prime Minister for a brief time in the eighteenth century, and the eighth Duke, Dorothy's great-uncle, had been a prominent politician in the nineteenth century, holding most of the top offices of state and three times declining offers of the premiership. Although for most of his career he held the courtesy title of Lord Hartington, he was known familiarly as Harty-Tarty. Of great political rectitude, his love life was irregular. In his youth he had been madly in love with a not particularly high-class courtesan known as Skittles. Later he had a thirty-year affair with the German-born Duchess of Manchester, whom he eventually married when she became a widow and who became known as 'the Double Duchess'.

Dorothy's father, Victor, had also been an active politician – as a member of the House of Commons for seventeen years and then as Governor-General of Canada and later Colonial Secretary. Her mother, Lady Evelyn Fitzmaurice, was of equally famous lineage. She, too, had a Prime Minister in her ancestry (Lord Shelburne) and her father had had a career of great distinction – Governor-General of Canada, Viceroy of India and Foreign Secretary.[1]

When Victor succeeded to the dukedom in 1908 it was with no great enthusiasm. At the time he was having a successful career in the House of Commons and did not want to exchange this for the less vital ambience of the House of Lords. He was also appalled at the thought of becoming entangled in the complexities of the massive Devonshire estates (as well as Chatsworth, Hardwick Hall in Derbyshire, Bolton Abbey in Yorkshire, Compton Place in Eastbourne and Lismore Hall in Ireland). For seventeen years he and his family had been living happily and comfortably in Holker Hall, a delightful house set in idyllic Lakeland country, and he dreaded moving from there into the cavernous splendours of Chatsworth.

Dorothy was eight when this move was made, and it is not recorded what she thought of her new lifestyle, which consisted for much of the time in travelling from one stately home to another in special trains along with nannies, governesses and numerous domestic servants including grooms with their ponies. She was one of seven children, and it seems they were a happy family and not upset by the continual changes of venue. As with most children of the aristocracy they were brought up more by their nannies and governesses than by their parents. Victor was a dutiful but distant father, most of his time being taken up by politics and the Devonshire properties, but, if somewhat ponderous, he was kindly and approachable. Their mother, Evie, was of a different temperament. She tended to be domineering and sharp-tempered with a streak of parsimony, especially noticeable in the treatment of her domestic staff but also felt at times by her guests, and her children were certainly not mollycoddled.

When Victor and Evie took over at Chatsworth there was a great change of atmosphere from that which had prevailed under Harty-Tarty and his Double Duchess. They had epitomized the 'fast set' of which Queen Victoria had so strongly disapproved – racing, gambling, frolicking and generally living it up. By comparison the new regime was lacklustre and even a little dull. But not entirely so. There were still splendid occasions of which Dorothy must have had a view from the sidelines, as when the King and Queen were entertained in Devonshire House at the traditional banquet before Derby Day. And then there were the Christmases at Chatsworth which were celebrated on a princely scale with a house full of visitors and an army of domestic servants working day and night to attend to their needs – tramping along interminable corridors, climbing innumerable stairs and preparing huge meals which then had to be transported two hundred yards to the dining-room, yet apparently enjoying every minute of it. Much later a former cook recalled: 'These days it's hard to explain to anyone how satisfying it was for us. It was just lovely hearing voices once again in all the bedrooms and children playing in the corridors. It was like one big family coming home again. We all felt part of it and loved it.'

A particular delight was the Christmas party for the staff. This is recalled by a retired housemaid: 'That was really something, I can tell you . . . The family and the gentry all came, of course, and we could invite two guests as well. There must have been three hundred of us there. Mrs Tanner, the cook, used to do the food wonderfully, and the dancing went on till three or four in the morning.'

With the outbreak of the First World War the Devonshire lifestyle had to be severely curtailed. Men of military age were enlisted, petrol and some foods were rationed, and the Duchess (not perhaps without some satisfaction) inaugurated a regime of strict austerity.[2] But in 1916 the Duke was persuaded to become Governor-General of Canada. For this he was well qualified: his success in politics was ascribed to his simplicity and straightforwardness and freedom from any form of ostentation or pretence. He was also a good mixer and without any snobbery. However, in spite of the fact that there was a war on and Canadians were by nature democratic, Victor decided that his governorship should not lack style. And so, U-boats notwithstanding, he set out across the Atlantic accompanied by a large retinue of cooks, maids, valets and liveried footmen as well as a quantity of china, plate, furniture and pictures.

He and most of his family were to be in Canada for five years, a period later described by Dorothy as being 'of idyllic happiness'. He got on well with Canadian politicians, established easy rapport with Canadian people and carried out his duties with dignity without being stuffy and aloof. The children especially had a wonderful time. They mixed freely and easily with others of their own age and it was totally taboo ever to pull rank. Dorothy, who was sixteen at the time of their arrival, was able to lead the kind of life she enjoyed most: outdoor, energetic, social and without too much intellectual pressure. She had grown up to be warm-hearted and gregarious but also had a strong will and a temper that could be explosive.

In 1919 there was excitement in the family when the Duke's eldest daughter, Lady Maud, became engaged to one of his aides-de-camp, who then returned to England, and his place was taken by a Captain Harold Macmillan, not long out of the battlefields of Europe where he had been three times wounded. Shy, bookish and somewhat graceless, the new arrival did not impress all the Cavendish family, but the Duke was delighted with him, admiring his scholarship and enjoying his conversation. Lady Dorothy, too, was much taken by him.

At the age of nineteen she was impressionable and ready to fall in love, and she found the wounded warrior with his diffident manner and erudite talk enchanting. Harold returned her love, and almost at once they became engaged.

It was an unexpected match as they seemed to have little in common: Harold shared none of Dorothy's outdoor tastes (apart from golf), and Dorothy, who was no reader, had none of Harold's academic interests. There is an inclination to think, in view of his later obsessive ambition, that Harold was making a worldly marriage to a rich duke's daughter, but it does seem he was genuinely and deeply in love with her. 'I am the happiest man there has ever been in the world,' he wrote to his mother. And later: 'I love her so much I hardly know what to do or say or think.' While Dorothy for her part wrote: 'I am so wonderfully happy. I didn't think that there could be anyone like he is in the world.'

Not many years earlier a duke and duchess would have been appalled at the thought of their daughter marrying the son of a middle-class publisher, but times were changing and dukes were coming to terms with democracy, and both Victor and Evie seem to have been sincerely pleased by the engagement and untroubled by the fact that Harold's grandfather was the son of a Scottish crofter.

The story of Harold's grandfather, Daniel Macmillan, is a truly remarkable one. He had been raised on a croft first on the Isle of Arran and later on the mainland, the tenth child in a family of twelve, and was to become in time the founder of a world-famous publishing firm and a friend of some of the greatest literary figures of the day. This he achieved through unrelenting toil and determination, first in a seven-year apprenticeship to a bookseller and bookbinder in the small Scottish town of Irvine, then as a bookshop assistant in Glasgow and London, then with his own bookshop in Cambridge and finally his own publishing firm in London. This feat is all the more extraordinary in the light of his lifelong struggle with ill health: at the age of twenty-one he was stricken with tuberculosis and knew that his lifespan was limited, but this only caused him to redouble his efforts. He was to die at the age of forty, his businesses flourishing and his faith in God undiminished. 'Thank God for my afflictions,' he said. 'It is only through suffering that we are made perfect.'

It was Daniel's second son, Maurice, who was the father of Harold, by the time of whose birth the family had become affluent and made more so by Maurice's marriage to a wealthy American widow, Nellie Hill, a lady of formidable character with great powers of command and a dominating influence in Harold's early life.

Harold was educated at Eton and Christchurch, Oxford, where he just had time to take a first in Honour Moderations (the first public examination at Oxford) before the outbreak of the First World War. Whereupon, like most young students at that time, he rushed to enlist and soon afterwards was immersed in the horrors of trench warfare. He was severely wounded in the Battle of the Somme, and his condition when he was brought back to England was critical. His life was probably saved by his mother pulling strings to have him removed from a military hospital to a private one in Belgrave Square. For the next two years he endured an agonizing but ultimately successful series of operations and treatments, but his wounds did not heal until 1920 and then not completely.

Harold and Dorothy's wedding was one of the grandest held in St Margaret's, Westminster, in the presence of a glittering congregation that included Queen Alexandra and the future King George VI as well as many of the leading literary figures of the day. They then set up house in London but in a different style to that which Dorothy had remembered from before the war, for by then Devonshire House in Piccadilly was being demolished to make way for a motor car emporium, and Lansdowne House in Oxford Street was to be replaced by the department store Selfridges. Harold had an ample income from the family firm, and their circumstances were affluent but not grandiose; their house in Chester Square was considered at the time modest but respectable. They could have settled down to an unruffled family life, but Harold sought more than this.

He had always had leanings towards a political career and these had been stimulated by his experiences during the war. Partly by direct contact with the men under his command and, more especially, by the task of censoring their letters home he had had his first insight into the lives of the poor – their brutal hardships, their insecurity and their indomitable cheerfulness in adversity – and he felt a compulsion to do something to better their lot. In seeking a constituency he asked for one predominantly industrial and working class and so was allotted Stockton-on-Tees, as tough and inauspicious a prospect for a Conservative as can be imagined.

Stockton had been at the heart of the Industrial Revolution. Once a thriving port for the transport of coal, it was the site of the country's (and the world's) first railway, and during the war it had enjoyed a measure of prosperity. In the years following, however, it had become one of the most depressed areas in Britain: unemployment stood at more than 25 per cent, and it was reckoned that some 80 per cent of the people were undernourished. But Harold was undaunted. Shy and diffident, he did not find it easy to communicate with the working class, and he was certainly no popular orator, but he forced himself to face up to the task.

It must be doubtful, however, that he would have had much success without the help he received from Dorothy. As a canvasser she was in a class of her own. She threw herself into the fray fearlessly and tirelessly and, ignoring all warnings, plunged into the darkest and murkiest streets. She was not afflicted by shyness, and her natural warmth and charm won all hearts. She might have been a duke's daughter but there was no grandeur about her (certainly not about her clothes – shapeless tweeds, pudding-bowl hat and sensible shoes), and she listened endlessly and with genuine concern to people's troubles, poured out sympathy and usually managed to cheer them up. 'Oh, she was wonderful,' a constituent later recalled. 'She knew everybody's face. She really made it for him. There was really no one like her. I would say that she was the greater part of his success here.'[3] And a notable success it was to win Stockton for the Conservatives in the 1924 election in the midst of a depression.

After the triumph at Stockton life for the Macmillans seemed to be burgeoning. Harold was a prosperous businessman and Member of Parliament; Dorothy was a prominent London hostess and by 1930 the mother of four children – one son and three daughters. But the clouds were gathering. Their marriage was foundering. The first onset of love had worn off, and it was becoming ever more evident how different were Harold and Dorothy in temperament and tastes. Whereas Dorothy was outgoing and passionate Harold was unemotional and withdrawn. And they had developed few interests in common. Harold could not be attracted by gardening or horses, while Dorothy had little taste for literature and, apart from the human aspect, no interest in politics.

Once in Parliament Harold became a serious and deeply committed politician. Such time as he had free from publishing he spent in the House of Commons or in conclave with colleagues, and this left little time for his wife and family. And he was not a good father; he was ill at ease with children and kept his distance from them. His son Maurice later recalled: 'He could be embarrassing when he tried to show affection . . . He could not cope with personal problems.'

Bored and dissatisfied, Dorothy became more and more stressed, and her situation was not helped by relations with her mother-in-law. Nellie had been delighted by Harold's engagement to Dorothy – the daughter of a duke was everything she could have hoped for – and in consequence had induced her acquiescent husband Maurice to leave the family home of Birch Grove to Harold in preference to his two elder brothers. This, however, proved to be a mixed blessing, as a proviso was added that Nellie should be allowed to live in part of the house during her lifetime, which meant in effect that she would be sharing it with Dorothy; this, as might be expected, led to friction. Nellie had been in many ways a wonderful mother to Harold, giving him at all times, as he put it, 'rock-like and unshakeable support', but she was also domineering and possessive, and this attitude continued after his marriage and was extended to Dorothy. As a mother-in-law Nellie tended to be all the things she should not have been – interfering, overbearing and all-pervasive. For Dorothy, left alone with her at Birch Grove while Harold was away in London, this was too much to bear and the sparks flew.[4]

At the same time Harold was finding their annual visits to Chatsworth a sore trial, particularly at Christmas when there might be assembled under one roof as many as 150 people (with domestic staff) including fourteen children under four. This was not his milieu, and he sought solitude in the recesses of the mansion; on top of this, he must have been aware that the Cavendish family regarded him as an outsider with his heavy, pontificating talk and lack of spontaneous humour. With his outdated clothes (including spats) and long drooping moustaches he was something of a figure of fun. Maurice later wrote that these visits must have been 'absolute hell' for his father.

By the end of the 1920s, then, the Macmillan marriage was under strain, with Dorothy chafing and frustrated and Harold aware of his shortcomings but at a loss as to how to put them to rights. And in 1929 Dorothy met Robert Boothby.

Robert Boothby was a close political colleague of Harold's. They were both Conservatives and unorthodox and on the left wing of the party. On all major political issues, notably the need for more positive action to combat unemployment, they were in full agreement and worked together harmoniously to goad the Conservative leadership into action. Between them there was affection and respect, and this in spite of the fact that as individuals they were as different as could be. Boothby was all the things Harold was not – ebullient, self-confident, hedonistic, oversexed – he lived life to the full with little thought to the consequences. By comparison Harold seemed at first sight colourless: introspective and cautious, his tastes were simple and ascetic and his pleasures in life were few (apart from shooting). Deeply intellectual, he seemed to learn about life from books rather than experience.

To Dorothy, caught in a loveless marriage, it seemed that Boothby could provide all the things she most craved – excitement, laughter and physical satisfaction. With him she became alive as she had not been before. It is not surprising that she should have fallen deeply in love with him. What is extraordinary is that he fell in love with her. She was not a great beauty and of no great intellect, and his sexual proclivities, then and even more so later, were ambivalent. But there was something compelling about her which he could not resist. 'She is the most formidable thing in the world,' he wrote later, 'a possessive, single-track woman. She wants me completely.' And: 'She has completely immobilised me for the last three years.'

In the circumstances of the affair there is an inclination to look on Boothby as a cad and a bounder, loose and fast-living, who heartlessly stole the wife of a close friend. But this is too obvious. For all his raffish ways, he was no Casanova. Weak of the flesh he certainly was and love affairs he had in plenty, but these were incidental and as often as not he was the victim rather than the villain. Certainly in the case of Dorothy it was she who made the running. It seems that at times he entertained thoughts of a deep and abiding love with a stable home and family, but in his heart he knew that temperamentally he was incapable of this. Perhaps the great tragedy of his life was that the nearest he came to it was with the wife of a respected friend and colleague.

The relationship was to have a number of strange twists. Perhaps the most extraordinary thing about it was its longevity. Most people, including Harold, thought it would blow over quite soon, but it was to last until Dorothy's death thirty-seven years later. It was also surprising to some people how open the affair was: little effort was made at concealment, Dorothy making long and clearly audible telephone calls to Robert every day and leaving his love letters around for all to see; they even went on holidays together. But although many people knew about the situation, no word of it appeared in any newspaper. Today journalists would have had a field day, but at that time they were less investigative, and the Edwardian convention still seemed to apply that so long as you kept out of the divorce courts you were not disgraced. It was also remarkable that relations between Macmillan and Boothby seemed to be unaffected. Certainly Harold was deeply upset; to be cuckolded so brazenly was a great dishonour, and it might have been expected that his feelings towards Boothby would have been bitter; but it seems they were unchanged, and their political collaboration continued, as before, on an amicable basis.[5] It may be that Harold appreciated that Dorothy and Robert's love for each other was heartfelt and he looked on the latter more as a fellow victim than a rival.

It is likely that at one time Harold was considering divorce, and Dorothy pleaded with him to grant her one, but his mother took a strong line against it, being convinced that it would have a damaging effect on his political career, which to her was of overriding importance. And so, great as was his anguish, Harold steeled himself to endure the situation and to keep up appearances as if nothing was happening. This was a courageous decision, and in time it had vital consequences; as a result of his humiliation and misery he was to acquire a new toughness and drive and a ruthless determination to succeed at all costs. At the time his political career was in the doldrums. He had made no great impression in the House of Commons, where his speeches tended to be diffuse lectures on political economy – carefully prepared and well informed but flat and uninspiring. Also his political persona was unprepossessing, even a little ridiculous. Many years later Baroness Asquith (formerly Lady Violet Bonham Carter) recalled him in scathing terms: 'He had long walrus moustachios, a high stiff collar, a limp damp handshake and pince-nez – no political sex appeal and certainly no other kind either.'

In 1929 his fortunes were at their nadir. As well as matrimonial troubles he also lost his seat at Stockton in the General Election of that year. And in 1931 he had a nervous breakdown and had to take refuge in a clinic in Bavaria. From here, however, he was able to return hurriedly in order to take part in another General Election campaign in Stockton. In this, Dorothy, in spite of being fully embroiled with Boothby at the time, gave him full support and, as always, played a key role, and Stockton was won back – no mean feat in a city still devastated by unemployment. But then came a disappointment, when on the formation of the National Government (see p. 156) he was left out while several of his contemporaries were given junior offices. The road to becoming Prime Minister and 'Supermac' was to be a long and thorny one, but he was utterly determined to tread it.

While the long-term effects of his wife's affair were to stimulate Harold with greater strength and ambition, they did the opposite for Boothby. Until then he had been the leading light of the younger Conservatives and regarded by many as a Prime Minister in waiting. But his character was flawed, and this became ever more apparent in the Dorothy affair, where he was shown to be weak, vacillating and fatally self-indulgent. At the same time he was having affairs with other women, becoming involved with them and then extricating himself, often on the initiative of Dorothy, who on one occasion pursued him across Europe to put an end to an attachment. In 1935 he did become married to a cousin of Dorothy's, Lady Diana Cavendish, but it came to an end almost at once and he went back to Dorothy. These entanglements did not put an end to his political career, and he was always to command attention in Parliament, but it was becoming recognized that he lacked soundness and gravitas and was no longer considered a contender for high office.

Between a husband suffering a nervous breakdown and a lover behaving chaotically and subject to moods of deep depression, Dorothy would seem to have maintained a reasonable level of stability. The strain of leading a double life must have been considerable: one day the gracious society hostess and mother of an apparently happy and unstressed family, the next consorting with a lover and planning divorce and even elopement. After ten years of married life, most of them unhappy, she was a different person to the uncomplicated girl she had once been. The warmth and joviality were still there, so, too, were the charm and personality, which, as a contemporary recorded, enabled her to 'light up a room' when she came into it. But other traits were emerging – selfishness, ruthlessness, perhaps even a streak of cruelty. Boothby, who was given to overstatement, once said of her (soon after saying that they were 'absolutely fixed' on each other) that she was 'the most selfish and possessive woman he had ever known'. While for her part Dorothy once cried out: 'Why did you ever wake me? I never want to see any of my family again. And without you life for me is going to be nothing but one big hurt.' The situation would seem to be that both of them felt trapped and lacked the strength to break free.

As may be inferred from this *cri de coeur*, Dorothy's relationship with her children was not entirely happy. She adored young children but tended to lose interest in them when they grew older, and she preferred girls to boys so that she had little rapport with her only son Maurice. Most poignant of all was the tragedy of her third daughter, Sarah. It has always been assumed (although not with complete certainty) that she was the daughter of Boothby. Certainly Dorothy always maintained that she was, but this may have been to bind Boothby more closely to her. And Boothby accepted that he was Sarah's father and cared for her and made provision for her. As will be seen later, everything in life was to go wrong for Sarah, including the affliction of many of the Cavendish family, that of alcoholism.

By the outbreak of the Second World War Harold's political career had not taken off. He had become an increasingly rebellious Conservative, and in consequence had been excluded from government office. It was not until

Churchill became Prime Minister in 1940 that this came his way and even then no more than as Parliamentary Secretary to the Ministry of Supply. In 1943, however, he had a notable promotion when he was appointed Minister Resident at Allied Forces Headquarters in Algiers. A few months earlier Anglo-American forces under General Eisenhower had invaded the French colonies of Algeria, Tunisia and Morocco, and Churchill felt the need for a representative on the spot to advise and report back, although it was not clear what his powers and responsibilities would be. Churchill described the post as 'a great adventure'. In the event it was to prove potent and far-reaching, involving not only North Africa but later Italy and the Balkans as well. In these years Harold found himself taking decisions involving thousands of lives, even the fates of nations. Richard Crossman, a member of his staff and future Labour Member of Parliament and minister, wrote of him at that time:

> Not even the Prime Minister in Britain enjoyed quite such unquestioned prestige as Harold Macmillan had earned for himself both in his own British staff and in Ike's entourage. And this exercise of great powers did not overawe him. He did not shrink from them, even revelled in them. At the same time came a great change in his political persona. Gone was the donnish intellectual pontificating on the sidelines, and in its place came the man of action – autocratic, resolute, scheming, duplicitous. Gone, too, was the diffidence and solemnity, replaced by humour and conviviality – a façade to some extent to cover the tension and anguish which were always there.

For nearly all this crucial period in Harold's career, Dorothy remained in England. She had much to occupy her there. Birch Grove had been given over to evacuees – a primary school from London – and Dorothy, in a cottage on the estate, was in her element with the young children she loved, giving them great care and attention. She also had growing family responsibilities with the appearance of the first grandchildren. And she still had a relationship with Robert Boothby.

His political career had taken a fatal blow in 1940 when, as a junior minister, some of his financial dealings before the war had been investigated by a select committee of the House of Commons and found to be 'contrary to the usage and derogatory to the dignity of the House and inconsistent with the standard which Parliament is entitled to expect from its members'.[6] In consequence he had been compelled to resign his office, although there were those who considered that he had been treated harshly. His constituents in Dundee, however, stood by him and he did not have to resign his seat in Parliament, where he was still a forceful speaker and debater. In time, too, he was to become a star performer on television.

During the long period that Harold and Dorothy were apart it seemed that their relationship began to mend – or at least become less tense. They corresponded regularly, Harold's letters being in the form of a diary of day-to-day events, clearly with future publication in mind, while Dorothy's were chatty and domestic. Their tone was affectionate but certainly not passionate. On the occasion when Harold had a narrow escape from death in a plane crash her letter to him seemed scarcely adequate:

> My dear Harold
>
> I was very disturbed this morning to hear of your accident . . . We all wondered where you were going in your aeroplane! They really are horrible things.
>
> Love, Dorothy

In April 1944, after a separation of sixteen months, Dorothy at last managed to join her husband in Algiers. He was overjoyed to see her, and the four months they had together were blissfully happy. As always Dorothy won all hearts by her warmth and informality and lack of condescension. She and Harold visited historic sites and went on picnics when Dorothy uninhibitedly would plunge into the sea 'in the buff', as she put it.

While he was 'Viceroy of the Mediterranean', as he came to be called, Harold's reputation as a politician had been greatly enhanced, but on his return to England at the end of the war he found himself out of touch with the political scene. For the past two and a half years he had been wielding autocratic powers. To return to the limitations of parliamentary democracy required adjustment. In the 1945 General Election, with the heavy swing to Labour, he stood little chance of retaining Stockton, where he was defeated heavily. However, after a few months the safe Conservative seat of Bromley in suburban London became vacant and he was adopted as candidate and in due course elected. But the Labour government seemed firmly entrenched in power and six years of opposition lay ahead of him, a sorry exchange for the 'viceroyalty of the Mediterranean'.

As well as adjusting to the political scene it was also necessary for Harold to adjust to the new family situation, which had changed greatly while he was away. Well might he have remarked: 'I felt myself almost a stranger at home.' Dorothy had moved back into Birch Grove where her two obsessions were her grandchildren and her garden. The liaison with Boothby continued, and on her visits to London she was in the habit of staying either with him or in a hotel rather than in the flat in which Harold was accommodated.

Of the Macmillan children, Maurice had served in the army throughout the war, for much of the time in an outfit known as the Phantom Signals. In the 1945 General Election he had courageously contested the Labour stronghold of Seaham in Northumberland, where he was overwhelmingly defeated by one of Labour's more vociferous stalwarts, Emanuel Shinwell. During the war he had married Katharine Ormsby-Gore, the daughter of Lord Harlech and a woman of strong character. Relations with Dorothy were strained, as she strongly resented what she considered her (and Harold's) cold-hearted treatment of Maurice, which was to become more marked when he showed the first signs of the alcoholism that would blight his life for many years. Of the daughters, the eldest, Carol, had married Julian Faber who became chairman of a firm of insurance brokers, and Catherine had married Julian Amery, the son of Leo Amery, a prominent politician and close friend of Harold's. Julian had had an adventurous war behind the lines with Albanian guerrillas and, later, as Churchill's personal representative with the Chinese generalissimo Chiang Kai-chek. In time he was to attain Cabinet rank and be the rising hope of right-wing Tories. The life of the youngest daughter, Sarah, was already becoming touched by tragedy. It seems that at the age of seventeen she had been told abruptly by a semi-intoxicated friend that she was Boothby's daughter. The shock of this was profound, and it is said she never really recovered from it.

In public the Macmillans still presented the appearance of a happy and united family, but underneath there was unease. Dorothy was a devoted grandmother but a difficult mother-in-law. And she was not always what she seemed to be. As well as being affectionate and benign she could also be wilful and temperamental. Her family loved her, but as they grew older and became more aware of her liaison with Boothby it caused them increasing distress.

Harold's term in opposition came to an end in 1951 when the Conservatives gained a small majority in the General Election and Winston Churchill again took office. In the government that was then formed Harold was appointed Minister of Housing, where he had a great success in achieving the Conservatives' target of 300,000 new houses (as opposed to Labour's 200,000) in just over two years. This performance marked him out for promotion, and high offices came to him in quick succession in the years following: Minister of Defence in 1954, Foreign Secretary in 1955, Chancellor of the Exchequer later in the same year and, finally, in 1957, Prime Minister.

It is ironic that Macmillan became Prime Minister following the least creditable incident in his career. Few have been able to make a plausible defence of his actions during the Suez affair – at first hawkish and militant and then, suddenly, in face of a run on the pound and the threat of oil sanctions, defeatist and submissive. When at the beginning of 1957 Eden's health broke down and he resigned the premiership, most people believed he would be succeeded by R.A. Butler, but it was found that the Cabinet and most Conservative Members of Parliament favoured Macmillan. The situation he took over was desperate. Britain's standing in the world had never been lower: she had been publicly humiliated and disgraced; her alliance with the United States had been seriously undermined and her finances were heading for bankruptcy. At home the

Conservative Party was divided and demoralized and the Labour Party was forging ahead in the polls. Seldom has a Prime Minister had to put together so many broken pieces, but Macmillan rose to the occasion with courage and acumen. It was to be his great achievement in the following years that Britain's position as a world power was to some extent retrieved, the US alliance was restored and the Conservatives won a convincing election victory.

In these successes Dorothy played a significant part. In every crisis she stood four-square behind her husband and kept up his spirits. As a wife she may have erred, but she never lacked for courage or sense of duty, and Harold was grateful for this and paid tribute to 'one without whose help I could have achieved nothing and who serves to remind me of the realities of life'. Left to herself, Dorothy would seldom have gone away from her garden, which was her solace and in whose tending she was a skilled practitioner: no dilettante, contenting herself merely with a little light weeding and deadheading, she got down to business in gumboots, digging, manuring and planting out. If the weather was cold she might strap a hot-water bottle round her midriff, and if the hours of daylight were too short she would don an illuminated miner's helmet and work into the night.

In the home Dorothy was delighted with the growing number of her grandchildren and loved to have them around her, but otherwise there was still stress. She was not an easy person to live with. Quentin Crewe, who was for a time the lover of Sarah Macmillan and close to Dorothy, has described the family ambience in the late forties as

> delightful but histrionic, at once divided and self-sufficient, full of shifting alliances and short-lived feuds. Family life was dominated by Dorothy, whose vitality, ardour, strong will and appetite for melodrama were felt everywhere at Birch Grove . . . Lady Dorothy's furies were dramatic, though seldom directed overtly at Harold himself . . . In her determination to do what pleased her and to do little that displeased her, she allowed her liking and disliking of people too free a rein, especially within her own family.

And her family had its tragedies. Not only Maurice but his three sisters, too, suffered from the Cavendish curse of alcoholism; although when he was forty, after a somewhat gruesome treatment, Maurice was cured of this affliction. By then, after four unsuccessful attempts, he had been elected to Parliament and in time, although not during his father's premiership, was to attain Cabinet rank before dying at the age of sixty-three. Dorothy and Harold's relationship with him had never been easy: they expected too much from him and were unsympathetic about his drink problem. Dorothy was also on bad terms with his wife, Katharine, who lived in a cottage on the estate, which gave rise to a number of clashes.[7]

The greatest tragedy in the Macmillan family concerned the youngest daughter, Sarah, who became increasingly unbalanced. She had several unhappy love affairs and after one of them became pregnant. When Dorothy learned of this she was appalled; she thought the birth of an illegitimate child would have a devastating effect on Harold's political career and ruthlessly – and perhaps brutally – coerced Sarah into having an abortion. Both Harold and Boothby were opposed to this. The latter wrote of it later: 'It was the one thing I could never quite forgive Dorothy, the one wicked thing she did. I think it was all part of her guilty conscience, but it killed Sarah.' Afterwards Sarah became ever more disturbed and later when she married she was found to be sterile. In consequence her alcoholism and depression intensified, her marriage broke down and she died at the age of thirty-nine.

When Harold became Prime Minister Dorothy was not unduly elated. 'I married a publisher,' she told a friend. 'Now look what I've got.' And when the crucial telephone call from Buckingham Palace came inviting Harold to meet the Queen, Dorothy, who was preoccupied with an unwell grandchild at the time, brushed it aside. 'And what do they want?' she said. Of course, the press was on to her at once with a flood of questions, and Dorothy lost no time in making it clear, although it might not have seemed necessary, that she had no interest in clothes and could not be looked on as a fashion plate.

At 10 Downing Street, however, she soon made her presence felt. The somewhat frigid atmosphere engendered by the Edens was dispelled. Her warmth and informality pervaded the place. Grandchildren were brought in, and their scooters and tricycles filled the entrance hall. These had to be removed when there were Cabinet meetings or when VIPs were expected, but even then Dorothy was liable to arrive in the midst of them in a battered old car laden with flowers and vegetables from Birch Grove. The permanent staff was delighted with the new atmosphere; those whose memories went back to the Baldwins and were to go on to the Wilsons declared that 10 Downing Street was at its happiest during the time of the Macmillans. Lord Hailsham (formerly Quintin Hogg), who saw Downing Street under many regimes, paid a heartfelt tribute to Dorothy as 'one of the most gracious of the ladies who occupied it, a wonderful help and inspiration to her husband, a charming hostess and a tireless worker'. On occasions the other side of Dorothy's character would come to the fore, as when she was driving to Birch Grove and finding her way blocked by a contingent of supporters of the Campaign for Nuclear Disarmament let loose at them a volley of basic English that left the chauffeur beside her awestruck. 'Wherever did you learn that language, milady?' he asked her. 'Mostly from the grooms,' replied the duke's daughter.

In 1958 Harold went on a much acclaimed tour of Commonwealth countries accompanied by Dorothy. Almost certainly she would have preferred to stay behind in her garden, but on this occasion she responded to the call of duty, getting out of her rustic clothes into an outfit more or less suitable to be at Harold's side throughout a tour covering some 35,000 miles with thirty-four stopovers.[8] And her support was invaluable. On his own Harold was apt to be tense and ill at ease, but Dorothy made all the difference, her charm and informality breaking down all barriers. At the end Harold paid her a warm tribute: 'Our success was largely due to the wonderful support which my wife gave to me throughout . . . she had at once conquered the hearts of the people by her own special gifts . . . This was her first experience of an almost royal progress, and it seemed to bring to the surface some of the hidden qualities of her deeply sympathetic character.'

In 1959 after his triumph at the General Election of that year Harold's prestige was at its height. At home he became known as Supermac, and abroad he soon established close relations with the new American president John F. Kennedy.[9] But then misfortunes and crises began to crowd in on him. A summit conference of world leaders, which he had been at great pains to organize, was broken off by the Russians when an American spy plane was shot down over Russia a few days before the conference was due to begin. Soon afterwards his reputation was badly dented by the so-called 'Night of the Long Knives' when he seemed to be driven into a panic by adverse opinion polls and summarily sacked one-third of his Cabinet. And in the following year his application to join the European Community was peremptorily vetoed by President de Gaulle of France. In his diary at that time he wrote: 'All our policies at home and abroad are in ruin.'

This was not the end of Harold's woe, for only a few months later came a crisis of a very different sort when his War Minister, John Profumo, became involved in a sex scandal said to endanger national security. In time this might have blown over, but, fatally, Profumo made an untrue statement in Parliament and had to resign in disgrace. The episode gave rise to an orgy of sleazy rumours in the popular press with speculations about the peccadilloes of other ministers. This was a situation with which the asexual Macmillan was unable to cope, and in Parliament he was seen to be blundering and inept.

Outside Parliament, too, he came under violent attack. This was the 'Swinging Sixties', which was not only the era of the Beatles and the miniskirt but also a time of seething unrest. Everyone seemed to be protesting about something. Mockery of the Establishment was particularly popular, and Harold was a prime target and an easy one, with his old-world mannerisms, seeming aristocratic languor and his bumbling off to the grouse moors in antique outfits.

The year 1963 had been an *annus horribilis* for Harold, but it is possible he might have survived it, for he was nothing if not resilient. But then fate struck another blow when he suffered a major health crisis requiring an urgent prostate operation. This did not prove as serious as he expected, but it so weakened him at the time that, combined with failing hearing and eyesight, he felt obliged to resign, which he might not have done had he known that twenty-three years of mostly active life still lay ahead of him.

During all the torments of 1963 Dorothy, predictably, had been a tower of strength. She had never been politically minded and seldom had a grasp of the political issues of the day, but she was full of practical good sense and was shrewd and intuitive about people – and usually accurate in her judgement of them. Over the years she and Harold had evolved a new relationship: pragmatic, affectionate, unsentimental; flowers and token gifts were not exchanged and anniversaries went unheeded. Boothby was still around[10] but played a less dominant role in her life. She had become convinced that her mission was to give full support to Harold and protect him from those who might seek to take advantage of him. And her efforts were greatly appreciated. In the six volumes of his memoirs he did not make frequent mention of Dorothy, but tributes were paid to her and these were warm and heartfelt:

'She has not spared herself since I became PM. She has been all over the country for simple and friendly meetings for women of all types. Now (when they come together at their conference) very many of them know her personally. Neither Mrs N. Chamberlain nor Lady Churchill, nor Clarissa Eden, attempted anything of the kind.'

And again: 'Even the troublesome things like formal entertaining she somehow made agreeable. She carried out all these duties with a combination of dignity and simplicity which is difficult to describe but which many still remember.'

And at the time of the Profumo affair, when she was especially supportive, he wrote: 'Without her constant daily affection I might have succumbed to melancholy brooding in the midst of all these troubles.'

She also coped efficiently and graciously with difficult occasions – the visits to Birch Grove of President de Gaulle and President Kennedy, for example, with their enormous retinue of security guards and sundry difficulties.[11] In the normal course of events they should have been entertained at Chequers, but Dorothy had taken a dislike to the place and never used it.

Rightly, her efforts did not go unrewarded, and soon after Harold's retirement she was created a Dame of the British Empire.

The happier relationship between Harold and Dorothy continued into retirement but was tragically cut short when, after only two years, Dorothy died suddenly of a heart attack while changing into her gardening clothes at Birch Grove. Harold was heartbroken. Agonizing as their relationship had sometimes been, he was desolate without her. Birch Grove seemed cold and empty and the loneliness, which had always been part of him, intensified.

Harold was to survive her by twenty years. In spite of serious war wounds and a life of exceptional stress, he lived to the age of ninety-two. And this epilogue was by no means unfruitful. He resumed his position in the family publishing business, produced six volumes of memoirs and on his rare and carefully orchestrated public appearances – whether in the House of Lords,[12] on prominent occasions or on television – he never failed to make a great impression. During his life Harold had played many roles – the gallant soldier, the political intellectual, the man of action, the Machiavellian politician, the patrician grandee – but perhaps that which he played with the greatest finesse was the elder statesman, humorous, benevolent and infinitely wise. But this, too, was a performance. Underneath he was a lonely, saddened and nervous old man. By her death Dorothy, for all aberrations, had left him depleted. On the last occasion he spoke of her he said: 'She filled my life. I thought in everything I did of her . . . She was devoted to me . . . I had my reward . . . in doing what was difficult I had my reward in the end.'[13]

Notes

1. He was also the author of the famous and controversial 'Lansdowne Letter', written in the middle of the First World War and urging a negotiated settlement with Germany in order to save European civilization.

2. She had a particular penchant for nettle soup, which would have been economical except that the Chatsworth head gardener insisted on growing the nettles in his greenhouses rather than gathering them from the highways and byways.

3. Having won all hearts, Dorothy had a relapse when she dozed off during the counting of the votes.

4. One of her daughters later recorded once coming across her sticking pins into an effigy of Nellie.

5. Some thirty years later, when he was Prime Minister, Macmillan was to recommend Boothby for a peerage.

6. The matter, which was of some complexity, concerned claims for compensation by Czech citizens resident in Britain whose cause Boothby had advocated in the House of Commons without revealing that he had an expectation of financial benefit from the matter.

7. On one occasion Dorothy was heard instructing a member of her staff to be sure to bolt all the doors in case Katharine was to come in and remove the furniture.

8. Her dress could be unpredictable. On one occasion she startled the immaculately garbed ambassador's wife with whom she was to appear on a television programme by wearing a beautiful blouse covered with Cavendish jewellery above the roughest of old skirts. 'Oh, it's all right,' she said. 'On television they only ever photograph your top half.'

9. This may have been facilitated by the marriage of Billy Hartington, Dorothy's nephew, to Kennedy's sister, Kathleen. The former was killed in Normandy in 1944 and the latter in an air crash in 1946.

10. It was not until after Dorothy's death that he felt free to marry Wanda Senna, a woman of Sardinian origin, thirty-three years his junior, who gave him great comfort in his last years.

11. One caused by de Gaulle was that a supply of his blood type had always to be at hand in the case of an assassination attempt; as there was no room for it in the domestic fridge another one had to be brought in.

12. For a time he had refused to take a title as he did not want to prejudice the political career of his son, Maurice. But in 1984 on his ninetieth birthday and after Maurice's death he accepted the title of Earl of Stockton.

13. Quoted from Alistair Horne, *Macmillan 1957–1986*.

15

FROM VIOLET ATTLEE TO
AUDREY CALLAGHAN

I quickly found that Mary Wilson possessed all the virtues of charm,
modesty, frankness and humour, guided by compassion and an acute
awareness of life's realities. She was at once immensely kind and friendly
and a human being to whom one instantly warmed. – Sir Robert
Lusty, Mary Wilson's publisher

VIOLET ATTLEE

Violet Attlee came from a prosperous, conservative, middle-class family,
like her husband Clement, the first Labour Prime Minister to have an
overall majority in Parliament. She and her twin sister, Olive, were the youngest
of eleven children.

In 1921, when she was twenty-five, she went in a holiday party to Italy that
included Clement Attlee. In the course of the holiday, which lasted for over a
month, they fell in love and became engaged and were married in the following year. It seemed a suitable if not particularly romantic match: both were
looking for a partner, the disparity in their ages (thirteen years) was not too
great, and they came from similar backgrounds. Their lifestyles as adults,
however, had been different. For Violet it had been a quiet, respectable existence with her parents in the salubrious atmosphere of Hampstead, but for
Clement life had been rougher.

After a private education at Haileybury College and University College,
Oxford (where such politics as he had were on the right wing of the Conservative
Party), Clement had been called to the Bar and seemed set to follow in his
father's footsteps as a stolid and successful solicitor. Then in 1905, at the age
of twenty-two, he paid a visit to the Haileybury Boys' Club in Stepney in East
London, and this made a profound impression on him. He marvelled at the
boys' courage and cheerfulness amid appalling living conditions and felt a
strong compulsion to help them. Soon afterwards he took over as manager of

the club, which with his private income he was in a position to do. From then on he became more and more involved in the affairs of Stepney, taking on the governorship of schools and hospitals, children's homes and lunatic asylums. At the same time he was drawn into politics.

The intense hardships of the Eastenders shocked him deeply. The more he saw of sweated labour, the depredations of slum landlords and the harsh administration of the Poor Law the more he was convinced that there was something fundamentally wrong with the capitalist system and was drawn towards socialism. And so he joined the Fabian Society, essentially middle class and based in Bloomsbury, and the newly formed Independent Labour Party (ILP), which was primarily working class and more strongly socialist. Here, as a well-to-do bourgeois, he might have felt out of place, but he was convinced that it was where he belonged, and overcoming his natural shyness and reticence took a full part in all their activities – orating at street corners, marching in processions, leading delegations and helping with the feeding of striking dock workers.

This life was interrupted by the outbreak of the First World War, which posed a problem for him as the ILP was strongly pacifist, opposed to anything in the nature of a capitalist war. But he knew he had to go and fight, so he obtained a commission in an unfashionable infantry regiment and served with distinction against the Turks at Gallipoli and in the Middle East and then against Germany on the Western Front. In the course of his service he was wounded severely and rose to the rank of major.

With the coming of peace and with this impressive record he might have been beckoned by new opportunities, but he at once returned to Stepney, making his home there and resuming his previous activities. By then he was a figure of considerable stature and in 1920 was elected Mayor.

Before becoming engaged to Violet Millar he had insisted on her coming to listen to him speak on Hampstead Heath so that she would have some idea of what she was in for. However, he did not expect her to live in his house in Stepney, which he described later as 'a barracks of a place overlooking a coal wharf'. Instead he found a house in nearby Woodford from where he could continue his work in Stepney. This became ever more demanding, and in the same year as he was married (1923) he was elected Labour Member of Parliament for Limehouse and, at the same time, appointed Parliamentary Private Secretary to the Labour leader Ramsay MacDonald.

These were difficult years for Violet. She did not take easily to Stepney and never felt at home in Woodford. Her interest in politics was limited, and she particularly disliked General Elections, of which there were three in the first three years of her marriage. She did not shirk her duties, however, and spent many hours at street corners and in bleak assembly halls and knocking on doors in search of votes. All of these she could endure, but what oppressed her were the long evenings she had to spend alone while Clement was occupied in Parliament. In the second year of her marriage she had a difficult pregnancy followed by a severe bout of postnatal depression. The advice of her doctors was that she should have no more children, but this she ignored and had three more over the next seven years. After the birth of the last she became seriously ill with a nervous disease and had to go into hospital for several weeks. Her condition, however, improved when in 1931 they moved out of the house in Woodford into one in the more congenial (and more Conservative) neighbourhood of Stanmore. At the same time, having no part in the formation of Ramsay MacDonald's National Government (see p. 156), Clement was able to spend more time at home.

This was not to last for long, however, as his political career continued to advance. In 1931 he was elected deputy leader of the Labour Party and four years later its leader. His election came as a surprise in some quarters, as there were others with more outstanding qualities, but it was perhaps his ordinariness and plainness that brought him into favour. At the time the party was in the mood for a leader as different as possible from MacDonald, and this he certainly was – unemotional, practical and blunt (and unlikely to be led astray by high-born ladies).

Attlee's rise to national fame had been rapid and unexpected, and there was a price to pay for it – the heavier strain on Violet. When Clement was at home he was an ideal family man: patient, understanding, handy around the house and if not exactly fun-loving at least ready to join in anything that was going on. But his public duties were becoming ever more demanding, and he had, too, to consider the family finances, which were coming under strain. There were few luxuries in the Attlee household at that time: minimal domestic help and modest holidays in the less expensive boarding-houses. There were times when consideration had to be given to leaving politics.

With the coming of the Second World War Attlee joined Churchill's coalition government first as Lord Privy Seal and then Deputy Prime Minister, standing in for Churchill during his long and frequent journeys abroad.

During the war Violet's life was domestic and unpretentious, caring for her young family and her husband when he was able to get home. In addition she took on war work with the Red Cross and Young Women's Christian Association. The Labour landslide in the election of 1945 took her completely by surprise. Later she said she had been flabbergasted by it. She was quite unprepared to become a Prime Minister's wife and move into 10 Downing Street and Chequers. In time she was able to cope with the situation capably, entertaining prestigious people and attending state ceremonies. But her main task, which she performed admirably, was to provide her husband with the quiet, untroubled relaxation which was essential to him in the stressful post-war years. There were times, though, when she came under great strain. She often had the feeling that civil servants and government colleagues were conspiring to keep her at a distance. It did not take much to make her feel inadequate and resentful. Clement did all he could to soothe her and make her feel wanted. One task she particularly enjoyed was driving him to his various appointments all over the country, which she tended to do at great speed and not always with total safety; there were a couple of minor collisions in the years ahead.[1]

Attlee was Prime Minister from 1945 to 1951 and remained leader of the Labour Party for four years following this. By then he and Violet had moved into a modest, manageable house near Great Missenden in Buckinghamshire known as Cherry Cottage. Here Violet was perfectly happy, leading an undemanding life, performing nearly all her own domestic chores and, with occasional inexpert help from Clem, most of the gardening. And she still loved to drive him everywhere.

She died suddenly in 1964 at the age of sixty-eight from a brain haemorrhage. Clement, who was to outlive her by nine years, missed her sorely. Despite succumbing occasionally to the stresses of her life and perhaps not being always in total sympathy with the Labour Party, she had been a devoted and supportive wife, and her husband's considerable political achievements would not have been possible without her.

CLARISSA EDEN

When Anthony Eden married Clarissa Churchill, Winston's niece, in 1952 he was fifty-five and she some twenty-three years younger. His first marriage had long been failing and had finally ended in divorce in 1950. Other family tragedies, too, had been crowding in on him, notably the death in action of his eldest son in the last weeks of the Second World War.

At that time he was a widely acclaimed Foreign Secretary and with good looks, considerable charm and a conciliatory manner he was popular with both friends and opponents and was generally accepted as heir-presumptive of Winston Churchill as leader of the Conservative Party and Prime Minister. But with family troubles, frail health and shaky finances he was badly in need of strong feminine support. This Clarissa was to give him, but in the four years that followed she would see the collapse of his career and the near ruin of his reputation.

In the first year of their marriage he came close to death when an operation for gallstones went seriously wrong and it was necessary for him to undergo a further operation in the United States by a specialist surgeon. This saved his life; and when, two years later, Churchill at last stepped down he succeeded to the premiership, and in the ensuing General Election the Conservative majority was increased.

But a major crisis arose in the Middle East when President Nasser of Egypt nationalized the Suez Canal – regarded in Britain as a vital link to the Empire and Commonwealth – and Eden became convinced that he should be withstood and, if necessary, overthrown in the same way as Hitler should have been in the days of Appeasement. This led him into bellicose and dubiously honourable action. How much this was due to his judgement being impaired by ill health is uncertain, but, extraordinarily, Eden, the man of peace, integrity and fine diplomacy, was led into a desperate undertaking. When the Suez operation ended in ignominious withdrawal he had no option but to resign, which he was able to do on grounds of his health, which had again taken a turn for the worse.

During this momentous crisis, Clarissa, the youngest Prime Minister's wife to date, stood squarely behind her husband. The strain must have been devastating, and well might she have remarked that during her twenty-one months in Downing Street the Suez Canal flowed through her drawing-room.

Against all odds Eden was to live a further twenty-one years, still respected in some quarters but bitterly reviled in others. But at all times Clarissa provided him with care, comfort and diversion and he found a domestic contentment which had been notably lacking in his earlier life.

ELIZABETH DOUGLAS-HOME

When in 1936 Lord Dunglass, heir to the Earl of Home (pronounced Hume), married Elizabeth Alington, few would have expected that one day this shy, self-effacing Scottish nobleman would become Prime Minister. Since 1923 when Lord Curzon had been denied the premiership because he was a member of the House of Lords it seemed that that office would never again be occupied by a nobleman. But politics is full of surprises.

Elizabeth was the daughter of Cyril Alington, Dean of Durham, who had been headmaster of Eton while Alec Dunglass was at school there.[2] Being six years younger she had made little impression on him then, but they met again, when Alec was twenty-six, fell in love and were married three years later.

It was to be a supremely happy marriage. Both were strong characters, if somewhat shy, deeply devoted to one another and with strong Christian convictions. During the next fifty years Elizabeth would see Alec through many vicissitudes, perhaps the greatest of which occurred four years after their marriage when, because of an injury to his spine, he was struck down and had to spend over a year flat on his back, cocooned in plaster. His recovery was for some time in doubt. As he himself said afterwards: 'I looked over the edge and had a glimpse of the infinite.' It must be doubtful that he would have survived but for the loving and imaginative care of Elizabeth.

But recover he did, and when after the war the Labour government had run its course and the Conservatives took office his career took off with conspicuous success. Churchill appointed him Secretary of State for Scotland, Eden promoted him to Commonwealth Relations, and then in 1970, to everyone's surprise – not least his own – Harold Macmillan appointed him Foreign Secretary. This caused something of an uproar, particularly among the intellectual left but also in his own party. Could this diffident, unprepossessing-looking aristocrat undertake such heavy responsibilities from the House of Lords? Alec himself was doubtful, but Macmillan was convinced that he could and so, strongly, was Elizabeth. When questioned by the press she stated firmly (with undertones of Lady Macbeth) that as far as she was concerned he was able enough for any post in the government, even that of Prime Minister. Macmillan's instinct about Alec proved well founded and at a time when the Cold War was at its bleakest (which included the Cuban Missile Crisis) he was to prove himself an outstanding Foreign Secretary.

Much more was in store for him. When in 1963 Macmillan's health seemed to have collapsed and he resigned suddenly, there was no agreement in the party as to which of the younger men should succeed him. The man who eventually emerged with most support was the one least expected and certainly the least ambitious for the post. Alec himself had great doubts about accepting it, as he was by then fifty-six and it would mean giving up his historic title. But once he became convinced that it was his duty (and Elizabeth had no small part in this) he did not hold back.

Alec and Elizabeth were to be in Downing Street for no more than a year, but it was long enough for them to become greatly loved and respected by the staff there. Alec was the first aristocratic Prime Minister since Lord Salisbury at the beginning of the century, but he was also one of the humblest and friendliest. And Elizabeth, too, played her part in creating a special atmosphere. Basically shy and seeming at times rather formidable, even intimidating, she nevertheless had a heart of gold, and her touch was unerring. There were tears when they left after the General Election of 1964, which the Conservatives lost by a whisker.

However, this was not the end of Alec's political career, and when after the 1970 election a Conservative government was returned under Edward Heath he resumed his role for four years as Foreign Secretary. But that was his last fling. He then took a life peerage and, perhaps more than any other Prime Minister of that time, became a greatly loved and venerated elder statesman. Elizabeth died in 1990, predeceasing him by five years.

MARY WILSON

No Prime Minister's wife has been a more unwilling occupant of 10 Downing Street than Mary Wilson. She had no love for politics, and living in a temporary flat above a set of offices, historic though they might be, had no appeal for her. She endured it as best she could and tried hard to do what was expected of her, but the strain of it sometimes showed.

Mary came from a happy, stable family.[3] Her father was a Congregationalist minister, who had started his working life at the age of twelve in a Lancashire cotton mill. He was a loving father but a strict one, and Mary had a rigorous Puritanical upbringing (no alcohol or any kind of gambling and five times to chapel on Sundays). His ministry involved constant changes of location. Mary was born in Diss in Norfolk, but the family then moved to Nottingham and later to the Lake District. She was to claim that she had moved house twelve times before she married. At school (mainly a boarding-school in Kent for the children of Nonconformist clergy) she was a bright pupil but not especially academic and probably would not have gone to university even if her parents could have afforded it. Instead she took a course in shorthand and typing and found a job with Lever Brothers, a large commercial firm in Port Sunlight in Lancashire.

She first met Harold Wilson when he paid a chance visit to a local tennis club. He was still at school at the time and until then had shown some diffidence in the company of young women, but the sight of Mary playing tennis was too much for him. It was, he said later, love at first sight. Certainly he lost no time in taking up tennis. He also told Mary that one day he would marry her and become Prime Minister, which Mary, no doubt, took with a pinch of salt.

Harold came from a lower-middle-class family of Yorkshire origin, whose finances fluctuated. His father was an industrial chemist who had made a good living during the First World War but in the inter-war years had been subject to unemployment. At grammar school Harold had shown few signs of the brilliant academic career that lay ahead of him but enough ability to win an open exhibition to Jesus College, Oxford.

His career at Oxford was unexpected. Remarkably for a future Prime Minister he took little interest in politics. While contemporaries like Edward Heath, Roy Jenkins and Denis Healey were making names for themselves in the Oxford Union, Harold held aloof and took part in few activities outside his college. All his efforts were concentrated on his academic studies, and here he was outstandingly successful. In his second year (1936) he won the prestigious Gladstone Memorial Prize for an English essay, and in his final examinations he gained a first in Modern Greats (philosophy, politics and economics) said to be the most outstanding for several years. This led to a scholarship as well as a junior lectureship at New College, and the prospect of a university career opened up before him.

It might have been that during his time at Oxford he would have forgotten the girl in the tennis club, but this was not the case; he was at great pains to maintain the connection and in 1938 he and Mary became engaged and were married on New Year's Day 1940. Mary loved the idea of a life at Oxford. Later she recalled: 'I thought it was wonderful. My idea of heaven. I can tell you there is nothing I would have liked as much as being a don's wife . . . very old buildings and very young people. There is everything anyone could want, music, theatre, congenial friends, all in a beautiful setting and within a fourpenny bus ride; it symbolised so much for me.'

These dreams were not to be realized, nor, for the time being, was the one of having at last a settled home. By then the Second World War had broken out, and Harold had registered for National Service. Instead of being drafted into the armed services, however, he was co-opted into the Civil Service, for which he would be mainly based in London, and this meant for Mary an unsettled life, sometimes in temporary accommodation in London, sometimes back in Oxford, sometimes taking refuge from the bombing with her in-laws in the country, especially after the birth in 1943 of her first baby, a son, Robin.

Harold served in the Civil Service with marked distinction, so that it was open to him at the end of the war to make it his permanent career, but this he decided against. By then he had set his sights on politics and was seeking a seat in Parliament as a Labour candidate. In 1945 this came his way, and in the General Election of 1945 he was elected member for Ormskirk in Lancashire. From then his career took off spectacularly. He was appointed a junior minister immediately, with no time on the back benches, and only two years later, at the age of thirty-one, he became President of the Board of Trade.

But this success was gained at a price. It had required abnormally hard work and long periods away from home; the strain on Mary, especially since the birth of a second son in 1948, was almost unbearable, and there was a danger of their marriage breaking up. That it was saved was due to Harold spending more time with her, taking her on some of his trips abroad and at last providing her with a pleasant permanent home in Hampstead Garden Suburb.

The Wilsons' lifestyle there surprised some people, not so much for of its simplicity and plainness as for its narrowness. Certainly Mary had friends among her neighbours and took part in local affairs, but Harold held aloof from both social and political activities. There was at that time in Hampstead a group of young Labour politicians that gathered round the new leader of the Labour Party, Hugh Gaitskell. This included such high flyers as Roy Jenkins, Tony Crosland and George Brown; but Harold had no inclination to join them. This was perhaps partly owing to personal antagonism between himself and Gaitskell but also to his nature.

Although highly intelligent with a mind as sharp a knife, Harold was no intellectual; he had little interest in abstract ideas. As Richard Crossman, one of his strong supporters, put it he was 'unreflective and unphilosophical'. There was a streak in him of great simplicity. In childhood he had been an enthusiastic boy scout – the movement's outdoor activities and simple code of honour making a great impression on him – and much of that ethos was to remain with him for life. Similarly his aesthetic tastes had not matured; he had little interest in art or music. He adored Gilbert and Sullivan, some of whose operas he knew by heart, and he enjoyed hymns and hearty, folksy songs but nothing much more. This did not leave him with many interests in common with

Mary, whose abiding passion was poetry and whose general tastes were considerably more sophisticated. She had practically no interest in politics, certainly not in run-of-the-mill, everyday politics: the machinations, jockeying for place, the 'art of the possible' – all those things in which Harold excelled – for these she felt a strong aversion. About one subject only did she feel deeply: that of unilateral disarmament; so much so that she threatened to vote Liberal if Labour did not agree to it.

There was nevertheless much in common between them. Their religious practices and beliefs were similar, both having been brought up in Nonconformist families, although in Harold's case this took the form mainly of good works, while in Mary's it was more doctrinal with much soul-searching over sin. Mary was devoted to her father and had the deepest respect for him, but in later life her own feelings became more relaxed. 'I've never worried much', she said, 'about so-called sin in personal relationships. I don't care for religious attitudes and ideas of morality which seem to depend on intolerance of one kind or another.' They were bound together, too, by their common taste for the simple pleasures of life. Unlike some Labour leaders they had no hankering for gracious living – expensive meals, rare wines and exotic holidays abroad. Their preference for food was of the plainest, and one wine was as good as another. And they were in total agreement as to holidays – always in the same place in the Isles of Scilly off the Cornish coast. After their first visit there in 1952 they fell in love with the place and built their own bungalow, which they visited two or three times a year. For Mary particularly it was an idyllic place, quite simply 'the most beautiful in the world'. The boating, the bathing, the walking and, above all, the relief of getting away from the hurly-burly of London and becoming temporarily part of the friendly, unobtrusive island community was one of her greatest delights.

Such a lifestyle made Mary a soft and easy target for the sharp-witted satirists of *Private Eye*, who in 'Mrs Wilson's Diary' portrayed her cruelly and inaccurately as a humdrum suburban housewife with a taste for such things as British tonic wines, HP Sauce and Magicoal fires. All of which snobbery Mary took with good humour and told a friend with some satisfaction that if they only knew the reality they could have made much more of it.[4]

In 1963, when he was forty-seven, Harold became leader of the Labour Party on the sudden death of Hugh Gaitskell, and a year later he was Prime Minister. This sudden rise to the top was in spite of the fact that he was something of a loner in the Labour Party and deeply distrusted by some. This was particularly the case with the intellectuals who had gathered round Gaitskell, but even such hoary old Labour warriors as Emanuel Shinwell and Aneuran Bevan regarded him as 'unprincipled' and 'a sheer absolute careerist out for himself alone'.

It is certain that he would not have gone as far as he did without strong support, someone behind him on whom he could rely entirely and with the zeal and political know-how to keep him on the rails and sustain him in good times and bad. With most Prime Ministers this has been the role of their wives, but it was one which Mary was incapable of filling; it was not in her nature. However, early in Harold's career there had appeared on the scene someone with all the necessary qualities.

Marcia Williams (later Lady Falkender) had been a typist in Transport House, the Labour Party headquarters, but had the ambition and steely will to go much further. In 1956 she became Wilson's secretary and soon saw her way to political fortune by attaching herself firmly, and at time fanatically, to his bandwagon. She quickly made herself indispensible and established a powerful hold over him that was never to be broken. From secretary she graduated to being political adviser, where she proved to be shrewd, strong-willed and combative. In order to get her way she was quite ready to resort to tantrums and strong language. She did not mind what she said to Wilson nor who heard her say it, and visitors were aghast to witness her screaming and calling him 'a silly little boy'. The one person who seemed quite unfazed was Wilson himself; indeed he seemed rather to relish it. He recognized in her a kindred spirit, someone to whom, in the words of a colleague, 'politics were meat and drink and the very air that was breathed' and who 'at her best had a political mind capable of testing and matching his own'. It seemed that she stimulated him and brought out new talents, for it was notable at that time that his political persona underwent a change. Until then his parliamentary performances had tended to be competent but prosaic. Now, as Shadow Chancellor confronting Harold Macmillan, they became humorous and lethally scathing.

It was to be expected that such a relationship would set tongues wagging. There were many who had no doubt that there was a sexual relationship between them, and these suspicions were heightened when Marcia's marriage broke up and she subsequently became pregnant. Mary, as always, behaved with decorum and dignity. She must surely at first have been uneasy and felt that she was being supplanted, but later she came to realize, as did others close to them, that there was no physical love – it was no more than a 'political marriage' – and that Marcia posed no threat to her. In time they became friends and Marcia went out of her way to be helpful. She was always to cause resentment among Wilson's other close colleagues, but most of them came to the conclusion that with all her bad temper and abrasiveness she was essential to the well-being of Wilson and so, too, to the Labour Party.

For Mary the move into 10 Downing Street was traumatic. It meant giving up the house in Hampstead where she had been living for the past fourteen years and moving once again into temporary accommodation. She had grown to love the quiet, unpretentious life with friends and family and not too much politics. In Downing Street it was very different: the flat was not her own, being mainly under the control of the Ministry of Works, and there was little privacy, with ministers and officials and sundry hangers-on dropping in at all times. It was not the life for her, but she strove to do her duty: she entertained parliamentary wives, she was at Harold's side during elections, establishing great rapport particularly with working-class wives, and she attended party conferences, which bored her to death but during which she endeavoured to put on a brave face.[5]

But there were times when her spirits sank low and she had difficulty in keeping going. Her great solace then, as it had always been, was her poetry. Mary had been writing poetry since childhood. It had provided her with a private world into which she could retreat at times of tension. A particular happiness while she was at Downing Street was a friendship she struck up with the Poet Laureate John Betjeman, who was a great admirer of her work. They became very fond of each other, corresponding copiously and mildly flirtatiously and making assignations in St James's Park, and they went on an expedition together to Mary's birthplace in Norfolk. It was all entirely innocent. It was a 'literary marriage' in much the same way that Harold's and Marcia's was a political one.

In 1970 Mary published a selection of her poems. Inevitably they were received with condescension by the literary cognoscenti, but they were an instant popular success, selling an incredible 75,000 copies, almost unheard of for a slim volume of poetry and said to be the largest sale of verse since Byron. No doubt they were given a boost by her being the wife of the Prime Minister, but it is probable that people connected with her poems – heartfelt, nostalgic and readily intelligible – more readily than with most other modern poets.

When in the General Election of 1970 the Labour Party was defeated unexpectedly by the Conservatives under Edward Heath, Mary could not but have mixed feelings. Certainly she grieved for the setback to Harold, but at the same time welcomed moving out of Downing Street, although not back to Hampstead but to a house in Westminster; and when four years later Harold became Prime Minister again she stayed put there. She also put pressure on Harold to keep to his intention of retiring, which he did, somewhat suddenly, in 1976. At the time this took many people by surprise and there was much speculation, most of it scandalous, as to the reasons for it. Only later did the true reason become known: Harold's awareness of the onset of Altzheimer's disease.

He was to live for another nineteen years – years of torment for Mary as she watched his once brilliant mind gradually disintegrate and he became less and less capable of doing anything for himself. At the same time, too, his reputation came under attack, sometimes from unexpected quarters. Wild and sometimes fantastic rumours were spread abroad about shady business transactions and even secret deals with the Russian KGB. During all these travails Mary never faltered. She faced up to devoting her life almost entirely to looking after him, to seeing to his needs as well as providing him with the opportunity of doing those things of which he was still capable. Saintly indeed she was, which did not come as a surprise to some people. A few years earlier, her publisher, Sir Robert Lusty, had quickly became aware of how much more there was to her than met the eye. 'I quickly found', he wrote, 'that Mary Wilson possessed all the virtues of charm, modesty, frankness and humour, guided by compassion and an acute awareness of life's realities. She was at once immensely kind and friendly and a human being to whom one instantly warmed.'

AUDREY CALLAGHAN

During the two and a half years that James Callaghan was Prime Minister his wife Audrey made no great impact on public attention, but she should not be underestimated. Behind the scenes she was competent and masterful, and that she was able to stay out of the limelight for most of the time was a mark of her success, as this was something she had been determined to do. Like other wives she was loyal and supportive, and but for her it is likely that Jim's political career would have ended sooner than it did. Like some others, too, she was an excellent household manager (as well as being a good plain cook, which not many of them were) and coped admirably with her family responsibilities, which included ten grandchildren. But what distinguished her from nearly all others was that she had had a notable career of her own, for the most part in local government. At an early age she had been elected to Lewisham Council and had subsequently been an alderman of the old London County Council. As a local councillor her main interests had been in education and all matters affecting children; later she was to become Chairman of the Board of Governors of Great Ormond Street Hospital, where she was active in bringing about beneficial reforms, notably in the provision of facilities for mothers to stay at the hospital while their children were patients.

Audrey came from a different background to Jim. Her father was a well-to-do businessman and she was brought up in comfortable circumstances, while Jim came from a working-class family that had known poverty, his father being in the lower ranks of the Navy, eventually rising to become Chief Petty Officer.[6] They had first met when they were both teaching in a Baptist Sunday school and were married ten years later, in 1938, by which time Jim was a tax officer in the Inland Revenue and Audrey had taken a degree at the London School of Economics as well as a diploma at a polytechnic in domestic science.

For a time during the Second World War Jim saw service in the Navy, at the end of which he was elected to Parliament as Member for Cardiff in the Labour landslide of 1945. In time he was to hold all the main offices of state until becoming Prime Minister after the sudden resignation of Harold Wilson in 1976.

At that time the Prime Minister's flat in 10 Downing Street had been unoccupied for two and a half years, as Mary Wilson had refused to move back into it when Harold became Prime Minister for the second time. Rather strangely, in 1976 it was Jim who was unwilling to move in, preferring their modest house in south London; but Audrey saw that this was impractical and, as so often, she had her way and immediately set about refurbishing the flat, which she did with considerable taste, winning praise from discerning critics.

In the performance of the duties of a Prime Minister's wife Audrey scored highly. She was conscientious and tactful and discreet in all her utterances and, much as she may have disliked them, she put on a brave face for official entertainments. But in one respect she could not compete with most other premiers' wives: she had no dress sense – even less than Lady Dorothy Macmillan. On smart, prestigious occasions she was wont to appear in ill-fitting, unfashionable clothes, sometimes embellished by what an American journalist called 'dime-store jewellery'. She was bored by clothes and thought they did not matter, but, of course, they do, if only because the wrong ones bring one into the limelight when fashion journalists have a field day in finding fault with them. Somewhat belatedly Audrey realized this and attempted some improvements but with little success.

After her brief occupancy of 10 Downing Street Audrey still had plenty to occupy her: all those things that interested her most – her charities, her grandchildren, her small mixed farm in Sussex where she and Jim raised pigs, grew apples and other crops, probably not very profitably but with great satisfaction. In old age health problems encroached, including a hip replacement, and these were exacerbated when at the age of seventy-two she was mugged in a street in South London and her assailants were made to realize that old ladies are not necessarily easy targets when Audrey retaliated vigorously. Tragically, at the end of the century she was incapacitated by Altzheimer's disease. Jim nursed her devotedly, and when it became necessary for her to go into a home he visited her every day and did all he could to comfort her.

Notes

1. This was a task she guarded somewhat jealously. When on one occasion she was not at the station to meet him off the train from London and a neighbour offered him a lift home, he replied, not perhaps altogether jokingly, that he would get no supper if she did (private source).

2. Her mother was Hester Lyttelton, youngest of the fourth Lord Lyttelton's fifteen children (see p. 81). By coincidence Elizabeth's younger brother Giles was to be a colleague and close friend of Harold Wilson at University College, Oxford, and he named his eldest son after him.

3. Mary was her second name. For the early part of her life she was known by her first name, Gladys.

4. Later one of her chief tormentors, John Wells, was to sponsor her for the chair of Professor of Poetry at Oxford.

5. There was an occasion during one of these when, unusually, she was seen to be making notes, and the media, anxious to know what was suddenly interesting the Prime Minister's wife, turned a long-distance camera on them, only to find that they were a shopping list.

6. He had been keen to go with Captain Scott to the South Pole but was dissuaded by his wife. If he had gone Jim would not have been born.

16

DENIS THATCHER

He was always a fund of shrewd, calm and penetrating comment. And
he very sensibly saved this for me rather than the outside world.

I could never have survived a minute without him. – Margaret Thatcher
on Denis

One of the most loyal, disciplined and delightful men I have ever
met. – Sir Robin Butler, Cabinet Secretary and head of the Civil Service

At the beginning of 1975 Denis Thatcher was approaching his sixtieth birthday and retirement as a director of the large multinational company
Burmah Oil. He had been a successful and affluent businessman and was looking forward to a retirement with some business commitments but with plenty
of time for his favourite occupations of golf, watching rugby and 'messing about
in boats'.

But on 11 February his wife Margaret was elected leader of the Conservative
Party, and all their future prospects were transformed. At that stage, however,
he could hardly have foreseen that for more than ten years he would be resident in 10 Downing Street, in attendance at high-level conferences all over
the world and supporting and keeping in place one of the country's most
dynamic and controversial Prime Ministers. At first sight he would have seemed
little qualified for such a role. Shy, politically unsophisticated and quite a male
chauvinist, he might have been expected to have been out of his element. Few
would have predicted the great success he was to have.

Denis's upbringing was conventional middle class. His father was born in
New Zealand but had been brought to England as a child, where he later become
manager of a thriving family business, the Atlas Preservative Company, manu-
facturing mainly wood preservatives and paint. Denis had a public-school
education at Mill Hill, north London, where he was happy but not particularly
distinguished. This was followed not by university but by a course in business
management, after which he was taken into the family firm, where at the age of

twenty-four he became works manager. By then, though, the Second World War was looming and Denis, anticipating it, joined the army and was commissioned, rather to his disappointment, into anti-aircraft defence. In time, however, his organizational skills were recognized and he was appointed a staff officer. He served with distinction in Italy, being mentioned in dispatches, and was awarded the MBE. With the coming of peace he returned to the family business where he became managing director, replacing his father who had died during the war.

As well as returning to a challenging job Denis also returned to a broken marriage. In 1942 he had had a whirlwind wartime romance with Margot Kempson, and they had been married just before he left for Italy. Margot was a charming and beautiful woman and they had been deeply in love, but their tastes and backgrounds were different – Denis's suburban and industrial, Margot's rural and horsy – and during the time Denis was abroad she had fallen out of love with him. They were divorced after four years of marriage. This Denis took hard, as, contrary to appearances, he was shy and sensitive, and a failed marriage was a great blow to his self-confidence. For a time he avoided female company and resigned himself to a single life, but this did not last long.

In 1949, when he was thirty-four, he was introduced to Margaret Roberts, the Conservative candidate for the local constituency of Dartford. The daughter of a Lincolnshire grocer, she had won a scholarship to Oxford and was bent on a career in politics. At twenty-three she was one of the youngest parliamentary candidates and one of very few women, but by her verve and intellectual prowess she had overcome Conservative prejudices and had made a deep impression in Dartford. She had made an impression, too, on Denis, but there was no question of love at first sight: both were too engrossed in their careers at the time and neither was of a particularly romantic nature. The more they saw of each other, however, the more they were drawn to one another. Margaret had been persuaded that she would not get far in politics without a husband, and it seemed to her that a reasonably wealthy middle-aged man would best suit her purposes. Denis, for his part, found that he was overcoming his aversion to matrimony and was falling under the spell of a compelling personality. After a courtship of two years they were married in 1951, soon after Margaret had stood for Dartford (a safe Labour seat) for the second time.

The Thatchers settled into married life in comfortable circumstances in Swan Court, Chelsea. For the time being it was necessary for Margaret's political career to be put on hold, especially when in 1953 she gave birth to twins. After putting on a brave show in two elections in Dartford she expected that now she would be given a safe seat, but it was to be seven years before one came her way. In the meantime she was not one to let the grass grow under her feet. At Oxford she had taken a degree in chemistry and she now set about qualifying for the Bar, which she did without difficulty and was taken into chambers in the Inner Temple. At the same time Denis was fully occupied with the affairs of the Atlas Preservative Company, which was forever expanding. He worked all hours and took numerous trips abroad, but he insisted on keeping his weekends free not so much for his family but for refereeing rugby matches; this was an abiding interest of his, and he became one of the top referees in the country. Later he described refereeing as 'the most rewarding experience of my life'.

In 1958, when she was thirty-two, Margaret was adopted as candidate for the safe Conservative seat of East Finchley in north London, and in the following year a General Election took place. In her campaign Denis was supportive but not particularly active. He would do no door-to-door canvassing, and although he appeared on Margaret's platforms he never spoke from them. He was prepared to visit the constituency in the evenings and at weekends (even giving up refereeing for this) but not during working hours. Margaret, of course, went into battle at full blast, never letting up for a minute, and won the seat comfortably with an increased majority.

With Margaret in Parliament life in the Thatcher household became ever more intense. It was necessary for her to be in the House of Commons at all hours of the day and night, Denis's workload was still increasing and there were two young children to be cared for. The services of a nanny had been obtained, but the children also needed parental attention, and the brunt of this fell on Margaret. Denis was never at ease with children; in their company he felt constrained and often irritable, and even in adulthood there was no intimacy between them.[1] However, Margaret and Denis had already come to an understanding about a design for living: they would go their own ways and pursue their own career without interference from the other; Denis would subsidize Margaret and give her moral support but would be involved minimally in politics; Margaret, for her part, would take charge of domestic affairs and would have no say in the management of Atlas. This arrangement was to work well. There was no resentment between them and no competition. Margaret did not complain about Denis's long absences abroad, nor about the time he spent refereeing rugby matches, while Denis made no objections when Margaret was away at nights in the House of Commons.

The pressure on Margaret became even greater when after only two years in Parliament she was appointed a junior minister and so had to rotate between their new home in Kent, East Finchley, Parliament and the Ministry of Pensions. There was some relief from this after three years when, after the General Election of 1964, Labour was returned to office.

By then, though, the strain was beginning to tell on Denis. The responsibility of running a large private company on which not only his immediate family but also his mother and two aunts depended for financial stability was proving onerous. He was showing signs of a nervous breakdown and was warned by his doctor that it was essential for him to let up and take a long break, advice which he had the good sense to accept, and he went off for a holiday of several months to his favourite country, South Africa. During this time he was able to give deep thought to the future and came to the conclusion that he could no longer go on as before and that a buyer should be found for Atlas Preservatives. There had already been enquiries, which he had rejected, but he now followed these up, and in the following year (1965) a sale was arranged to Castrol Oil for £530,000 with Denis retained as a director. A year later Castrol itself was taken over by Burmah Oil, and Denis assumed he would be out of a job, but again he was appointed to a directorship, which he retained until his retirement ten years later.

During the six years the Conservatives were in opposition Margaret had little respite from her routine as she was appointed one of the Opposition spokesmen on Treasury affairs, which pleased her as it was a step towards what was then her ultimate goal, the post of Chancellor of the Exchequer. In 1970 the Conservatives under Edward Heath were returned to office and Margaret was appointed Minister of Education, where she came in for strident abuse in the press for her decision to abolish free milk in schools – abuse which pained Denis more than it did her. Four years later she was again in opposition, but any idea that this would mean a let-up was dispelled the following year when to general surprise, not least her own, she was elected leader of the Conservative Party. This was a notable triumph. In the teeth of some fierce opposition she had prevailed over the grandees of the party and became the first woman leader. There were many who considered that she had little chance of staying the course. How wrong they were.

All this occurred at around the same time as Denis retired from Burmah Oil, and far from the quiet life he had been expecting he found himself in a maelstrom: their house in Chelsea was constantly overrun by politicos and besieged by the press, and security men from Special Branch watched out for their safety. And more was in store for them. In the succeeding years all attempts to displace Margaret came to nothing, and when the Conservatives gained an overall majority in the General Election of 1979 Margaret became Prime Minister and she and Denis moved into 10 Downing Street.

By then Denis was already evolving for himself a role as consort. Generally his aim was to keep as far in the background as he could. 'So long as I keep the lowest possible profile and neither write nor say anything', he once said, 'I avoid getting into trouble.' And so he decided at once that he would give no interviews to the media. He had acquired a strong aversion to journalists, whom he had found intrusive and untruthful, and the worst culprit in his eyes was the BBC ('bearded lefties, pinko socialists, overmanned, overpaid and unpatriotic'). 'Vipers', he called members of the press, but much as he might despise them he was always careful to be scrupulously polite and, although at times under extreme provocation, never lost his temper.

Although Denis felt it a great honour to move into 10 Downing Street, he was to find, as had many Prime Ministers' consorts before, that life there was no picnic. Conditions in the attic flat at the top of the building were cramped and claustrophobic, and there was little privacy; civil servants, politicians and secretaries pervaded the place and their sitting room was often the scene of high-powered, overwrought conferences extending deep into the night. And meals could not be depended on: often they were meagre and makeshift; a member of Margaret's staff once said that Denis seldom knew whether he would have a hot supper, a cold one or none at all. In contrast to this were conditions at Chequers, where life was spacious and luxurious and which Denis loved dearly.

If Denis was successful in coping with the press he was less at ease when it came to an essential task of a Prime Minister's consort – that of entertaining and being entertained by what he called 'the great and the good'. He had always been shy, his social graces were not polished and small talk did not come readily. Nevertheless, he did not duck out. He could not attend all the occasions required of him, as he had an active life of his own but, he later claimed, if he was available he went and was always there on the big occasions. At meetings of world leaders he was a somewhat incongruous figure among the elegantly dressed female spouses from Europe and the Africans and Asians in their flowing brightly coloured robes. As always he was cooperative, but he did draw the line at becoming involved in all the activities laid on for them, as these had a distinctly feminine flavour; attending fashion shows, kindergartens and hospitals were not for him and he usually managed a visit to a local factory over which he could cast an expert eye. Occasions he particularly found a trial were Commonwealth Heads of Government Meetings (CHGM), as one of his stronger prejudices was against what he regarded as the 'tinpot dictators' of Africa and Asia who were constantly attacking Western colonialism and at the same time asking for financial aid, much of which then disappeared into prestige projects and private Swiss bank accounts. CHGM was transcribed by him into 'Coons Holidaying on Government Money', and when an Australian journalist once told him at one of the meetings that 'back home no one gave a monkey's tit about all of this' he was not unsympathetic.

When the Thatchers first moved into Downing Street Denis was able for a time to achieve his aim of being an invisible partner, as the spotlight was very much on Margaret, the first woman Prime Minister. But this was not to last. The sharp wits of *Private Eye* soon saw in him a figure of comedy. A few years before they had successfully made Mary Wilson a figure of fun, portraying her as a typical suburban housewife (see p. 213). Now they saw possibilities in depicting Denis as a boozy, saloon-bar buffoon. In a series of letters addressed to 'Dear Bill' from Denis he was shown to be endlessly seeking 'tinctures' and 'waterholes' and pronouncing far-right political opinions about 'coons' and 'pinkos'.

In some ways this image was not far off the mark: Denis was a heavy drinker and smoker, his talk was often interlarded with four-letter words and few were less politically correct. But he was no fool and was canny enough to realize that the mockery of *Private Eye* could rebound in his favour. If people were to regard him as a nincompoop out of the pages of P.G. Wodehouse they would not see him as a sinister power behind the throne. Better to be something of a joke than a Svengali. And so to some extent he played up to this image, restraining neither his language nor his drinking habits, and some of his off-the-cuff remarks exceeded anything from 'Dear Bill'.[2] But amid the bluff and the heartiness he was careful to maintain a certain style and bore in mind the words of his grandmother that gentlemen might be coarse but never vulgar. The success of the 'Dear Bill' letters led to the production of a play in the West End called *Anyone for Denis?* This was less good-natured, more bitter and more scatological. However, Denis and Margaret went to see it, and Denis was not unduly put out. Margaret, however, was deeply shocked.

It was not long before it became evident, especially to Margaret's inner circle, that Denis was doing an admirable job as Prime Minister's consort. It was certainly ironic that the first man to occupy this position should be a strong male chauvinist who would normally have been appalled at the idea of a woman premier. But to Denis Margaret was on a plane of her own; he loved and admired her above all others and had no doubt that she was one of the great women of all time and one of the greatest Prime Ministers and that it was up to him to give her all the support he could. This he did with great tact and judgement; he realized that he must not stick his oar in when it was not wanted. Someone close to Margaret later said of him: 'His greatest talent was for keeping out of Margaret's way. His second was being able to materialize at the exact moment when she needed him most.' He knew as well as anyone how great was the strain Margaret had to endure and how at times she became obsessed with fears and fantasies and, as he put it, 'divorced from what the hell is going on'. It was then that he stepped in and soothed her and brought her down to earth. Always his was the voice of calmness and common sense, and she listened to him when no one else could get through to her. She wrote later: 'He was always a fund of shrewd, calm and penetrating comment. And he very sensibly saved this for me rather than the outside world.'

In other ways, too, Denis was an admirable consort. Although most political functions bored him, his behaviour at them was courteous and considerate. As a host he always put nervous people at their ease and watched out for those who were being neglected and took them under his wing. And he never talked down to people or gave himself airs and never lost the common touch. Margaret was referred to as 'my woman' or 'the boss', and in addressing her she was as often as not 'sweetie' or even 'sweetie pie'.

In his years at Downing Street Denis was always fully occupied. As well as attending government functions he also retained a number of non-executive directorships, for which, with his Downing Street contacts and his own business experience, he was much in demand. But he did not take these lightly and was always diligent in mastering the details of the companies concerned and being well prepared for board meetings. And he was scrupulous about accepting hospitality or anything in the nature of a free hand-out. To avoid being compromised he was even known to refuse offers of free rounds of golf. At Downing Street there was usually a heavy postbag for him, which he attended to personally, answering each letter, even the most trivial, in longhand with a fountain pen (never a ballpoint). But however great the pressure he always managed to find time for his favourite occupations of golf and watching rugby matches followed by a get-together with cronies at a friendly bar.

After enduring three General Elections Denis began to think that the time had come for Margaret to step down, but he would not press her to do so. He knew how much the job meant to her, and he was firmly convinced that she was far the best Prime Minister available, but by 1990 he sensed that the end was near. He could see that the ambitious along with the dissatisfied and the disappointed were conspiring to bring her down, and he had a feeling that they would succeed. His great hope was that when the end came it would be dignified and benign, but sadly this was not to happen. In the leadership election of 1990 Margaret failed by only two votes to obtain the necessary majority, after which there were defections in the Cabinet, and she felt she must resign. Although he had been secretly wanting this for some time, Denis could not but be disgusted and tearful at the way it happened and the disloyalty of her colleagues.

Quitting the top job and settling into private life was an agonizing process for Margaret, and Denis did all he could to support and comfort her. Not that life was at all empty: their engagement books were as full as ever with invitations to speak pouring in from all over the world. And in retirement they did not change what had always been their way of life in going their separate ways. It was rare that they had a quiet evening together at home, nor did they much want one. When their daughter, Carol, suggested booking a table for them to celebrate some anniversary, Margaret firmly turned down the idea. 'What would we talk about?' she said.

The humiliation and bitterness of Margaret's resignation was something from which neither would recover completely, but there was much of which they could be proud. Margaret was the longest-serving Prime Minister of the twentieth century and her achievements were widely acclaimed even – if somewhat grudgingly – by her opponents. And Denis's part in them was being recognized more and more. Sir Robin Butler, Cabinet Secretary and head of the Civil Service, who had been in daily contact with them at Downing Street, wrote of him that he was one of the most loyal, disciplined and delightful men he had ever met. In her memoirs Margaret wrote that she could never have survived a minute without him. He came to be regarded with universal respect and affection, and when in the following year he was honoured with a baronetcy (a hereditary title which had for some time fallen into disuse) there was general approbation. Denis himself was delighted at the honour but told a friend at the time that he was equally delighted at being elected a member of Sunningdale Golf Club.

He had never found it easy to talk emotionally. Like many Englishmen his true feelings were usually masked by a front of badinage. But to his daughter, Carol, when she was writing his biography, he spoke for once from the heart: 'For forty wonderful years I have been married to one of the greatest women the world has ever produced. All I could produce – small as it may be – was love and loyalty.' He died on 26 June 2003 at the age of eighty-eight.

Notes

1. It was not until the twins were in their twenties that they came to know about their father's first marriage, and only then because a newspaper was about to publish details of it.

2. As when he was once asked by a Tory faithful if he had a problem with drink and he replied: 'Yes, madam, I have. There is never enough of it.'

17

NORMA MAJOR

Things like that just don't happen to people like us. – Norma Major
when she was about to move into 10 Downing Street

I've only ever thrown things twice. – Norma Major on life at
Number Ten

No Prime Ministers' wife has been more surprised to find herself in 10
Downing Street than Norma Major. 'Things like that just don't happen
to people like us,' she once said. Yet in less than twenty years she found herself
transposed from a modest single life as a teacher in south London to being in
the heart of government as wife of the Prime Minister.

Norma Johnson was born in Shropshire in 1942. Soon afterwards her
family was plunged into tragedy. Her father, who had served throughout the
war in the army, was killed soon after it ended in a motor-cycle accident.
Four months earlier her mother had lost a baby son when he was a few days
old. And so in 1945 Edith Johnson found herself alone with Norma and a
pension of £3 a week on which to survive. To this daunting situation she
responded courageously, taking as much work as she could manage, sometimes as many as three part-time jobs simultaneously. But Norma's childhood
was impoverished. At the age of four she was sent to a boarding-school run
by an army charity; this she found frightening and hard to endure. Later,
she attended a comprehensive school in Peckham, where, again, the going
was rough. At home, too, conditions were not easy. She and her mother lived
in a tenement flat in Bermondsey with shared washing and cooking facilities
and an outside toilet on a bomb-damaged balcony. However, there was, Norma
said later, a great spirit of community and she did not look back on her childhood with horror. Certainly their struggles and sacrifices paid off, for when
at the age of twenty-eight she met John Major she was a qualified teacher with
a car and flat of her own.

John well remembers their first meeting. It occurred when he was rallying
votes for a General London Council election and a fellow worker brought

Norma along to assist with transport. In his words: 'She was slender, a little above average height with mid-brown hair, shining brown eyes and a beautiful, curving, glamorous smile. Dressed in beige check suit, fawn blouse and white knee-length boots, she was stunningly attractive.'

John, always susceptible, fell for her at once. With Norma, too, it was love at first sight, and it was she initially who made the running. She invited him to a party to which he was unable to come and then to a gala performance of an opera at Covent Garden. Opera was Norma's great passion; several times she had queued through the night for tickets. In time John was to come to share her enthusiasm to some extent, but on this occasion he disgraced himself by falling asleep at the climax when Joan Sutherland was singing the mad scene from *Lucia de Lammermoor*. Nevertheless ten days later they were engaged, and six months afterwards they were married. During that time Norma found out about the life and origins of the man she was to marry.

John Major came from a somewhat bohemian background. His father, Tom Major,[1] had at one time been a performer in the music halls and circus, sometimes as a singer, sometimes a clown and sometimes a trapeze artist. He led a roving, uninhibited life, married at first to Kitty Grant, a woman five years older than himself, by whom he had no children – although there were several on the side. Until late in life John Major was to discover half-brothers and half-sisters of whose existence he had not formerly been aware. When Kitty died as a result of an accident Tom married a young dancer named Gwen who was twenty-six years his junior and described by her future son John as 'a cheeky, teasing, self-willed girl, often in trouble for misbehaviour and pranks. But she charmed her way out of every scrape.'

By the outbreak of the Second World War Tom and Gwen had two children and were not expecting to have any more, but then in 1943, after a gap of eleven years, when Tom was sixty-four and Gwen thirty-eight, she found herself pregnant again. The circumstances attending John's birth were dramatic. At the time Gwen was suffering from double pneumonia and pleurisy, which nearly killed her. John was born when she was still very ill, and he, too, became infected with a virus that almost proved fatal. However, he was to survive not only this illness but also the flying bombs which were then falling freely on London.

Later he would win a scholarship at a local grammar school where he did not distinguish himself and left as soon as he could at the age of sixteen with few O-levels and no interests apart from cricket and politics. For some years afterwards he led a somewhat aimless life, drifting in and out of dead-end jobs, sometimes being unemployed and drawing the dole.[2] Eventually he found a job with a bank that took him for a short spell to Nigeria where he was in a motor accident which resulted in a leg being broken in several places and a kneecap smashed beyond repair. Throughout this time his interest in politics continued to grow, and at the age of twenty-five, now back in England, he was elected member of Lambeth Council and two years later became chairman of the Housing Committee.

It was in the same year, 1970, that he met Norma, and after they were married they moved to John's newly acquired flat in Streatham – plain and serviceable but in Norma's opinion badly in need of embellishment. At this time, too, Norma's initiation into politics began, which until then had been only a minor interest. She was never to become obsessively political, but she was always ready to play her part in support of John.

The next stage in his career was the realization of his lifetime ambition to become a Member of Parliament at Westminster, and for this it would be necessary for him to fight at least one hopeless seat; and so he twice contested the safe Labour seat of St Pancras North before being chosen for the Tory stronghold of Huntingdon. This was a notable achievement, as the local councillor from Brixton was an unlikely choice for a large rural constituency. Norma deserves much of the credit for this success. A good-looking, hard-working and faithful wife was no longer as common in politics as it had once been. Safe seat though Huntingdon might have been, the Majors worked at it as if it were a marginal, and in the General Election of 1979 John, at the age of thirty-six, was returned with a majority of over 20,000. And now he was ready for the next advance up the greasy pole,[3] but even he, ever optimistic and with boundless self-confidence, could not have foretold that within only eleven years he would have reached the top of it.

With John in Parliament Norma was confronted with the realities of being a 'political widow'. While Parliament was sitting John was hardly ever at home in the evenings and often away until late into the night. Like other MPs' wives Norma found the loneliness of this difficult to endure. After only four years on the back benches John had been appointed to the Whips' office, where he came into close contact with his Conservative colleagues, among whom was an attractive and ambitious young woman MP, Edwina Curry. For a time he became besotted by her and she by him. Their affair was kept under wraps; had it become public it would have undoubtedly spelled the end of his career.[4] However, it did come to the attention of Norma, who behaved with great dignity and restraint and decided that she should forgive her errant husband. It did, of course, intensify her loneliness, but she was helped by having plenty to occupy her. By then she had two young children – eight-year-old Elizabeth and James, aged four – and she was heavily involved with charitable work; in particular she had become an active supporter of the National Society for Mentally Handicapped Children (MENCAP), for which she raised large sums of money. In addition, she found time to pursue her abiding interest in opera and set out to write a biography of the singer Joan Sutherland. Over the next ten years she embarked on detailed research, tracking down every performance the singer had given as well as every recording. It was a labour of love.

In the House of Commons John's career was advancing exceptionally rapidly.

After two years as Assistant Whip he had been appointed a junior minister and two years after that a Cabinet Minister, first as Chief Secretary to the Treasury and then, to everyone's surprise (not least his own), Foreign Secretary. At the time he did not welcome this. He had little experience of foreign affairs and the job he really wanted was Chancellor of the Exchequer. But he could not refuse, as it was a clear indication that Margaret Thatcher had marked him out as her successor.

If John was stunned by the appointment Norma was dismayed. It meant a very different lifestyle for the family. In the first place, they lost all their privacy. Security men accompanied them wherever they went, often with an armoured car, and in their country home near Cambridge every kind of electronic device was installed, and an unsightly caravan to house their guards was parked in the garden. In time the couple became used to these intrusions, but at first, as John later recalled, they made their life a misery. Second, the appointment meant a heavy increase in John's workload. The amount of reading matter a Foreign Secretary has to get through each day exceeds that of any other minister, and the red boxes were for ever piling up, even on their bed – something to which Norma took particular exception.

There was also for Norma an unwelcome increase in official entertaining. She had never enjoyed receptions, banquets and parties and would much rather have been running her household or attending to the affairs of MENCAP. But, like John, she soon adjusted to the job, and when it ended after no more than three months she had her regrets. John's departure from the Foreign Office – almost as sudden as his arrival – was occasioned by the resignation of Nigel Lawson as Chancellor of the Exchequer and the appointment of John in his place. There, too, he did not remain long. Within a year he was Prime Minister.

Her husband's accession to the premiership brought no great joy to Norma. She felt deeply sorry for Margaret Thatcher, and she was overawed at the thought of living in 10 Downing Street. Most Prime Ministers' wives in recent times have had similar reservations. Audrey Callaghan found it cold and unwelcoming, Lady Home claimed that it made her a grass widow and Mary Wilson said that it made her sick with fear, and she refused to move in when her husband became Prime Minister for the second time. Certainly the private flat on the top floor was not inviting. Margaret Thatcher had had little time or inclination to attend to décor and her husband even less. But Norma set to work with a will to make the apartment habitable, insisting on a new kitchen and redecoration throughout. She also obtained the loan of some fine pictures. The overall effect, someone remarked, was rather grand, in the style of a country house. In time Norma came to feel at home at Number Ten, but at first it was a struggle to keep her head above water. So many things demanded her attention, including an immense amount of mail, and she did not get secretarial help with this for some time. She always worried when she felt she was not in control of a situation.

Of course Norma's greatest problem as the Prime Minister's wife was the media, which never left her alone and was always ready to misrepresent her and catch her out. There was a tendency at first among journalists to regard her as a shrinking violet, but there they were wrong. She was, to use a cliché, 'her own woman'. John was later to pay tribute to her 'grace and charm through all the highs and lows of over a quarter of a century'. But he also said she was tougher than she looked, and Norma herself admitted to a temper that she could not always control ('I've only ever thrown things twice'). In time she came to terms with all the tittle-tattle in the tabloids about her fashion sense, her make-up, her household foibles and other trivia – but never completely. After she left Number Ten she was asked what she would do differently if she had the time again. She replied at once: 'I would not do any interviews.'

In the 1992 General Election, the winning of which was perhaps John's greatest triumph, Norma was, as always, constantly by his side, smiling and confident but making no speeches of her own or, indeed, any utterances of a political nature. The victory ensured another five years in Downing Street, and during that time Norma was more assured and at ease and was able to do more of those things she did best. She greatly extended her work for MENCAP, and with the kudos of Number Ten and the help of famous friends, particularly those connected with opera, she was able to bring money pouring in. She also finished her life of Joan Sutherland and set to work on a history of Chequers.

Few politicians have had such a meteoric rise as John Major, but, as is often the case, nemesis was lying in wait. In the mid-1990s it became evident that all was not well with the Conservative Party. It was said of it once that its secret weapon was its unity, but this had now disappeared. The root cause was the issue of union with Europe, over which opinions differed sharply and there was, in John Major's words, 'a proliferation of bickering, squabbling and back-stabbing'. Other factors were compounding the divisions: a small number of Tory MPs were found to have been acting disreputably, some in business deals, others in sex scandals. This so-called 'sleaze' was confined to a small minority of members, but at the time it did great harm to the party.

So, as the next General Election approached, John Major became aware that the Tories were doomed. At the same time there was a resurgence of the Labour Party, which had been remodelled to present a more attractive face to the electorate. It was to emerge as New Labour, although it might as well have been called 'New Conservative', as most of its new policies had been appropriated from the Tories.

Although by now with little hope of victory, John Major decided to go down fighting, so he campaigned as hard as ever. As always, Norma was by his side, but this time with a heavy heart; for her mother was mortally ill with cancer, and she could not conceal her anxiety. A reporter from *The Times* wrote scathingly: 'Norma Major's finely honed "celebrity smile" vanished abruptly yesterday to reveal a persistently glum expression. Whether she was suffering from first-day nerves or a wife's natural boredom . . . her gloomy countenance did little to lighten the Tory campaign mood.'

The reporter was unaware of the real reason for Norma's gloom, and when he was apprised he laid off. To add to Norma's woes a mole was discovered on her back which it was feared might be malignant. Medical opinion was that it should be removed at once, which was done quietly in Downing Street rather than in hospital so as not to attract attention. It was found to be non-malignant but for a time was painful.

Although weighted down by political pessimism and personal worries, John and Norma persevered. They hoped to keep a Labour victory within reasonable bounds, but this was denied them, and in the final count Labour had a landslide majority. All that remained then was for them to move out of Downing Street, which proved an emotional occasion as they were dearly loved by the permanent staff, many of whom were in tears when they saw them off.

A few days previously John had agreed warmly with someone who had told him that there were more things in life than politics and, as if to demonstrate this, he made straight for the Oval to watch a game of cricket. A short time later he announced his resignation as leader of the Conservative Party. Norma, too, could now devote herself to those things she enjoyed doing most. But first there was the matter of some 400,000 letters of sympathy to be confronted.

Notes

1. His proper name was Tom Ball. Major was his professional name. Later, when John went to grammar school he was deeply humiliated by being made to assume, albeit temporarily, the name of Major-Ball.

2. Surely the only Prime Minister to have done so.

3. See p. 70.

4. It was not revealed until some twenty years later when Edwina wrote of it in her autobiography.

18

CHERIE BLAIR

I started life as the daughter of someone, now I am the wife of someone, and I'll probably end up as the mother of someone. – Cherie Blair

When Tony Blair became Prime Minister it was likely there would be a new style of premiership. He and his wife Cherie are a remarkable partnership – both lawyers, strongly politically minded with much the same orientation to the left and deeply religious – Cherie Roman Catholic, Tony High Anglican. Their backgrounds, though, are different: Tony comes from a stable middle-class home and a private education, Cherie from a broken home and state schools. In temperament, too, there are differences: Tony is sociable and outgoing with populist tastes (particularly sport and pop music), while Cherie is shy (although less so than formerly) and unconventional, with an outstanding academic record and a high-powered career of her own. Downing Street had never seen anything like it.

Both Cherie's parents, Tony and Gale Booth, were second-line actors. As such, they were often on tour, and Cherie was born in the Lancashire town of Bury in 1954 when they were temporarily in residence there. Tony Booth had received a Roman Catholic and socialist upbringing, but this did not keep him from a loose-living lifestyle. A few years after Cherie was born he abandoned any ideas of setting up his wife and two daughters in a home of their own and deposited them with his mother Vera, a stalwart Liverpudlian with whom many of her errant family at times took refuge.

When Cherie was nine Tony made a complete break from Gale and cohabited with another woman by whom he was to have two more daughters.[1] By then he had become nationally famous through his part in the highly successful television series *Till Death Us Do Part*. The great cross Cherie had to bear in childhood was that hers was a broken home and her father the local Lothario.[2] It made a deep impression on her, but it did not prevent her from brilliant scholastic achievements.

At school it was soon evident that she had outstanding gifts of intellect and application. She romped through all examinations, usually in first place.

Four As at A-level led to a place at the London School of Economics, where she was to gain the highest first in Law awarded for several years. The LSE at that time was quietening down after a turbulent time in the late 1960s when the students had been continually demonstrating, engaged in sit-ins and pelting visiting speakers with missiles. While there Cherie did not stand out either for political extremism or for leadership qualities, only for intellect and hard work. But neither was she a recluse. It might have been expected that she would be somewhat diffident and awkward with men, as until then she had lived in an all-female environment both at home, where there were few male visitors, and at her schools, which had been single sex . But this does not appear to have been the case. A male fellow student later recalled: 'Cherie Blair was memorable in terms of her brightness and sociability and the fact that she was a student whom you studied with, who was good company, was helpful, encouraging and obviously had a very bright future. I mean she stuck out. There's no doubt about that.'[3]

After the LSE Cherie could have taken a year to become a Bachelor of Common Law at Oxford, but she decided to take her Bar finals immediately, in which she came top in the whole country. The next step was to become a pupil in chambers of a senior lawyer. There was strong competition for these pupillages, but Cherie had no difficulty and was accepted at once by Derry Irvine, QC. It was usual for lawyers to have only one pupil, and soon afterwards Irvine interviewed an engaging young lawyer, one Tony Blair, and was so struck by his freshness and idealism that, in spite of his mediocre academic record, he took him on as well.[4] This caused Cherie some annoyance at first, and there might have been jealousy between them, but instead there was mutual attraction, and this survived until the end of the year, when it was necessary for one of them to stand down. With her superior academic qualifications Cherie expected that she would be the one who would be retained. But in the event it was Tony who was chosen and she had to find a new master. This she had no difficulty in doing, but it must have dawned on her, not for the last time, that success in life depends not only on examination success; charm and persuasiveness also count.

A year later Tony and Cherie became engaged. For a time Cherie had held back. She was suspicious of middle-class males, whom she generally regarded as easygoing and lightweight; but she and Tony had been finding more and more in common – in particular an idealistic desire to change the world for the better through politics. They were married three years later, and their first home was in Hackney, where they became active members of the Labour Party. The ambition of both of them was to get into Parliament, but, as might have been expected, only hopeless seats were offered them at first.

In the run-up to the General Election of 1983 Cherie was the Labour candidate for the Tory stronghold of Thanet North, while Tony, who had just lost his deposit in a by-election in Beaconsfield, had at first no constituency at all.

But then at the last moment luck – of which throughout his career he has always had his full share – came his way. When polling day was a month off there were still a few constituencies without Labour candidates, one of which was Sedgefield in the North-East, a new seat but reckoned to be safe for Labour. Tony thought that he did not have much chance of being nominated; it seemed unlikely that in a predominantly working-class area with a strong mining constituency there would be much favour for a young lawyer from London, one that was middle class, intellectual and long-haired. But he decided that he had nothing to lose by trying, and somehow he was able to persuade a nucleus of people that his heart was in the North-East (he had lived there as a child) and that he had new and fresh ideas for reviving the Labour Party.

He was opposed by a stalwart working-class left-winger who had been wooing the constituency for some time, but in the end Tony scraped through against him by the narrowest of margins. In the General Election he had a majority of over 8,000, and so within four weeks of being out in the cold he found himself a Member of Parliament, one of the youngest, in a safe Labour seat. Down in Thanet North Cherie got nowhere.

Tony's election to Parliament altered the course of Cherie's life. It seems that she gave up at once all ideas of finding a seat for herself; for the time being there was room for only one MP in the family, and maybe she realized that Tony had political gifts she did not possess. Besides, her forte was the law, so it made sense for her to pursue a legal career which would also have the advantage of boosting the family finances, necessary in those days when an MP's pay was only just enough to live on.

She was, however, to give Tony full political support. Every weekend she would make the 250-mile journey to Sedgefield, where she played her part in wooing the constituents, and in this she was often found to be more adept than Tony. For all his charm and ebullience Tony was not always at ease in a working-class environment; it did not come naturally to him. Cherie with her working-class origins found it easier. Certainly at this time Cherie showed her mettle. During the week she was taking on more and more legal work; at the weekend she was the MP's wife and political activist; then in 1984 came a new role with the arrival of her first child. No wonder she expected that all domestic duties should be shared equally between her and Tony – something to which her husband readily agreed and in which field he was possibly the more proficient.

In 1994 the Labour leader John Smith died suddenly, and after a suitable interval the Labour Party set about electing a successor. Tony Blair, by then Shadow Home Secretary, was one of the favourites; the other was the Shadow Chancellor Gordon Brown. The two were good friends and were inhibited about standing against each other, but one had to prevail: Tony – eloquent and persuasive, with great flair if not great depth; Gordon – knowledgeable and imposing, with heavy punch but lacking in political sex appeal. After much backstairs deliberating the indications were that the party in general favoured Tony, and Gordon withdrew.

So in July 1994, at the age of forty-two, Tony Blair became leader of the Labour Party. One year later Cherie became a QC. Two years later after a landslide Labour victory at the polls they were ensconced in 10 Downing Street. At forty-four Tony was the youngest Prime Minister for more than two hundred years, while Cherie was a high-flyer in her own profession. They had three young children – with another to follow shortly after. For 10 Downing Street this was indeed a transformation.

Of the various problems to be confronted, the one Cherie addressed at once was that of her role as Prime Minister's wife. She had definite views about this. She would be the silent spouse. She would give no interviews, make no off-the-cuff remarks and try to give no impression that she was wielding undue influence behind the scenes. She would also not let up in her career at the Bar. Here she had already made great strides, but her ambitions were not yet fulfilled; and if achieving these meant taking on cases in opposition to the government, so be it. During official ceremonies and electioneering she would be at her husband's side and smile and make innocuous comments but, apparently, no more.

A difficult problem, as for all premier's wives, was how to deal with the media. Its appetite for photographs, interviews and titbits of information is inexhaustible. This was something about which Cherie felt strongly. As a child she had known what it was like to be the daughter of a celebrity, and she was determined that her children should have maximum protection from media intrusion. On this the press was not uncooperative, and a deal was struck whereby the children would not be photographed, in return for officially arranged photocalls; this agreement, by and large, has been honoured. Cherie has also been concerned about her own privacy. She might have had hopes that the media would be put off by her acting as a 'silent spouse', but she was to find that the more you shun publicity the more you attract it. She was not left alone. Journalists could not accept that such a highly intelligent and successful woman was not the power behind the throne. They loved to present her as 'the most powerful woman in the country' and were constantly on the look-out for any unguarded comments that might bear this out. Of course, Cherie has been aware of this and has generally watched her tongue carefully. She has also been aware of the danger of careless talk from friends and relations, and these have been told that they must say nothing, however trivial, or they will be dropped; and most, if not all, have complied with her request. The majority of journalists, too, it was found, could be made to keep in line. The Blairs knew how desperate they were for exclusive information; the competition among them for this was intense, and they were made to understand that it would only come their way if they did not print anything offensive or ask awkward questions in public. By the use of this tactic a form of censorship was imposed.

Both parents have attached great importance to their children being considered 'ordinary' and leading lives as normal as possible. The matter of schooling was a problem. It was, of course, out of the question that they should go to private schools, but it was almost as impossible that they should go to an inner-city comprehensive, so a compromise was reached whereby they went to a Roman Catholic school, grant-maintained and selective, in Fulham.

Since arriving at Number Ten there have, predictably, been changes in the Blairs' lifestyle. Certain expensive tastes have been developed. Cherie has smartened up her appearance considerably. When she first entered the public eye she was rather conspicuously dowdy, and the Labour agent at Sedgefield felt he had to comment on the fact. But as Prime Minister's wife she became much more clothes-conscious. Gone were the leggings and pixie boots and in their place came designer outfits[5] and a hairstyle which requires a hairdresser to accompany her (at her own expense) on trips abroad. Quite quickly she was transformed into a chic and fashionable figure.

The Blairs have also shown a taste for the opulent in their choice of holiday venues, preferring châteaux and palazzi to more humble establishments. But home life has a more democratic flavour. When in 2000 their youngest son Leo was born, Tony said he would take his share of caring for him (although he jibbed at paternity leave), and changing nappies in the middle of the night is only one of the tasks undertaken for the first time by a Prime Minister in office.

Most Prime Ministers' wives (especially those in the Labour Party) have found official entertaining a heavy burden, and there have been occasional signs of Cherie wilting under the strain,[6] but she and Tony have made it more congenial by their choice of guests, which usually includes a sprinkling of sportsmen, pop stars and television personalities, and the emphasis is on informality.

In the General Election of 2001 the Labour Party romped home to another sweeping victory over a demoralized Conservative Party. For a Prime Minister who had been in office for four years Tony's popularity rating was unprecedented. Cherie, too, was riding high: at the age of forty-five she had taken the birth of a baby in her stride (emerging from hospital and resuming work only three hours afterwards); her legal practice was flourishing; she was becoming a more assured figure in public and seemed to be finding greater enjoyment in life at the top. But nemesis was lying in wait. Nature had endowed her with great gifts, but these did not include sound judgement, particularly of character, and it had not gone unnoticed that she sometimes kept strange company. It was partly as a result of this that at the end of 2002 she found herself in hot water over the affair that the media dubbed 'Cheriegate'.

One of her more bizarre associates was Carole Caplin, a one-time topless model who had set herself up as a 'lifestyle guru' and advised Cherie on such issues as clothes, cosmetics and exercise, as well, so it was rumoured, as on more intimate matters. She was certainly an unusual confidante for a Prime Minister's wife, but, as far as was known, she was on the level with no sinister intentions.

But the same could not be said of her partner, Peter Foster, a bankrupt and a convicted fraudster facing extradition to Australia. Cherie should have given him a wide berth, but rashly she engaged him to act on her behalf in a property deal, which was discovered by the *Daily Mail*, who raised an outcry about it. However, although what Cherie had done may have been ill-judged, it was not illegal, and in time the matter might have subsided. But in a moment of madness she got the Downing Street Press Office to deny that she had had anything to do with the fraudster, but this was soon disproved by the production of emails between them, and she was forced to admit that she had been lying or, as she put it somewhat euphemistically, 'misleading'. With some courage she then made an emotional public apology, pleading that her mistakes had been due to having too many responsibilities and that what she had done was only to protect the privacy of her family. This of course gave rise to widespread press coverage, with shocked outrage being expressed by people, some of whom were not best known for their own veracity. Although in some quarters Cherie took a heavy battering she also had her supporters, one of whom wrote that 'for the first time she has emerged as a real human being, a hurt and proud woman'.

At the time of writing the uproar over 'Cheriegate' and Carole Caplin's influence is beginning to die down – Caplin was finally dismissed from Cherie's employment in the Blair household in autumn 2003 – but it may take further twists yet. Certainly Cherie has been left with egg on her face, but people have lived down greater scandals than this.

The media battering she has endured may have led Cherie, in October 2003, to come to the support of Betsy Duncan Smith, wife of Iain, at that time Leader of the Opposition, who, it was alleged, had been paying her for secretarial services she had not performed. 'I always feel sympathy with every woman who is trying to juggle a lot of tasks,' Cherie declared, adding: 'I always have sympathy for those hounded by the press.'

Notes

1. Later he was to have two more by another partner.

2. A libertine of historic reputation.

3. Quoted from Linda McDougall, *The Perfect Life of Mrs Blair*.

4. A fortunate choice as it was to land him in time on the Woolsack as Lord Chancellor.

5. As well, allegedly, as innumerable pairs of shoes.

6. As, for example, when a camera caught her in a deep yawn at the Jubilee concert at Buckingham Palace.

BIBLIOGRAPHY

Abse, Leo, *Tony Blair: The Man Behind the Smile*, Rubon Books, London, 2001

Adams, R.J., *Bonar Law*, John Murray, London, 1976

Aldington, Richard, *Wellington: Being an Account of the Life and Achievements of Arthur Wellesley, First Duke of Wellington*, Heinemann, London, 1946

Asquith, Margot, *Autobiography*, Thornton Butterworth, London, 1920

Avon, Lord (Sir Anthony Eden), *Memoirs: Full Circle*, Cassell, London, 1960

Ayling, Stanley, *The Elder Pitt: Earl of Chatham*, Collins, London, 1976

Baldwin, A.W., *The True Story*, Allen and Unwin, London, 1955

Battiscombe, Georgina, *Mrs Gladstone*, Constable, London, 1956

Bennett, Daphne, *Margot: A Life of the Countess of Oxford and Asquith*, Victor Gollancz, London, 1984

Betjeman, John, *Letters: Volume 2 (1952–84)* (ed. Candida Lycett Green), Methuen, London, 1996

Black, Jeremy, *Pitt the Elder*, Cambridge University Press, Cambridge, 1992

Blake, Robert, *Disraeli*, Eyre and Spottiswoode, London, 1966

Blythe, Henry, *The Fatal Passion*, Hart-Davis, London, 1972

Bolitho, Hector, *No. 10 Downing Street*, Hutchinson, London, 1957

Bonham Carter, Violet, *Winston Churchill As I Knew Him*, Collins, London, 1965

Brookshire, Jerry H., *Clement Attlee*, Manchester University Press, Manchester, 1995

Brown, Peter Douglas, *William Pitt, Earl of Chatham: The Great Commoner*, Allen and Unwin, London, 1978

Browne, Montagu, *Long Sunset*, Cassell, London, 1993

Bryant, Arthur, *The Great Duke*, Collins, London, 1971

Carlton, David, *Anthony Eden: A Biography*, Allen Lane, London, 1981

Cecil, Lady Gwendolen, *Life of Robert, Marquis of Salisbury* (4 volumes), Hodder and Stoughton, London, 1921–32

Cecil, Lord David, *The Cecils of Hatfield House*, Constable, London, 1973

Cecil, Lord David, *The Young Melbourne*, Constable, London, 1939

Churchill, Winston and Clementine Churchill, *Speaking for Themselves: Personal Letters of Winston and Clementine Churchill* (ed. Mary Soames), Doubleday, London, 1998

Churchill, Winston, *Great Contemporaries*, Collins, London, 1937

Clifford, Colin, *The Asquiths*, John Murray, London, 2002

Colville, John, *Fringes of Power*, Hodder and Stoughton, London, 1985

Courcy, Anne de, *Circe*, Sinclair-Stevenson, London, 1993

Crane, D., *Kindness of Sisters*, HarperCollins, London, 2002

Crewe, Lord, *Lord Rosebery*, John Murray, London, 1923

Davenport-Hines, Richard, *The Macmillans*, Heinemann, London, 1992

Derry, John W., *Charles, Earl Grey*, Blackwell, London, 1992

Dixon, Peter, *Canning*, Weidenfeld and Nicolson, London, 1976

Drew, Mary, *Catherine Gladstone*, Nisbet, London, 1919

Elletson, D.H., *Maryannery*, John Murray, London, 1959

Elton, Lord, *The Life of James Ramsay MacDonald*, Collins, London, 1939

Feiling, Keith, *Life of Neville Chamberlain*, Macmillan, London, 1946

Foreman, Amanda, *Georgiana, Duchess of Devonshire*, HarperCollins, London, 1998

Gash, Norman, *Lord Liverpool: The Life and Political Career of Robert Banks Jenkinson, Second Earl of Liverpool, 1770–1828*, Weidenfeld and Nicolson, London, 1984

Gash, Norman, *Politics in the Age of Peel*, Longman, London, 1953

Gray, Denis, *Spencer Perceval*, Manchester University Press, Manchester, 1963

Grigg, John, *Lloyd George: From Peace to War 1912–16*, HarperCollins, London, 1985

Grigg, John, *Lloyd George: The People's Champion*, Eyre Methuen, London, 1978

Grigg, John, *War Leader*, Allen Lane, London, 2002

Grigg, John, *The Young Lloyd George*, Eyre Methuen, London, 1973

Guedalla, Philip, *Bonnet and Shawl*, Hodder and Stoughton, London, 1928

Guedalla, Philip, *Lord Palmerston*, Ernest Benn, London, 1926

Harris, Kenneth, *Attlee*, Weidenfeld and Nicolson, London, 1982

Herbert, Lucy, *Mrs Ramsay MacDonald*, London, 1926

Hibbert, Christopher, *Wellington: Personal History*, HarperCollins, London, 1997

Hinde, W., *George Canning*, Collins, London, 1973

Holmes, Richard, *The Iron Duke*, Harper Collins, London, 2001

Horne, Alistair, *Macmillan: 1894–1956* and *1957–1986* (2 volumes), Macmillan, London, 1988–9

Jenkins, Roy, *Asquith*, Collins, London, 1964

Jenkins, Roy, *Baldwin*, Collins, London, 1987

Jenkins, Roy, *Churchill*, Macmillan, London, 2001

Jenkins, Roy, *Gladstone*, Macmillan, London, 1995

Kelch, Ray, *Newcastle, Duke Without Money*, Routledge and Kegan Paul, London, 1974

Lee, Elizabeth, *Wives of the Prime Ministers, 1844–1906*, Nisbet, London, 1917

Lloyd-George, Earl, *Dame Margaret*, Allen and Unwin, London, 1947

Longford, Elizabeth, *Byron*, Hutchinson, London, 1976

Longford, Elizabeth, *Wellington: Pillar of State*, Weidenfeld and Nicolson, London, 1972

Longford, Elizabeth, *Wellington: Years of Sword*, Weidenfeld and Nicolson, London, 1969

Mabell, Countess of Airlie, *Lady Palmerston and Her Times*, Hodder and Stoughton, London, 1922

MacCarthy, Desmond, *Lady John Russell*, Methuen, London, 1910

MacCarthy, Fiona, *Byron: Life and Legend*, John Murray, London, 2002

MacDonald, James Ramsay and Margaret MacDonald, *A Singular Marriage: A Labour Love Story in Letters and Diaries* (ed. Jane Cox), Harrap, London, 1986

MacLeod, Ian, *Neville Chamberlain*, Methuen, London, 1961

Macmillan, Harold, *Autobiography* (6 volumes), Macmillan, London, 1966–72

Macmillan, Harold, *The Past Masters*, Macmillan, London, 1975

Magnus, Philip, *Gladstone*, John Murray, London, 1954

Major, John, *John Major: The Autobiography*, HarperCollins, London, 1999

Major, Norma, *Chequers: The House and Its History*, HarperCollins, London, 1996

Marshall, Dorothy, *The Rise of George Canning*, Longman's Green and Co., London, 1938

Martin, Kingsley, *The Triumph of Lord Palmerston*, Allen and Unwin, London, 1963

Maurois, André, *Disraeli: A Picture of the Victorian Age*, John Lane, Bodley Head, London, 1927

McDougall, Linda, *The Perfect Life of Mrs Blair*, Politico's, London, 2001

Middlemas, E.K. and J. Barnes, *Baldwin: A Biography*, Weidenfeld and Nicolson, London, 1969

Minney, Rubeigh James, *Puffin Asquith*, Leslie Frewin, London, 1973

Montgomery Hyde, H., *Baldwin, the Unexpected Prime Minister*, Hart-Davis, London, 1973

Monypenny, William Flavelle and George Earle Buckle, *Life of Benjamin Disraeli, Earl of Beaconsfield* (6 vols), John Murray, London, 1910–20

Morgan, Austen, *Harold Wilson*, Pluto Press, London, 1992

Morgan, Austen, *J. Ramsay MacDonald*, Manchester University Press, Manchester, 1987

Morgan, Kenneth O., *Callaghan: A Life*, Oxford University Press, Oxford, 1997

Normington, Susan, *Lady Caroline Lamb*, House of Stratus, London, 2001

Ogden, Christopher, *Life of the Party*, Little, Brown, London, 1994

Owen, J.B., *The Rise of the Pelhams*, Methuen, London, 1957

Pemberton, W. Baring, *Lord North*, Longman's Green and Co., London, 1938

Petrie, C., *Lord Liverpool and His Times*, James Barrie, London, 1954

Pimlott, Ben, *Harold Wilson*, HarperCollins, London, 1992

Plumb, J.H., *Sir Robert Walpole: The King's Minister*, Allen Lane, London, 1960

Plumb, J.H., *Sir Robert Walpole: The Making of a Statesman*, Allen Lane, London, 1956

Prest, John M., *Lord John Russell*, Macmillan, London, 1972

Ramsay, A.A.W., *Sir Robert Peel*, Constable, London, 1928

Rentoul, John, *Tony Blair, Prime Minister*, Little, Brown, London, 2001

Rhodes James, Robert, *Anthony Eden*, Weidenfeld and Nicolson, London, 1986

Rhodes James, Robert, *Bob Boothby*, Hodder and Stoughton, London, 1991

James, Robert Rhodes, *Rosebery: A Biography of Archibald Philip, Fifth Earl of Rosebery*, Weidenfeld and Nicolson, London, 1963

Ridley, Jasper, *Lord Palmerston*, Constable, London, 1970

Roberts, Andrew, *Salisbury*, Weidenfeld and Nicolson, London, 1999

Rose, Kenneth, *The Later Cecils*, Weidenfeld and Nicolson, London, 1978

Rosebery, Lord, *Chatham: His Early Life and Connections*, Humphreys, London, 1910

Sampson, Anthony, *Macmillan*, Allen Lane, London, 1967

Schweizer, Karl W., *Lord Bute: Essays in Re-interpretation*, Leicester University Press, Leicester, 1988

Selden, Anthony, *10 Downing Street*, HarperCollins, London, 1999

Selden, Anthony, *Major: A Political Life*, Weidenfeld and Nicolson, London, 1997

Sherrard, Owen Aubrey, *Lord Chatham: Pitt and the Seven Years' War*, Bodley Head, London, 1952

Soames, Mary, *Clementine Churchill*, Cassell, London, 1979

Sorpel, John J., *Tony Blair: The Moderniser*, Michael Joseph, London, 1995

Stevenson, Frances, *Lloyd George: A Diary* (ed. A.J.P. Taylor), Hutchinson, London, 1971

Stevenson, Frances, *The Years That Are Past*, Hutchinson, London, 1967

Sylvester, A.J., *Life with Lloyd George*, Macmillan, London, 1975

Taylor, Stirling, *Robert Walpole and His Age*, Jonathan Cape, London, 1931

Thatcher, Carol, *Below the Parapet*, HarperCollins, London, 1996

Thatcher, Margaret, *Path to Power*, HarperCollins, London, 1995

Thatcher, Margaret, *The Downing Street Years*, HarperCollins, London, 1993

Thomas, Peter D.G., *Lord North*, Allen Lane, London, 1976

Thorpe, D.R., *Eden*, Chatto and Windus, London, 2003

Tilby, A. Wyatt, *Lord John Russell: A Study in Civil and Religious Liberty*, Cassell, London, 1930

Trevelyan, G.M., *Lord Grey of the Reform Bill*, Longman's Green and Co., London, 1926

Walker Smith, D., *Neville Chamberlain*, Robert Hale, London, 1967

Walpole, Spencer, *Life of Spencer Perceval*, Hurst and Blackett, London, 1874

Walpole, Spencer, *Lord John Russell*, Longman's Green and Co., London, 1889

Williams, Susan, *Ladies of Influence*, Allen Lane, London, 2000

Young, G.M., *Stanley Baldwin*, Hart-Davis, London, 1952

Ziegler, Philip, *Addington: A Life of Henry Addington, First Viscount Sidmouth*, Collins, London, 1965

Ziegler, Philip, *Melbourne*, Collins, London, 1976

Ziegler, Philip, *Wilson: The Authorised Life*, Weidenfeld and Nicolson, London, 1993

INDEX